SUPPORTING FRATERNITIES AND SORORITIES

IN THE CONTEMPORARY ERA

Culture and Society in Higher Education

Pietro A. Sasso and Joseph L. DeVitis, Editors

Culture and Society in Higher Education is a book series that analyzes the role of higher education as an incubator, transmitter, and transformer of culture. While examining the larger social, economic, and political connections that shape the academy, it seeks to revivify American colleges and universities and to re-explore their core purposes. In so doing, the series reaffirms our social contract and the common public good that should ideally drive the policies and practices of contemporary post-secondary education. Prospective book topics include, but are not limited to, such themes as the purposes of higher education, the worth of college, student learning, new forms of liberal education, race matters, feminist perspectives, LGBTQ issues, inclusion and social justice, student mental health and disabilities, drug-related topics, inclusion and social justice, fraternity and sorority life, student activism, campus religious questions, significant legal challenges, problems of governance, the changing role of faculty, academic freedom and tenure, political correctness and free speech, testing dilemmas, the amenities "arms race," student entitlement, intercollegiate athletics, technology and social media, and distance instruction.

Books in the Series:

Student Activism in the Academy: Its Struggles and Promise (2019)

Generally Speaking: The Impact of General Education on Student Learning in the 21st Century (2019)

Supporting Fraternities and Sororities in the Contemporary Era: Advancements in Practice (2020)

Foundations, Research, and Assessment of Fraternities and Sororities: Retrospective and Future Considerations (2020)

Joseph L. DeVitis is a retired professor of educational foundations and higher education. He is a past president of the American Educational Studies Association (AESA), the Council of Learned Societies in Education, and the Society of Professors of Education. He lives with his wife, Linda, in Palm Springs, California.

Pietro Sasso is faculty program director of the College Student Personnel Administration at Southern Illinois University Edwardsville. He is the recipient of the Dr. Charles Eberly Research Award from AFA and is the ACPA Men and Masculinities Emerging Scholar-In-Residence for 2017 to 2019. He serves on the board of the Center for Fraternity/Sorority Research at Indiana University.

Supporting Fraternities and Sororities in the Contemporary Era

Advancements in Practice

EDITED BY

*Pietro A. Sasso, J. Patrick Biddix
and Mónica Lee Miranda*

Myers
Education
Press

GORHAM, MAINE

Published by Myers Education Press, LLC
P.O. Box 424
Gorham, ME 04038

Myers Education Press is an academic publisher specializing in books, e-books and digital content in the field of education. All of our books are subjected to a rigorous peer review process and produced in compliance with the standards of the Council on Library and Information Resources.

LIBRARY OF CONGRESS CATALOGING-IN-PUBLICATION DATA AVAILABLE FROM LIBRARY OF CONGRESS.

13-digit ISBN 978-1-9755-0268-3 (paperback)
13-digit ISBN 978-1-9755-0267-6 (hardcover)
13-digit ISBN 978-1-9755-0269-0 (library networkable e-edition)
13-digit ISBN 978-1-9755-0270-6 (consumer e-edition)

Printed in the United States of America.

All first editions printed on acid-free paper that meets the American National Standards Institute Z39-48 standard.

Books published by Myers Education Press may be purchased at special quantity discount rates for groups, workshops, training organizations and classroom usage. Please call our customer service department at 1-800-232-0223 for details.

Cover design by Sophie Appel

Visit us on the web at **www.myersedpress.com** to browse our complete list of titles.

Contents

Dedication

To Tau Delta Phi Fraternity and Mario P. Sasso,
for inducting me into your diverse brotherhood that
has enriched and shaped my perspectives as a scholar and educator.
(PAS)

To William Raimond Baird,
the "first author" of fraternity research,
whose 1879 foundational reference remains useful today.
(PB)

Para Mami y Papi, por su amor, apoyo, y ejemplo de integridad, resistencia, y humildad.
To the Founders of Omega Phi Beta Sorority, Inc. for creating a Latina-oriented sorority dedicated to serving and educating through our diversity. For creating a platform for women, especially women of color, like me, to find their voice and speak truth to power.
(MLM)

Preface

Pietro A. Sasso, Joseph DeVitis, J. Patrick Biddix,
and Mónica Lee Miranda

Ever since the medieval universities were founded, young people
have done whatever it takes to gain acceptance, to break with their
past lives, to achieve a sense of power, to carve out a society of
their own that isn't quite what their tutors and teachers had in mind.

—HANK NUWER

THE DEVELOPMENT OF this text initially was inspired when Dr. Sasso was a young master's student at the University of Rochester, when the venerable Dr. Charles Eberly introduced him to a copy of the text *The Administration of Fraternal Organizations on North American Campuses: A Pattern for the New Millennium* by Dr. Dennis Gregory (2003). Dr. Gregory has so graciously authored a foreword denoting change in the more than 15 years since the original text was published. His initial inspiration for this is noted and appreciated.

This text is also inspired by the pyre of fraternity that appears innate, primarily by newly initiated members. When Dr. Sasso was a campus-based professional as a fraternity/sorority advisor and traveling chapter consultant for his own fraternity, this provoked a sense of revelry, as it appeared as a baptism. However, in the vein of ritualistic references, Dr. Sasso eventually experienced burnout of those same fires and washed his hands akin to Pontius Pilate. He later transitioned from campus professional to a faculty identity and, during this time, he watched several generations of his own students enter and exit the

profession of fraternity/sorority advising as a revolving door. The reasons for this are reflected and reinforced by many of the challenges acknowledged in this text.

Moreover, the father of Dr. Sasso unexpectedly passed during the development of this
text, which delayed its release and progression. His father was also a member of the same
fraternity, Tau Delta Phi, and he affiliated at Rutgers University-Newark. These events
reignited his pyre for fraternity, as several of the fraternity brothers of Dr. Sasso served as
pallbearers and others appeared randomly at the funeral services. He had not communicated with or seen many of them in several years or even since college. This funeral, as a
death metaphor, is accurate with regard to the fraternity/sorority experience. Even in death
as in life, the concept of fraternity for collegiate men and women continues to promulgate
impactful developmental experiences. Also, this narrative example potentially exemplifies
the ethos of the conceptualization of fraternity and conjures affirmative sentiment despite
many of the challenges contained in this text.

In soliloquy and in unison, the editors of this text have carefully curated chapters that
have attempted to help us reconstruct the meaning of the fraternity/sorority experience.
We continue to have instances that draw national scrutiny from student protests and sit-ins
over the existence of fraternities at Swarthmore College or the continued announcement of
the annual closures of a chapter for sexual assault, substance abuse, or hazing. The general
meaning of "fraternity" and "sorority" should facilitate bonds of mutual support. Ideally,
fraternity/sorority life on college campuses should not foster the founding values and goals
of service, philanthropy, education, leadership, identity development, cultural awareness,
and brotherhood/sisterhood. Unfortunately, we see, all too often, the negative attributes
often associated with such actions as hazing, misuse of drugs, superficial relationships,
herd mentality, and other injurious behaviors that hinder human development (e.g., sexism, racism, ableism, and classism). Ideally, fraternity/sorority life on college campuses
should not foster the negative attributes often associated with the aforementioned challenges along with those described within this text. Yet those characteristics have pervaded
any number of fraternities and sororities, painting a still life of degradation and dishonor
as media headlines provide face validity to these claims.

At the same time, fraternity/sorority groups can instill a form of monolithic conformity, a severe obstacle to human growth, rather than openness to new and different ideas
(DeSantis, 2007). This helps us understand that we need to continue to be our own agents
of change. Among the chief intentions of this book is to demonstrate how *all* such groups
can exist with a greater sense of purpose—one befitting colleges and universities that truly
seek to shape lives that matter.

With that aspiration in mind, higher education professionals should strive to assist in
the integration of fraternity and sorority experience with student development and student
success. For example, institutional culture seems to have a profound effect on academic
success. Those colleges that stress the life of the mind often compensate for fraternities and
sororities that "place too much emphasis on social involvement" (Pike, 2000, p. 136). An
integration of intellectual and social life should be the ultimate aim. Both higher education

institutions and the fraternity/sorority community need to assure the public that they are living up to their ideals. Our sincere wish is that this text, balanced with chapters that serve to challenge and support the community, will serve to direct campus life in that more productive direction.

Note: This text uses a number of terms interchangeably. Most notably, the collective terms *Greek* and *fraternity/sorority* appear throughout this text to denote fraternity/sorority systems or campus communities. There is no consistency within this text as the authors used professional vernacular from several academic disciplines and institutional types. In respect to academic freedom, authenticity of the author voice, and other culturally-based organizations the use of such terms were left in deference to the chapter authors.

References

DeSantis, A. D. (2007). *Inside Greek U: Fraternities, sororities, and the pursuit of pleasure, power, and prestige*. Lexington, KY: University Press of Kentucky.

Pike, G. R. (2000). The influence of fraternity or sorority membership on students' college experiences and cognitive development. *Research in Higher Education, 41*(1), 117–139.

Foreword: Looking Back

Dennis E. Gregory

IN 2000 WHEN I transitioned from being a student affairs administrator to a faculty member after 25 years of service, I began to cast about for topics upon which to do research, publish, and present. I was not new to presenting at conferences and had published articles on my dissertation and other topics before that time, but developing a scholarly research agenda and picking topics about which I knew, in which I had an abiding interest, and where I knew material was needed posed an interesting conundrum. Legal issues of various types were a fertile area for exploration, issues around student conduct were near and dear to my heart, and fraternal organization issues were of profound interest. As I examined the material on these topics, I found that fraternal organizations—while many aspects related to them had been researched in depth, particularly issues of hazing, alcohol, and other types of substance abuse—was a topic on which there was a dearth of broad publication. In fact, *Baird's Manual of American College Fraternities*, which was originally published by William Raimond Baird in 1879, and has been edited many times (Anonymous, 2010; Anson & Marchesani, 1991; Baird, 2015), is now in the public domain and digitized by Google. Yet this was the only general reference book on fraternal organizations that I was able to find. The latest issue at the time of that writing was the 1991 edition, and it was dated even then.

This book, while a marvelous resource, was really a source for facts and figures on individual fraternal organizations and contained no analysis of institutions or themes surrounding the modern fraternal organization. As a result, I began the task of creating an edited book on the topic of modern fraternal organizations for college men and women. I sought authors whom I knew and who had broad knowledge about such organizations (e.g., leadership, legal issues, and the like) and others who were recommended to me because of their specific expertise on the topic assigned to them. While writing chapters in such a book as well as editing it were a challenge, we thought it came together well. *The Administration of Fraternal Organizations on North American Campuses: A Pattern for the New Millennium* was published in 2003 by College Administration Publications (Gregory, 2003b).

I was very pleased when the coeditors of this text contacted me to let me know that they were putting together a text on college fraternal organizations, and especially pleased when they asked me to write this foreword and a chapter for the book. To the best of my knowledge, since my book was published in 2003, there has been but one other scholarly, book-length, broad-based exploration of these organizations and the issues being faced by them, the changes and growth which have transpired since 2000, and their current status.

Male fraternities, in particular, remain lightning rods for criticism and negative publicity. The North-American Interfraternity conference has faced defections from several large and prestigious fraternities due to organizational and leadership issues. The number of high-profile hazing and alcohol-related deaths spiked in 2017, with 70 deaths since 2000 (Cooper, 2017). The "rape culture" that is alleged to exist within the fraternity system at the University of Virginia was examined as part of the now-debunked and defaming gang rape allegations put forward in the article in *Rolling Stone* magazine. One has only to do an internet search to find articles in several popular media outlets, including *The Atlantic Monthly* (Flanagan, 2014; Flanagan, 2017), *The BBC News* (Cooper, 2017), and *The New York Times Magazine* (Kang, 2017), regarding hazing deaths and negative perceptions about fraternities. In an article on the Great Value College website, the authors ask, is joining a fraternity or sorority a good idea? (n.d.). While the article briefly describes the positive and negative aspects of joining a fraternal organization, the author notes that, "In fact, there has been at least one hazing-induced death each year since 1975 and 82 percent of those deaths were connected to binge drinking"(para. 5). *The Chronicle of Higher Education* studied what happened when universities suspended Greek organizations after hazing deaths (Zamudia-Suaréz, 2017).

A number of primarily small private universities have removed fraternal organizations from their campuses (Schonfeld, 2014), and new calls for the elimination of all fraternal organizations continue to occur in the media (Giacobbe, 2015; Wade, 2017). To say that the case against fraternal organizations is resounding is a profound understatement.

All of the above make this new book critically important for the understanding of, and ability to work with, fraternal organizations in the near and distant future. While, of course, the status of men's social fraternities, particularly those relating to the NIC (North-American Interfraternity Conference) are the most at risk, women's sororities' fates may also attach themselves to the fate of the men's organizations. In my book (Gregory, 2003a) we also addressed issues around HBCU (historically black colleges and universities) organizations, NPC (National Panhellenic Conference) organizations, and what we called the "emerging organizations." These were ethnic-focused organizations focused on LGBTQ students and other similar groups. These organizations have grown and thrived during the 15 years since the writing of the book and have become a very important part of those campuses with strong Asian, Latino, Native American, and other minority populations. It is important that the "Divine Nine" NPHC (National Pan-Hellenic Council) organizations and other organizations of growing importance be considered by Greek Life professionals and scholars as they go about their duties.

While Freedom of Association has been seen as the strong bedrock upon which the existence and growth of fraternal organizations at public institutions can be based, even here there are some cracks in the foundation of such a perception. In a case from the University of Pittsburgh (*Pi Lambda Phi v. University of Pittsburgh*, 2000) the Third Circuit Court ruled that some fraternal organizations do not deserve association protection because their actions, recruitment practices, and other aspects of their operations make them unqualified for such protection. This case has been cited favorably by several other circuits and a number of district courts, but has not garnered Supreme Court attention at this point. However, given the challenges facing fraternity groups, it is possible that an all-out effort to remove such protection may have a negative effect on fraternal organizations writ large.

At the time my book was written, individual campus oversight programs were in vogue (Gregory, 2003a). While they have faded from focus on many campuses as individual fraternal and national/international organizations have introduced their own programs, one of the best that I referred to in the first chapter of the book was from the University of Maryland, College Park. In the Maryland Plan, university officials noted seven purposes that they believed should be shared by all fraternal organizations. These include (a) complementing the academic mission of the college or university; (b) developing leadership among members; (c) service to the community; (d) developing character among members; (e) developing the whole person; (f) building community; and (g) developing lifelong friendships (Greek Life, 1995; Gregory, 2003a). These foci are still at the heart of the fraternal experience and are common to the student development agenda of most campuses. However, our organizations, in many cases, do not live up to those lofty ideals.

Instead, the problems that were pointed out in 2003 still persist and, in some cases, have increased. These include alcohol abuse, hazing, anti-intellectualism, lack of student development within chapters and across campus Greek systems, sexism, racism, and lack of appreciation for diversity (although some gains have been made in these areas, sexism and racism remain large problems) (Gregory, 2003a).

Finally, in 2003, I proposed what I called a "comprehensive worldview" approach for the management of fraternal organizations. Here I noted that management of fraternal organizations ranged along a continuum from campuses in which fraternal organizations existed without much oversight at all (due to lack of staff, lack of financial support, and other factors) to the far end of the spectrum in which campus leaders still believe that *in loco parentis* is still in play regarding fraternal organizations. Neither of these management directions are helpful. I proposed a 10-point plan which, if implemented, could create significant improvement in fraternal organization systems. While some of these proposed elements were carried out, many fell by the wayside; piecemeal approaches taken by individual organizations and individual campuses still prevail. Examining what is necessary for the greater good of fraternal organizations and their host campuses and making needed compromises and concessions take a greater political will than existed then and now. Fifteen years later those vital adjustments still do not exist. To use the vernacular, "it ain't getting any better."

I hope that the ideas and perspectives generated by and reported in these texts will have more influence than did those put forward in 2003. The two texts by Sasso, Biddix, and Miranda (research/foundations and supporting the movement) that follows contains more 35 chapters with about 60 authors. They provide the opportunity for the authors to address many issues around fraternal life and American campuses that host them. Many of those chapters address and update topics that were originally discussed in Gregory (2003) book and thus expand the coverage of the subject. Specific topics include sexual assault; First Amendment issues (e.g., when protected expression becomes unprotected action); recruitment; risk management; the history of various fraternal groups; and a number of other very provocative and interesting topics. The group of authors who are engaged in this process is outstanding, and their amount of experience related to fraternal organizations totals hundreds of years. I encourage readers to take full advantage of the opportunities provided by this text and to take the advice of these authors to heart in order to improve the fraternal experience of all future participants—and to fulfill the promise of the organizations and their founders.

Dennis E. Gregory, EdD

References

Anonymous. (2010). *Baird's manual of American college fraternities*.

Anson, J. L., & Marchesani, R. F. (Eds.). (1991). *Baird's manual of American college fraternities*, 20th ed. Baird's Manual Foundation.

Baird, W. R. (2015). *Baird's manual of American college fraternities, Volume 8*. Arkose Press. ISBN-10: 1343727626

Cooper, K. (2017, November 17). The deadly problem with US college fraternities. *BBC News*. Retrieved from http://www.bbc.com/news/world-us-canada-42014128

DeSantis, A. D. (2007). *Inside Greek U: Fraternities and sororities and the pursuit of pleasure, power, and prestige*. Lexington, KY: The University of Kentucky Press.

Flanagan, C. (2014, March). The dark power of fraternities. *The Atlantic*. Retrieved from https://www.theatlantic.com/magazine/archive/2014/03/the-dark-power-of-fraternities/357580/

Flanagan, C. (2017, November). Death at a Penn State fraternity. *The Atlantic*. Retrieved from
    https://www.theatlantic.com/magazine/archive/2017/11/a-death-at-penn-state/540657/

Giacobbe, A. (2015, July 14). Is it time to ban Greek life? Colleges make a case against
    sororities. *Teen Vogue*. Retrieved from https://www.teenvogue.com/story/banning-
    college-greek-life-sororities

Greek life: A foundation for the future. (1995). College Park, MD: University of Maryland Col-
    lege Park Division of Student Affairs.

Great Value Colleges. (n.d.). Is joining a fraternity or sorority a good idea? Retrieved from
    https://www.greatvaluecolleges.net/faq/is-joining-a-fraternity-or-sorority-a-good-idea/

Gregory, D. E. (2003a). The dilemma facing fraternal organizations at the millennium. In D.
    Gregory (Ed.), *The administration of fraternal organizations on North American campuses:
    A pattern for the new millennium*. Asheville, NC: College Administration Publications.

Gregory, D. E. (2003b). Creating a comprehensive worldview approach to the management
    of fraternal organizations. In D. Gregory (Ed.), *The administration of fraternal organi-
    zations on North American campuses: A pattern for the new millennium*. Asheville, NC:
    College Administration Publications.

Kang, J. C. (2017, August 9). What a fraternity hazing death revealed about the painful search for
    an Asian American identity. *The New York Times*. Retrieved from https://www.nytimes.
    com/2017/08/09/magazine/what-a-fraternity-hazing-death-revealed-about-the-painful-
    search-for-an-asian-american-identity.html

Pi Lambda Phi Fraternity, Inc. v. University of Pittsburgh, 229 F.3d 435 (3d Cir. 2000).

Schonfield, Z. (2014, March 10). Inside the colleges that killed frats for good. *Newsweek*. Re-
    trieved from http://www.newsweek.com/inside-colleges-killed-frats-good-231346

Wade, L. (2017, May 19). Why colleges should get rid of fraternities for good. *Time*. Retrieved
    from http://time.com/4784875/fraternities-timothy-piazza/

Zamudio-Suaréz, F. (2017, November 7). What happened after 3 universities suspended Greek
    life. *The Chronicle of Higher Education*. Retrieved from https://www.chronicle.com/
    article/What-Happened-After-3/241699

PART ONE:

CHALLENGES

CHAPTER 1

New Member Education

Brian Joyce

Introduction

The outcomes of fraternity and sorority membership is an infrequently studied aspect of campus culture, with conflicting views on the impact that fraternal organizations have on their members' personal, academic, and professional development. However, there is even less scholarship fully exploring the differences and outcomes specifically within fraternity and sorority new member education programs.

New member education can often be referred to as pledging, even though most fraternities and sororities have moved away from this term. Pledging is described by Cokley and Wright (1995) as the process of becoming a member of a fraternity or sorority. The pledging process "seeks to acquaint or orient the prospective new member as to the rules, cultures, and beliefs of the group or organization" (p. 5). Many fraternities and sororities have opted instead to recruit prospective members into the organizations as new or associate members, where new members have all the rights and responsibilities of initiated members as a way to reduce the power dynamics inherent within fraternities and sororities and to diminish hazing behaviors associated with the traditional pledging process.

In this chapter, the author will analyze the outcomes of fraternity and sorority membership, the goals of new member education, the differences in race and gender, and the role that alcohol plays in the new member process.

New Member Education Outcomes

Fraternities and sororities have numerous positive effects on the involved student. Members of fraternities and sororities were more involved on campus (Astin, 1993), worked more effectively in groups (Pike & Askew, 1990), possessed increased leadership development skills (Kuh & Lyons, 1990), possessed greater ties to the college or university (McClure, 2006), spent substantially more time participating in co-curricular activities (Asel, Seifert, & Pascarella, 2009), facilitated increased levels of volunteerism and community service (Asel, Seifert, & Pascarella, 2009; Hayek, Carini, O'Day, & Kuh, 2002), and developed increased learning and intellectual development (Astin, 1993; Pascarella & Terenzini, 2005). Students' participation in high impact student organizations like fraternities and sororities facilitated a positive student experience and growth in student learning and personal development (Astin, 1999; Chickering & Reisser, 1993).

Joining a fraternity and sorority provides students an opportunity to join an exclusive network of successful members and alumni/ae. The North American Interfraternity Conference (NIC), the umbrella organization for 74 international and national men's fraternities, highlighted these networking opportunities as one of the primary benefits of membership (NIC website, n.d.). Fraternity men account for 50% of the Top 10 Fortune 500 CEOs. Fraternities also lay claim to 44% of all United States presidents and 31% of United States Supreme Court justices (NIC website, n.d.).

Although there are documented incidents of positive effects on the student experience, fraternities and sororities are highly scrutinized and debated facilitators of student involvement that simultaneously encourage skepticism on their true value toward student growth and development. For example, fraternity and sorority members did not experience the same gains in cognitive outcomes as compared to non-Greek peers (Martin, Hevel, Asel, & Pascarella, 2011), even contributing negatively in some cases, particularly in the first year of college (Pascarella, Edison, Nora, Hagedorn, & Terenzini, 1996). Pike (2003) demonstrated that fraternity and sorority members eventually made positive gains in the senior year of college, but these gains were often in spite of the fraternity and sorority culture, not because of it.

While fraternity and sorority members have higher self-efficacy than their non-affiliated peers, which normally has a strong link to positive academic achievement, fraternity and sorority members' academic performances suffered. Thompson, Oberle, and Lilley (2011) compared self-efficacy, academic effort, GPA, and test scores between 186 fraternity and sorority members and non-affiliated students enrolled in undergraduate psychology courses. While membership in a fraternity or sorority indicated higher self-efficacy and greater academic effort, academic performance did not significantly differ.

There has been significant debate about the overall value of fraternities and sororities in the academic environment (Kuh, Pascarella, and Wechsler, 1996). Hevel, Martin, Weeden, and Pascarella (2015) found no statistically significant general effects on critical thinking, moral reasoning, inclination to inquire and lifelong learning, and psychological well-being. On a positive note, fraternities and sororities did not negatively influence students' educational outcomes, but the findings do not bode well for advocates for fraternities and sororities, who claim the organizations are effective facilitators of student educational outcomes (Hevel et al., 2015).

The Goals of New Member Education

Understanding and measuring fraternal brotherhood can help scholars develop a better understanding of the value of fraternities. McCreary and Schutts (2015) conducted focus group interviews with 14 fraternity undergraduates about brotherhood. The authors identified four themes of brotherhood including solidarity, shared social experiences, sense of belonging, and accountability (McCreary & Schutts, 2015). The need to belong is a valuable and essential component of fraternal life.

In a similarly constructed study in terms of methods and focus as the brotherhood study, Cohen, McCreary, and Schutts (2017) conducted focus groups with sorority women to explore the conceptualization of sisterhood. The sorority women who participated described sisterhood based on shared experiences, support and encouragement, belonging, accountability, and common purpose. As with the previous study, sense of belonging was an essential component of sororities and did not differ by gender.

The need to belong can be so strong that it leads to disastrous results, including hazing, when new member education programs are enacted recklessly. However, a purposeful and intentional new member education process can lead to positive results. When a conceptual leadership framework was used within a fraternity new member education program, there was a significant increase in leadership practice scores in pre- and posttests administered (Posner, 2004). In a quantitative study of 258 participants, fraternity and sorority members were more likely than non-members to believe that new member activities should be positive and had more positive beliefs overall about the purpose of the new member process (Cokley, Miller, Cunningham, Motoike, King, & Awad, 2001).

Asel, Seifert, and Pascarella (2009) suggested a four-year developmental model for fraternities and sororities wishing to develop members academically and developmentally. Many national fraternities and sororities have developed such programs over the years. Lambda Chi Alpha abolished pledging in 1972, developing instead the associate member program, which promoted an anti-hazing culture that gave new members all of the rights and responsibilities of initiated members (n.d.). Lambda Chi went on to develop the True Brother initiative in 2007, which served as a four-year, comprehensive, values-based programming model. Sigma Phi Epsilon created the Balanced Man Program, a four-year, non-pledging, non-hazing developmental program based on equal rights and responsibilities, continuous development, accountability, living the ritual, and mentoring (n.d.). Beta Theta Pi created the Men of Principle Initiative in 1998 to focus on academics, recruitment, risk management, and leadership (n.d.). Zeta Tau Alpha utilized the Links Membership Enrichment Program to offer meaningful, enriching programming during each year of a sister's collegiate journey (Zeta Tau Alpha, n.d.). These are just some of the many positive examples of four-year developmental programs that are productive and meaningful ways of conducting new member education in a purposeful and intentional way.

Differences in Race and Gender

Attitudes about the new member process differ based on race and gender (Cokley & Wright, 1995). In general, sorority women are less supportive of hazing than fraternity men (Ellsworth, 2006). Men were far more likely to believe that new members should undergo a challenging or difficult process to join a fraternity than women reported (Cokley & Wright, 1995). However, male students reported being far more likely to report activities prohibited by law than women.

There were vast racial differences in terms of the culture of new member education. Ninety-four percent of White students disagreed that physical requirements should be part of new member activities (Cokley & Wright, 1995). However, alcohol-related hazing was far more common in traditionally, predominantly White fraternities and sororities than their peers in culturally based groups (Allen & Madden, 2012). Kimbrough (2009) outlined the differences in hazing practices of Black pledges as a humbling process. Black pledges were often made to stand in single file lines, dress alike, and march in a group (Kimbrough, 2009). The results of Cokley and Wright's (1995) study suggested that Black students were more likely than White students to agree that activities such as dressing alike, eating the same food, undergoing mentally or psychologically challenging activities, and subservient behavior should be present in new member activities for fraternities and sororities. However, the pledging process, as it had been known since the 1920s, was banned by all historically Black fraternities and sororities in 1990 (Kimbrough, 2009). In its place was an intensive education period lasting only a few days known as membership intake (Kimbrough, 2009).

The outcomes of fraternity and sorority membership differed by race as well. Hevel, Martin, Weeden, and Pascarella (2015) determined that fraternity and sorority membership had a significant negative influence on White students' critical thinking skills, but had no effect on students of color. In their study, fraternity and sorority membership was correlated with significantly lower levels of moral reasoning for students of color but was significantly higher for White students than for students of color in fraternities and sororities.

In general, students who attended more racially diverse institutions had more racially diverse friends (Park & Kim, 2013), but membership in a fraternity indicated a negative net gain in the value of openness to diversity (Pascarella et al., 1996) and rates of interracial interaction and friendship (Park & Kim, 2013). Fraternities and sororities promoted close personal friendship through tight bonds and activities for members only. In terms of creating racial diversity, the selectivity and exclusive nature of the fraternity and sorority selection process made creating a racially diverse environment a challenge.

The Role of Alcohol in New Member Activities

The single greatest predictor of binge drinking in college is membership in a fraternity (Wechsler, Davenport, Dowdall, Moeykens, & Castillo, 1994). Specifically, fraternity members drink more heavily and more often than non-members (Wechsler, Dowdall, Davenport, & Castillo, 1995). Sorority members are also more at risk for engaging in binge drinking and experiencing the negative repercussions of drinking than non-members (Wechsler, Kuh, & Davenport, 1996). This is particularly true for those members living in the fraternity or sorority house. Sixty-nine percent of residents of a fraternity house and 45% of residents of a sorority house labeled partying and drinking as important activities to them (Wechsler et al., 1996). Fraternity and sorority house residents reported more alcohol-related problems (a hangover, did something they regretted, missed a class, forgot where they were or what they did, etc.) than non-residents and non-members (Wechsler et al., 1996).

At least some of the drinking issues occurring within fraternities and sororities can be attributed to a continuity of drinking patterns prior to college. Students who drink heavily in high school often continue that pattern in college (Borsari & Carey, 1999). Two thirds of fraternity house residents who binge drink in college were binge drinkers in high school (Wechsler et al., 1996). There is a self-selection process that occurs within group membership where potential new members seek out an organization that espouses their own values and beliefs. Experience with heavy drinking and a positive attitude toward heavy drinking environments can lead new college students to seek out fraternities (Borsari & Carey, 1999).

The negative trends in alcohol use among fraternity and sorority members were often even more complicated by the new member process. In a qualitative study with four fraternities, members asserted that their new member processes were dry or alcohol-free (Kuh & Arnold, 1993). Active members of the fraternities were often intoxicated at events, including events that included hazing, but they required new members to abstain unless otherwise directed by the actives to drink, underscoring the power differential between actives and new members (Kuh & Arnold, 1993). This system created a double standard and ironically inflated the influence of alcohol in the socialization of new members (Kuh & Arnold, 1993). Kuh and Arnold found that, "alcohol, which was already viewed as a desirable commodity by 18-year-olds, became even more desirable when it was withheld" (p. 331).

Of course, the new member process is not always dry. The new member processes of fraternities and sororities encourage a socialization of alcohol use that dictates cultural norms of irresponsible and dangerous usage (Wechsler et al., 1996). Numerous studies suggested the strong cultural influence of alcohol in fraternities and sororities is related to the socialization of new members, not just the recruitment of individuals with preestablished negative alcohol behaviors (Asel, Seifert, & Pascarella, 2009; Kuh & Arnold, 1993). According to Kuh and Arnold (1993), students just arriving at a college or university and immediately recruited into a fraternity and sorority are most susceptible to the persuasive peer pressure of fraternities whose "excessive use of alcohol during new member socialization may be so deeply embedded in the psyche of some groups" (p. 333). Alcohol is often used to foster intimacy and unity in group socialization processes, particularly among college men, because of the normative culture of binge drinking in college communities (Nezlek, Pilkington, & Bilbro, 1994).

Conclusion

The fraternity and sorority new member education period is the central group socialization process for fraternity and sorority members. Scholars present conflicting views on the overall value of fraternities and sororities. At best, fraternities and sororities are not a detriment to the learning and development of its members, but there is not strong evidence to suggest that the organizations are adding to members' holistic development. The new member process in particular, and unfortunately sometimes the entire experience, is one that is inextricably intertwined with high-risk alcohol abuse. Untangling alcohol from its deeply rooted influence on the new member experience is and should remain the primary goal of the fraternity and sorority community.

References

Allan, E. J., & Madden, M. (2012). The nature and extent of college student hazing. International Journal of Adolescent Medicine and Health, 24, 83–90.

Asel, A. M., Seifert, T. A., & Pascarella, E. T. (2009). The effects of fraternity/sorority membership on college experiences and outcomes: A portrait of complexity. Oracle: The Research Journal of the Association of Fraternity/Sorority Advisors, 4(2), 1–15.

Astin, A. (1993). What matters in college? Four critical years revisited. San Francisco, CA: Jossey-Bass.

Astin, A. (1999). Student involvement: A developmental theory for higher education. Journal of College Student Development, 40(5), 518–529.

Beta Theta Pi. (n.d.). Men of Principle Initiative. Retrieved from http://beta.org/about/men-of-principle-initiative/

Borsari, B. E., & Carey, K. B. (1999). Understanding fraternity drinking: Five recurring themes in the literature, 1980–1998. Journal of American College Health, 48(1), 30–37.

Chickering, A. W., & Reisser, L. (1993). *Education and identity* (2nd ed.). San Francisco, CA: Jossey-Bass.

Cohen, S., McCreary, G., & Schutts, J. (2017). The conceptualization of sisterhood within the collegiate sorority: An exploration. *Oracle: The Research Journal of the Association of Fraternity/Sorority Advisors, 12*(1), 32–48.

Cokley, K., Miller, K., Cunningham, D., Motoike, J., King, A., & Awad, G. (2001). Developing an instrument to assess college students' attitudes toward pledging and hazing in Greek letter organizations. *College Student Journal 35*(3), 451–462.

Cokley, K., & Wright, D. (1995). *Race and gender differences in pledging attitudes* (ERIC Research Report Accession No. ED 419 999).

Ellsworth, C. W. (2006). Definitions of hazing: Differences among selected student organizations. Oracle: The Research Journal of the Association of Fraternity Advisors, 2(1), 46–60.

Hayek, J., Carini, R., O'Day, P., & Kuh, G. (2002). Triumph or tragedy: Comparing student engagement levels of members of Greek-letter organizations and other students. *Journal of College Student Development, 43,* 643–663.

Hevel, M. S., Martin, G. L., Weeden, D. D., & Pascarella, E. T. (2015). The effects of fraternity and sorority membership in the fourth year of college: A detrimental or value-added component of undergraduate education? *Journal of College Student Development, 56*(5), 456–470.

Kimbrough, W. M. (2009). The membership intake movement of historically black Greek-letter organizations. *NASPA Journal, 46*(4), 603–613.

Kuh, G. D., & Arnold, J. C. (1993). Liquid bonding: A cultural analysis of the role of alcohol in fraternity pledgeship. *Journal of College Student Development, 34,* 327–334.

Kuh, G. D., & Lyons, J. W. (1990). Fraternities and sororities: Lessons from the college experiences study. *NASPA Journal, 28,* 20–29.

Kuh, G. D., Pascarella, E. T., & Wechsler, H. (1996). The questionable value of fraternities. *Chronicle of Higher Education, 42*(32), A68. Retrieved from https://www.chronicle.com/article/The-Questionable-Value-of/97441

Lambda Chi Alpha. (n.d.). History. Retrieved from https://www.lambdachi.org/aboutlca-2/history-2/

Martin, G. L., Hevel, M. S., Asel, A. M., & Pascarella, E. T. (2011). New evidence on the effects of fraternity and sorority affiliation during the first year of college. *Journal of College Student Development, 52*(5), 543–559.

McClure, S. M. (2006). Voluntary association membership: Black Greek men on a predominantly white campus. *The Journal of Higher Education, 77*(6), 1036–1057.

McCreary, G., & Schutts, J. (2015). Toward a broader understanding of fraternity: Developing and validating a measure of fraternal brotherhood. *Oracle: The Research Journal of the Association of Fraternity/Sorority Advisors, 10*(1), 31–50.

Nezlek, J. B., Pilkington, C. J., & Bilbro, K. G. (1994). Moderation in excess: Binge drinking and social facilitation among college students. *Journal of Studies on Alcohol, 55*(3), 342–351.

North American Interfraternity Conference. (n.d.). Fraternity statistics. Retrieved from http://www.nicindy.org/fraternity-statistics.html

Park, J. J., & Kim, Y. K. (2013). Interracial friendship and structural diversity: Trends for Greek, religious, and ethnic student organizations. *The Review of Higher Education, 37*(1), 1–24.

Pascarella, E. T., Edison, M., Nora, A., Hagedorn, L. S., & Terenzini, P. T. (1996). Influences on students' openness to diversity and challenge in the first year of college. *Journal of Higher Education, 67*(2), 174–195.

Pascarella, E. T., & Terenzini, P. T. (2005). *How college affects students: A third decade of research* (Vol. 2). San Francisco, CA: Jossey-Bass.

Pike, G. R. (2003). Membership in a fraternity or sorority, student engagement, and educational outcomes at AAU public research universities. *Journal of College Student Development, 44*(3), 369–382.

Pike, G. R., & Askew, J. W. (1990). The impact of fraternity or sorority membership on academic involvement and learning outcomes. *NASPA Journal, 28*(1), 13–19.

Posner, B. Z. (2004). A leadership development instrument for students: Updated. *Journal of College Student Development, 45*(4), 443–456.

Sigma Phi Epsilon. (n.d.). Balanced Man Program. Retrieved from http://sigep.org/the-sigep-experience/programs/balanced-man-program/

Thompson, J. G., Oberle, C. D., & Lilley, J. L. (2011). Self-efficacy and learning in sorority and fraternity students. *Journal of College Student Development, 52*(6), 749–753.

Wechsler, H., Davenport, A., Dowdall, G. W., Moeykens, B., & Castillo, S. (1994). Health and behavioral consequences of binge drinking in college. *Journal of American Medical Association, 272,* 1672–1677.

Wechsler H, Dowdall G. W., Davenport A, Castillo S. (1995). Correlates of college student binge drinking. American Journal of Public Health, 85, 921–926.

Wechsler, H., Kuh, G., & Davenport, A. (1996). Fraternities, sororities, and binge drinking. *NASPA Journal, 33*(4), 260–279.

Zeta Tau Alpha. (n.d.). Programming. Retrieved from https://zetataualpha.org/about/programming

CHAPTER 2

Fraternity and Sorority Liability and Risk Management

Gregory S. Parks and Sarah J. Spangenburg

THE YEAR 2017 was a challenging one for fraternities, vis-à-vis hazing. The deaths of Timothy Piazza, Maxwell Gruver, and Andrew Coffey sparked a national dialogue and call for reform. In light of these efforts, this chapter explores the different ways that liability arises in the context of fraternity and sorority hazing. While this chapter is not an exhaustive presentation of the ways that liability can potentially arise in hazing cases, it ultimately addresses several ways that liability exists and a more fruitful path forward with respect to risk management.

Hazing Liability

Under negligence theory, a party may be civilly liable where they fail to behave with the level of care that someone of ordinary prudence would have exercised under the same circumstances. To establish a prima facie case of negligence, a plaintiff must show (a) the existence of a legal duty that the defendant owed to the plaintiff; (b) the defendant's breach of that duty; (c) injury to the plaintiff; and (d) proof that defendant's breach caused the injury.

Individual Liability

In some instances, individual actors are civilly liable for hazing. For example, in *Kenner v. Kappa Alpha Psi Fraternity* (2002), Santana Kenner sought membership into Kappa Alpha Psi Fraternity at the University of Pittsburgh. During two chapter meetings that month, members of the fraternity "engaged in psychological and physical hazing of Kenner and other initiates" (p. 180). A few months later, Kenner was told to attend a chapter meeting at a member's apartment. When he arrived, Kenner was greeted by four chapter members who beat him more than two hundred times on the buttocks with paddles. After he was beaten, Kenner noticed his buttocks were numb and his genitals were swollen. He checked into the hospital the next day because he had blood in his urine and swelling in his genitalia. "As a result of the beating, Kenner suffered renal failure, seizures, and hypertension requiring three weeks of hospitalization and kidney dialysis" (p. 180).

Kenner filed a negligence action against individual members and the national fraternity. The defendants moved to have the matter dismissed, which the trial court granted. On appeal, the court held that the individuals did, in fact, owe a duty to Kenner. "Renal failure and the possibility of death" were both found to be foreseeable harms of the initiation process (p. 183). The court went on to state that it is in the public's interest to establish a duty to perform safe intake procedures. Kenner established a prima facie case against one of the individual defendants, and the summary judgment for that defendant was reversed and remanded for trial. He established this prima facie case by setting forth facts alleging that the defendant knew there was a moratorium on hazing; he failed to adequately address this issue at interest meetings for prospective members; he "did not understand the new . . . intake process"; and he "did not take steps to find out what [hazing] activity had occurred after an informational meeting he had conducted" (p. 184). Had he "been more engaged in the [intake] process," Kenner would not have sustained his injuries (p. 184). The court found that these factors were sufficient to survive the defendant's motion to dismiss (2002).

Chapter Liability

Fraternity and sorority chapters can also be held liable for hazing. For example, in *Quinn v. Sigma Rho Chapter of Beta Theta Pi Fraternity* (1987), the Illinois Court of Appeals found that a fraternity chapter owed a duty of care to a pledge who suffered neurological damage from excessive consumption of alcohol during an initiation ceremony. During the ceremony, each pledge had to drink 40 ounces of beer from a pitcher, 8 ounces of whiskey, and additional liquor purchased by the fraternity members. After William Quinn lost consciousness from extreme intoxication, fraternity members brought him back to the fraternity house and left him on a hardwood floor. After sleeping for approximately 14 hours, the plaintiff awoke, found that he "could not properly use his hands or arms," and was taken to a hospital (p. 1195). Quinn alleged in his complaint that he "suffered neurological damage to his arms and hands necessitating the attention of a hospital, doctor, and physical therapist and causing partial disability" (p. 1195). The defendant moved to dismiss, which was granted by the trial court. On appeal, the court determined that the chapter created a legal duty when it required the plaintiff to drink excessive amounts of alcohol in order to become a member, because it was foreseeable that injuries would occur.

National Organization Liability

Some courts are still reluctant to hold national fraternities liable for the actions of chapters. They recognize that it is difficult for national fraternities to monitor the daily actions of every chapter and hold that a chapter involved in hazing is not enough to place liability on the national fraternity outright (*Prime v. Beta Gamma Chapter of Pi Kappa Alpha*, 2002). Among the ways that a national fraternity or sorority can be held negligent for hazing can be through respondeat superior, where the conduct of members can be imputed to the national organization. In addition, negligence can be imputed to national organizations by who they hire, who they retain, or how they train employees. These principles also apply to acts or omissions of nonprofit organizations, including churches, when the organization "solicits volunteers to perform projects on its behalf" (*Allen v. Zion Baptist Church of Braselton*, 2014, p. 611). Lastly, a national organization may be held civilly liable for failing to employ research, data, and best practices to reduce hazing. While there are no published court opinions that analyze these legal doctrines in the context of hazing, a savvy lawyer might seek to employ them.

Respondeat Superior

In the past, cases have relieved nationals from liability for the actions of a chapter if they demonstrated that they were not controlling the local members or had no knowledge of their actions. In contrast, national fraternities that involved themselves with chapters in an effort to control hazing were punished with liability if something went wrong (Sunshine, 2004). In order to address this, courts have been adopting respondeat superior as a theory of liability that can be applicable to national fraternities for their chapter hazing incidents.

Respondeat superior is a theory of liability that holds a master is vicariously liable for the servant's actions vis-à-vis master–servant agency (Sunshine, 2004). Over time, respondeat superior has extended to include national organizations and the local members as their agents, holding the national liable for the locals' actions. Respondeat superior takes away the incentive of national fraternities to disengage from chapters so they are not deemed liable. Instead, the issue becomes "not whether the employer did in fact control and direct the employee in the work, but whether the employer has the right" (p. 131). This prevents national fraternities from turning a blind eye to their locals. In such a context, the master or principal can be held liable regardless if it authorized the actions or not.

In *Ballou v. Sigma Nu* (1986), Sanford Ballou, a University of South Carolina, Sigma Nu pledge, died during the last night of pledge night called "hell night" in which he was left unconscious inside the fraternity house after a night of heavy drinking. At trial, the jury entered a verdict in favor of the father, and the fraternity appealed. The lower court decision was affirmed. Sigma Nu had admitted that the members of its chapters were agents but argued that the actions of these members were outside the scope of the agency relationship. The court rejected the national's argument, stating that the scope of agency includes not only actual authority—that is, specific powers granted to a third party by a principal to act on its behalf—but also apparent authority—that is, where a reasonable third party would understand that an agent had authority to act. The court further noted that Sigma Nu set out the guidelines for the initiation of new fraternity members and allowed supplementation of that initiation process. As such, the chapter exercised its apparent authority in creating hell night as part of its initiation process and that this was supposedly in furtherance of their goal to admit new members, meaning that these actions were under the scope of the agency relationship.

Negligent Hiring

The analysis begins at the initial decision to hire an employee. Factors to consider in weighing whether an employer took reasonable care in making its hiring decision can include the reasonableness of the investigation conducted by the employer into the employee's background, in light of the job for which the employee is hired, and the risk of harm or injury to third parties (Green, 1998). The employer can protect itself from claims of negligent hiring by ensuring that the applicant is competent and qualified to do all related job duties (Lienhard, 1996). After all, courts agree that hiring despite actual knowledge of the dangerous propensities of an employee may be sufficient to constitute a breach of the employer's duty to hire fit employees; many courts are willing to find a breach of employer duty where a reasonable investigation into the background of the employee would have alerted the employer of the danger.

Negligent hiring cannot be invoked where there is no duty owed by the employer. Thus, first it must be established whether the employer owed a duty to the plaintiff to exercise reasonable care in hiring and retaining employees. While the threshold is constantly changing, the court in *DiCosala v. Kay* (1982, pp. 517–518) posed it as "whether a reasonably prudent and careful person, under the same or similar circumstances, should have anticipated that an 'injury to the plaintiff or to those in a like situation would probably result' from his conduct." This means that an employer's duty extends not only to customers but anyone reasonably foreseeable that could be injured. [1] Once a duty to the plaintiff is established, the plaintiff in a negligent hiring action has the burden of proving: (a) that the defendant employed the tortfeasor; (b) that the employee was unfit or incompetent for his position; (c) that the employer knew or should have known that the employee was unfit or incompetent; (d) that an act or omission of the employee actually caused the plaintiff's injuries; (e) that the employer's negligence in hiring or retaining the employee proximately caused the plaintiff's injuries; and (f) that the plaintiff was actually harmed (Minuti, 1988).

The first element, employment, should not be difficult to prove. Things like the payment of wages, the power to hire and terminate, and the power to control the individual's conduct can indicate an employment relationship (*Dovell v. Arundel Supply Corp.*, 1966). The second and third elements will be highly fact-based, focused on whether the employee was able to perform the job in a safe and competent manner, whether the person was properly licensed to perform job duties, whether there was anything in his background (criminal or character) that would have indicated he had dangerous tendencies; then whether the employer knew or should have known this information from a reasonable inquiry (*Jones v. Toy*, 1985; Minuti, 1988; *Murray v. Modoc State Bank*, 1957). A potential employee's character, reputation, and prior employment references are considered not only important but admissible as evidence when showing that the employer possessed evidence of the employee's unfitness (Minuti, 1988). The fourth and fifth elements of causation are also intertwined. The evidence of unsuitability in the employee's background must be related to the harm caused. For example, in *Argonne Apartment House Co. v. Garrison* (1930), an employer was not found liable for negligent hiring when his repairman, hired despite a conviction for intoxication, committed theft. Finally, the plaintiff must have actually suffered harm from the employee's inability to properly do the job. Simply hiring someone incapable of doing a job, while not a sound business decision, is not a tort. That decision must cause actual harm to a person.

Negligent Retention

The differentiating factor between negligent hiring and negligent retention is when the employer knew of an employee's unfitness for a position. If, after taking reasonable steps during the hiring process, the hiring decision is made, a shift into negligent retention can occur. An employer may be negligent for retaining an unfit or incompetent employee if, during the course of employment, the employer "becomes aware or should have become aware of problems with an employee that indicated his unfitness," and the employer fails to address that employee's violent propensities (*Garcia v. Duffy*, 1986, pp. 438–439). Through post-hiring conduct or facts that come to light after the hiring decision was made, actual or constructive notice by the employer of an employee's risks to others triggers a response requirement (*Yunker v. Honeywell, Inc.*, 1993, p. 424). Employers have a duty to not only screen potential employees but to continually monitor them for events that indicate they might be harmful or unqualified. [2] Courts emphasize that the length of the employee's relationship with the employer is important when analyzing negligent retention (*Witover v. Celebrity Cruises*, 2016).

Negligent Training

Negligent training is different than the other negligence actions in that it focuses on the duty an employer has to train their employees in a reasonable way that will allow them to perform their job responsibilities without causing harm to themselves or others. In order for a third party to demonstrate a prima facie case for negligent training, the plaintiff must show that: (a) the employer owed a duty to prevent harm to the plaintiff resulting from the tortious acts of an employee; (b) that this duty was breached by the employer; (c) that the breach of this duty was a proximate cause of the plaintiff's injuries; and (d) that the act of the employee would be considered a tort (*Brijall v. Harrah's Atl. City*, 2012; *Okeke v. Biomat USA, Inc.*, 2013). The employer is not necessarily required to anticipate the injuries that a third party would sustain as a result of their training, but the injury to the third party must have been a foreseeable result of their failure to train their employee properly and there must be a direct relationship between the improper training and the injuries sustained (*Clark v. Knochenhauer*, 2015; *Employer—Employee*, 2017). It is not enough for a plaintiff to point out the flaws in the employer's training program; the plaintiff must establish a breach of duty in training its employee that is causally linked to the plaintiff's harm. Additionally, some states require the plaintiff to demonstrate more than the prima facie elements of negligence; in New York, in order for a plaintiff to state a claim for direct negligence,

> [the] plaintiff must show: (1) that the tort-feasor and the defendant were in an employee–employer relationship; (2) that the employer knew or should have known of the employee's propensity for the conduct which caused the injury prior to the injury's occurrence; and (3) that the tort was committed on the employer's premises or with the employer's chattels. (*Tsesarskaya v. City of New York*, 2012, p. 463–464)

Some courts also hold that a plaintiff must take an extra step in demonstrating that an employer has negligently trained an employee. The plaintiff must provide testimony on the proper standard of care for the specific training that the employer is providing. One example is the recent decision made by the Supreme Court of Iowa in *Alcala v. Marriot International, Inc.* (2016) in which the court held that the plaintiff needed proof of the standard of care or of breach of the standard of care in regard to the defendant's training in order to establish a claim for negligent training. The court based its reasoning on decisions of other jurisdictions that have held that negligent training claims fail if there is not testimony to demonstrate the training standard for the employment that is in dispute (*Alcala v. Marriot International, Inc.*, 2016). Since the plaintiff's burden to establish a negligent training claim can vary between states, when an employee seeks to establish that negligent training occurred, it is vital to understand the state law on the subject.

Technologically Feasible/Artificially Below Standard Solutions

A fraternity or sorority national organization may contend that they have made their best effort to reduce hazing within their ranks. They may indicate that their approach has been consistent and on par with other similarly situated organizations in their industry. In essence, fraternities and sororities may defend their risk management and hazing reduction practices by noting that they have employed the "state of the art" or customary practices in the "Greek" community. This argument is not unlike many made by manufacturers in tort product liability cases. However, for fraternities and sororities this argument may be unavailing.

Under general principles of tort law, a manufacturer bears strict liability for injury resulting from its product, if the product's design is "defective" (Urban, 1990). "A product is defective in design if (1) the foreseeable risks of the design exceed the benefits, or (2) the product is more dangerous than an ordinary consumer would expect when used in a reasonably foreseeable way" (*Clay v. Ford Motor Co.*, 2000, p. 669). Courts use this risk benefit test to determine if the risks of the design were foreseeable, and factors that the court considers include:

> [T]he nature and magnitude of the risks in light of the intended and reasonably foreseeable uses of the product; the likely awareness of the product's users of those risks; the likelihood that the design would cause harm in light of its intended and reasonably foreseeable uses; and the extent to which the product conformed to any applicable product standards that were in effect when it left its manufacturer. (p. 669)

When considering the second option to prove product defect (reasonable consumer expectations), courts have held that "proof that a product could have feasibly and practicably been designed more safely is proof that the product failed to meet reasonable consumer expectations" (*McCathern v. Toyota Motor Corp.*, 1999, p. 810). Under this approach, a plaintiff "must present evidence from which the jury could find the availability of a safer practicable alternative design" (p. 810).

A party that has a tort claim brought against it may defend itself by providing evidence as to the state-of-the-art practice in its industry and its conformity to such practices.

> [S]tate-of-the-art evidence . . . is properly admissible to establish that a product is not defective and unreasonably dangerous because of a failure-to-warn . . . of dangers that were not known to [the manufacturer] or knowable in light of the generally recognized and prevailing scientific and technical knowledge available at the time of the manufacture and distribution. (*Fireboard Corp. v. Fenton*, 1993, 1172).

However, this evidence must be weighed against the standard of care for such manufacturers. The standard of care attributed to a manufacturer is that of an "expert in [the] field . . . [who] has a duty 'to keep abreast of scientific knowledge, discoveries and advances'" and "'is under a duty to make tests to ascertain the nature of its product[s]'" (*George v. Celotex Corp.*, 1990, p. 28). Courts have held that "'[i]n this scientific age the manufacturer undoubtedly has or should have superior knowledge of his product'" (p. 28).

Although courts are to consider a manufacturer's compliance with industry standards, it has been held that courts "must also remember that those standards may sometimes merely reflect an industry's laxness, inefficiency, or inattention to innovation" (*Elliott v. Brunswick Corp.*, 1990, p. 1508). Therefore, a manufacturer may not solely rely on industry practice in fulfilling its duties. In fact, to allow a manufacturer to rely solely on industry practice would allow the industry to set its own standard of care. Furthermore, "the industry may be lagging behind in its knowledge about a product, or in what, with the exercise of reasonable care, is knowable about a product" (*George v. Celotex Corp.*, 1990, p. 28). Overall, courts have agreed that customary practice and state of the art in an industry may be an artificially low bar when determining these cases (*Favalora v. Aetna Casualty & Surety Co.*, 1962; *Townsend v. Kiracoff*, 1982).

Hypothetical: Zeta Zeta Zeta Fraternity (Tri-Zeta) has had decades of hazing issues fraught with physical violence and excessive alcohol use. Tri-Zeta's approach to addressing this issue was to use a little research, data, and best practices here and there but to more generally throw ideas against the wall and hope they stick. In an effort to address the issue, Tri-Zeta hired Eric to be its national Risk Management Director. Eric had never been trained in risk management and had no degree in the area nor any certificates. In fact, Eric knew very little about risk management; he had been hired because he was a close friend and supporter of Tri-Zeta's National President. Eric's on-the-job training consisted of looking information up on Google and catching whatever information he could at various student affairs and Greek-life conferences. Eric played a critical role in developing Tri-Zeta's risk management policy.

At the local level, each of Tri-Zeta's college chapters was assigned a local advisor who was an alum of Tri-Zeta. Advisors had to go through web-based training once a year. The training was an hour and consisted of 30 PowerPoint slides that provided basic information about fraternity and sorority-related liability issues, including hazing. Advisors were never tested on their knowledge. Aaron served as advisor to Big State University's Tri-Zeta chapter.

Three pledges to the Tri-Zeta chapter at Big State University died one evening as a result of hazing. Their estates sued Tri-Zeta, claiming, among other things, that Tri-Zeta hired Eric and knew or should have known that he was unqualified for the Risk Management Director job when they hired him and, nonetheless, retained him. They also claimed that Tri-Zeta inadequately trained both Eric and Aaron, and that Tri-Zeta's conduct was the proximate cause of their sons' deaths.

Rethinking Risk Management

In response to the escalating threats associated with hazing, fraternities and sororities created and adhere to risk management rules (Kimzey, 1997). Contemporarily, the roots of risk management started in 1921 with economist Frank H. Knight, when he established that risk arises from randomness but is affected by knowable probabilities. More influential risk management research began after World War II, as it has been associated with market insurance and protection of companies from losses (Dionne, 2013). With regard to hazing, the fraternity and sorority industry may have "risk" management all wrong. Consider that in February 2002, U.S. Secretary of Defense Donald Rumsfeld responded to a question at a U.S. Department of Defense news briefing about the lack of evidence that would link the Iraqi government with supplying weapons of mass destruction to terrorist groups. He noted:

> Reports that say that something hasn't happened are always interesting to me, because as we know, there are known-knowns; there are things we know we know. We also know there are known-unknowns; that is to say we know there are some things we do not know. But there are also unknown-unknowns—the ones we don't know we don't know. And if one looks throughout the history of our country and other free countries, it is the latter category that tend to be the difficult ones.

The question for the fraternity and sorority industry is whether they are grappling with known-knowns, known-unknowns, or unknown-unknowns. In short, are they dealing with "risk" or something else much more challenging?

Decisions that have multiple outcomes with differing, measurable values imply that individuals are making choices with risk. Knight (1921) emphasizes that risk involves possibilities that can be measured and includes more information than ambiguous situations, giving organizations the potential to make a better decision. The numerical probability of occurrence of a group of instances can be reached through calculations or from knowledge of past experiences (Knight, 1921). While this arrival at a decision does not create complete certainty, decisions can be made based on the odds of a specific outcome (Schendel, 2007). Conversely, ambiguity is a situation in which an individual cannot know or measure the probability of an event. Because of the unique attributes of a situation, it is improbable to create a group of outcomes that could occur (Knight, 1921). This type of uncertainty involves a lack of information that makes organizations less confident when making a choice. This unmeasurable uncertainty, commonly referred to as Knightian uncertainty, emphasizes aversion from making decisions when the outcomes cannot be estimated. The first branch of ambiguity is asymmetric knowledge, where one group knows more than the other, leaving a party uncertain in their decision. Often this situation occurs in an unpredictable corporate environment, where there are many extraneous organizational variables that impact decision makers (Miller, 1992).

Regarding hazing, so little appears to be known about its root causes that it seems less like the management of "risk" and more like the management of "ambiguity." This distinction seems critical to how fraternities and sororities deal with hazing and how they could address it more effectively. In unfamiliar contexts, individuals tend to attempt to draw conclusions and feel a lack of confidence when past knowledge does not clarify the situation. When decision makers know they are missing information, they attempt to rule out the unknowns, but if uncertainties still exist the situation is ambiguous. Individuals will attempt to create more confidence in their decisions by converting a nonquantitative situation into a measurable risk. Individuals can handle risk by diversifying, avoiding the regret of negative outcomes from past risky decisions, and emotionally separating themselves from the choice process. Being rational in decision-making involves an individual making selections that best reach the goal, regardless of what this outcome is. One perspective, the coherence view of decision-making, emphasizes the importance of logical reasoning and the process (Reyna & Farley, 2006).

Knight highlights the combination of perception and inference in eliminating uncertainty. First one must obtain knowledge by being conscious of the circumstances in which the decision is being made, then they must infer what the future situation will produce statically (Knight, 1921). Then the decision maker can create probabilities in order to alter this static outcome. In situations where information is missing, organizations should try to transition from the ambiguous uncertainty to a choice only involving risk. To make this transition, decision makers can rely on past information that assists in estimating. Retrospective trends help individuals convert ambiguity to risk, giving them a level of confidence in their choices. However, organizations still resist these risky decisions because the probabilities used are from the past and create a new type of uncertainty influencing decisions. Foresight leads to additional issues in accuracy because of the time it takes to produce these predictions and the distance from when the past situation occurred (Knight, 1921). Reduction of risk in one area can lead to an increase in uncertainty in others, referred to as trade-off risk management (Miller, 1992).

Through flexibility individuals can adapt to change, rather than avoid it, and increase internal responsiveness for the future (Miller, 1992). Uncertainty can be continuously managed through information production that permits the creation of models (Knight, 1921). Information production allows individuals to draw inferences based on patterns that can reduce risk when converted to models predicting future outcomes. Through diversification, decision makers rely on the "pattern" of randomness to assure that at least one of their risky decisions will provide a positive result. The more diverse decisions an individual makes, the more likely the possibility of an outcome benefiting the decision maker (Knight, 1921). For insurance companies, this method is utilized with the assumption that dealing with groups, rather than individual cases, will lessen the amount of risk possible. Organizations purchase insurance to protect against property losses, and the insurance company chooses to diversify the companies they provide for to lessen their losses and having to cover the cost (Miller, 1992).

After using knowns to convert ambiguous situations to decisions only involving risk, organizations can use models, diversification, and risk avoidance to manage uncertainties and have confidence in making these decisions. By creating self-insurance or setting aside resources to cover the costs of a poor decision, individuals utilize risk avoidance to manage uncertainties (Miller, 1992). Additionally, they can use specialization to transfer the risk to someone with more knowledge of the situation, using the judgment of other individuals more suited to make a certain decision (Knight, 1921). Evidently the most common method for dealing with risk is securing better knowledge of the future and consolidating the imminent risks to give the burden to those more capable of choosing a course of action.

If hazing is a complex issue with a multitude of factors that undergird and propel it, the only way to begin to address it is to: (a) develop a depth of understanding about it; (b) consider the variety of elements that drive it; and (c) understand how those elements interact with one another. Here, the authors employ three tools toward this end—that is, sensemaking, design thinking, and the socio-ecological model. Sensemaking, first conceptualized by Karl E. Weick, consists of structuring the unknown, as well as putting stimuli into frameworks in order "to comprehend, understand, explain, attribute, extrapolate, and predict" (1995, p. 4). Design thinking has been employed as another process for better understanding the world around us and, especially, the challenges within organizations. Design thinking draws upon logic, imagination, intuition, and systemic reasoning to explore innovative problem-solving (Coakley, Roberto, & Segovis, 2014). While sensemaking and design thinking provide processes for innovative problem-solving, the socio-ecological model provides a framework within which processes might fit. Under systems thinking "the system of any individual concept, or that concept's 'ecology,' is made up of content and context, where content is defined as the set of symbolic or informational variables in a conceptual space" (Cabrera, Colosi, & Lobdell, 2008, p. 303). Building on this theory, Urie Bronfenbrenner defined human development "as the person's evolving conception of the ecological environment, and his [sic] relation to it, as well as the person's growing capacity to discover, sustain, or alter its properties" (Ungar & Richter, 2013, p. 348). Bronfenbrenner's ecological systems model consists of four environmental levels, with each level impacting differently the development of each person: (a) the microsystem; (b) the mesosystem; (c) the exosystem; and (d) the macrosystem (Onwuegbuzie, Collins, & Frels, 2013). Specifically, identify factors that emerge from the individual, small groups, the organization, and the broader culture.

Conclusion

This chapter aimed to offer insight into the ways that liability can arise in the context of hazing in fraternities and sororities. While it is not exhaustive, the reader should now understand that liability in these circumstances is possible in many different ways, and actors that allow hazing to occur can be held liable one way or another. This should encourage those that can deter hazing to institute methods and policies that aim to eliminate hazing within fraternities and sororities. This can be done through a more systematic approach to understanding the problem and employing research, data, and best practices.

Notes

1. Additionally, another commentator laid out the following components for any third party person injured by an employee: (1) the employee and the plaintiff were in places where each had a right to be when the wrongful act occurred; (2) the plaintiff met the employee as a direct result of the employment; and (3) the employer received some benefit, even if only potential or indirect, from the meeting of the employee and the plaintiff (North, 1977).
2. For additional discussion and cases, see Witover v. Celebrity Cruises, 161 F. Supp. 3d 1139, 1148 (S.D. Fla. 2016); Gaughan v. Crawford, 2009 WL 631983, at *1 (March 10, 2009); Poplin v. Bestway Express, 286 F. Supp. 2d 1316, 1318 (M.D. Ala. 2003); Cruz v. New York, 24 F.Supp.3d 299 (W.D.N.Y. 2014); Mumford v. Carnival Corporation, 7 F. Supp. 3d 1243 (S.D. Fla. 2014); Peterson v. Miranda, 991 F. Supp. 2d 1109 (D. Nev. 2014).

References

Alcala v. Marriot Inter., Inc., 880 N.W.2d 699 (Iowa 2016).

Allen v. Zion Baptist Church of Braselton, 328 Ga. App. 208, 761 S.E.2d 605 (2014).

Argonne Apartment House Co. v. Garrison, 42 F.2d 605 (D.C. Cir. 1930).

Ballou v. Sigma Nu General Fraternity, 291 S.C. 140 (S.C. 1986).

Brijall v. Harrah's Atl. City, 905 F. Supp. 2d 617 (D.N.J. 2012).

Cabrera, D., Colosi, L., & Lobdell, C. (2008). Systems thinking. *Evaluation & Program Planning, 31*, 299–310.

Clark v. Knochenhauer, No. MMXCV146011914, 2015 WL 7941283, at *3 (Conn. Super. Ct. Nov. 12, 2015).

Clay v. Ford Motor Co., 215 F.3d 663 (6th Cir. 2000).

Coakley, L. A., Roberto, M. A., & Segovis, J. C. (2014). Meeting the challenge of developing innovative problem-solving students using design thinking and organizational behavior concepts. *Business Education Innovation Journal, 6*, 34–43.

Department of Defense News Briefing Transcript. (Feb. 12, 2002). Retrieved from http://archive.defense.gov/Transcripts/Transcript.aspx?TranscriptID=1939

DiCosala v. Kay, 91 N.J. 159, 450 A.2d 508 (1982).

Dionne, G. (2013). Risk management: History, definition, and critique. *Risk Management and Insurance Review, 16*, 147–166.

Dovell v. Arundel Supply Corp., 361 F.2d 543 (D.C. Cir. 1966), cert. denied, 385 U.S. 841 (1966).

Elliott v. Brunswick Corporation, 903 F.2d 1505 (11th Cir. 1990).

Employer—Employee, 30 C.J.S. § 205 (2017).

Favalora v. Aetna Casualty & Surety Co., 144 So.2d 544 (La. App. 1962).

Fireboard Corp. v. Fenton, 845 P.2d 1168 (Colo. 1993).

Garcia v. Duffy, 492 So. 2d 435 (Fla. Dist. Ct. App. 1986).

George v. Celotex Corp., 914 F.2d 26 (2nd Cir. 1990).

Green, R. M. (1998) *Negligent hiring: An emerging theory of employer liability for employee misconduct*. Philadelphia, PA: The American Law Institute.

Jones v. Toy, 476 So.2d 30 (Miss. 1985).

Kenner v. Kappa Alpha Psi Fraternity, Inc., 808 A.2d 178 (Pa. Super. Ct. 2002).

Kimzey, S. (1997). The role of insurance in fraternity litigation. *Review of Litigation, 16*, 459–490.

Knight, F. H. (1921). *Risk, uncertainty, and profit*. Mineola, NY: Dover Publications, Inc.

Lienhard, R. (1996). Negligent retention of employees: An expanding doctrine. *Defense Counsel Journal, 63*, 389–395.

McCathern v. Toyota Motor Corp., 985 P.2d 804 (Or. Ct. App. 1999).

Miller, K. D. (1992). A framework for integrated risk management in international business. *Journal of International Business Studies, 23*, 311–331.

Minuti, M. (1988). Employer liability under the doctrine of negligent hiring: Suggested methods for avoiding the hiring of dangerous employees. *Delaware Journal of Corporate Law, 13*, 501–536.

Murray v. Modoc State Bank, 181 Kan. 642, 313 P.2d 304 (1957).

North, J. C. (1977). The responsibility of employers for the actions of their employees: The negligent hiring theory of liability. *Chicago-Kent Law Review, 53*, 717–730.

Okeke v. Biomat USA, Inc., 927 F. Supp.2d 1021 (D. Nev. 2013).

Onwuegbuzie, A. J., Collins, K. M. T., & Frels, R. K. (2013). Foreword to using Bronfenbrenner's Ecological Systems Theory to frame quantitative, qualitative, and mixed research. *International Journal of Multiple Research Approaches, 7,* 2–8.

Prime v. Beta Gamma Chapter of Pi Kappa Alpha, 47 P.3d 402 (Kan. 2002).

Quinn v. Sigma Rho Chapter of Beta Theta Pi Fraternity, 507 N.E.2d 1193 (Ill. App. Ct. 1987).

Reyna, V. F., & Farley, F. (2006). Risk and rationality in adolescent decision making: Implications for theory. *Psychological Science in the Public Interest Archive, 7,* 1–44.

Schendel, Dan. (2007). Risk and uncertainty. *Strategic Entrepreneurship Journal, 1,* 53–55.

Sunshine, J. S. (2014). A Lazarus Taxon in South Carolina: A natural history of national fraternities' respondeat superior liability for hazing, *Charlotte Law Review, 5,* 79–138.

Townsend v. Kiracoff, 545 F.Supp. 465 (D. Colo. 1982).

Tsesarskaya v. City of New York, 843 F. Supp. 2d 446 (S.D. N.Y. 2012).

Ungar, M., Ghazinour, M., & Richter, J. (2013). Annual research review: What is resilience within the social ecology of human development. *Journal of Child Psychology and Psychiatry, 54,* 348–366.

Urban, D. A. (1990). Custom's proper role in strict liability actions based on design defect. *UCLA Law Review, 38,* 439–488.

Weick, K. E. (1995). *Sensemaking in organizations.* Foundations for organizational science. Thousand Oaks, CA: Sage Publications.

Witover v. Celebrity Cruises, 161 F. Supp. 3d 1139 (S.D. Fla. 2016).

Yunker v. Honeywell, Inc., 496 N.W.2d 419 (Minn. Ct. App. 1993).

CHAPTER 3

Mental and Emotional Health: Understanding the Present, Enhancing the Future

Monica G. Burke and Aaron W. Hughey

I stared out of the window of the psychiatric ward in utter disbelief that my freshman year of college had ended after only two months. I went to American University with so much hope. College was going to be the place where I moved forward with my life. A setting where I could meet new people, make new friends, and finally get out of my small town. I was also hoping to no longer be haunted by my bipolar disorder that plagued me in high school. Unfortunately, the change to a new environment brought out the worst episodes I had ever seen.

—ROSS SZABO (2018)

ALTHOUGH THIS KIND of experience is certainly not commonplace among college students who choose to become involved in the Greek system on campus, the mental and emotional well-being among this cohort has come under increasing scrutiny in recent years (University of Michigan, n.d.). Mental and emotional health is a core component for all human beings that is essential for our overall health and functioning. When our mental and emotional health is in a good state, we manage our basic cognitive and social skills; recognize, express, and modulate our emotions; are flexible and able to cope with adverse life events; function in social roles; and modulate a harmonious relationship between our body and mind (Galderisi, Heinz, Kastrup, Beezhold, & Sartorius, 2015).

However, mental health issues can occur when an individual experiences diminished capacities—cognitive, emotional, attentional, interpersonal, motivational, or behavioral—that interfere with their enjoyment of life or adversely affect interactions with society and the environment (Stephens, Dulberg, & Joubert, 1999). These issues can be manifested in various ways, such as feelings of low self-esteem, stress, or excessive worrying; recurrent frustration or irritability; and burnout (Stephens et al., 1999). In reality, mental health is a dimension of the Greek community that has not been closely examined in the past (Scott-Sheldon, Carey, & Carey, 2007).

For college students, life is filled with new opportunities to grow and learn. However, anxiety, fear, worry, disappointment, sadness, and anger are as much a part of life as joy, passion, curiosity, delight, and contentment, as growing and learning often involve unpleasant as well as pleasant emotions (Burke, Sauerheber, Hughey, & Laves, 2017). Along with freedom and independence, college students must manage multiple experiences and stressors—that is, academics, social belonging, expectations, relationships, finances, and pressures regarding future success—which place them at a greater risk for poor mental and emotional health maintenance. Consequently, stress and anxiety have been identified as common emotions college students experience that impact them behaviorally, cognitively, and physiologically. Among all the mental and emotional conditions associated with the college student population in general and the Greek life community in general, depression is most often cited as a potential concern (McNamara, 2016).

Furthermore, as Szabo and Hall (2018) note,

> The stigma surrounding mental health is less now than it was in the decades before it. I think part of the reason this is more discussed is because we have learned more about the brain in the past two years than we did in all of the thousands of years before that. People are willing to share their stories and organizations are running effective promotional campaigns. Colleges are seeing their counseling centers flooded with students who need help and research is teaching us more about the issues students are facing. I think this combination of decreased stigma and more research is leading to this topic being discussed as much as it is. (para. 7)

Whereas the number of college students who seek counseling for mental and emotional concerns has increased dramatically in recent years (Rudavsky, 2018), it is unclear as to whether this percentage is mirrored in the Greek community. Indeed, research into the mental and emotional health of members of the Greek community has been somewhat inconclusive (National Council on Disability, 2017). This gap in knowledge is reiterated by Reifman (2011), who noted that the (potentially) attitudinal/behavioral differences seen years later between college alumni who did and those who did not participate in the fraternity/sorority system reflect their pre-college personalities and not the actual experience of being in a Greek organization; therefore, any research purporting to show effects of fraternity/sorority participation should be taken with caution. Still, the statistics are cause for concern, as Arroyo (2015) points out:

> Fraternities and sororities aren't perfect, but they have the potential to equip their members to handle mental health challenges better than other parts of a college campus ... Fraternity and sorority chapters are affected by suicide, substance abuse, mental health disorders and other extreme issues. (para. 1)

In fact, in Spring 2018, the National College Health Assessment (American College Health Association, 2018) reported that about one-third (33.2%) of college students identified stress as a primary cause for impaired academic performance at some point in their past year, with anxiety (26.5%) also noted as an influence. In total, more than half of the students (57.6%) reported more than average or tremendous stress and overwhelming anxiety (63.4%) within the last 12 months. Some students have reported being diagnosed with post-traumatic stress disorder (PTSD) because of their involvement with Greek organizations on campus, as observed in the following account posted by Osby (2015):

> Looking back, I never would've associated PTSD with pledging a BLGO [Black Greek Letter Organization], but with so many failed attempts at controlling the underground hazing process and so many eager college students seeking new experiences and their desire to belong, it all makes sense. Many kids have died trying to pledge, and I wonder how many more mental casualties there have been, caused by those who perform ritualistic hazing processes. How many emotional scars have been left on the hearts of those who chose to walk away? I've never been to war, but I bear the scars of someone who survived the terror of an organization that wasn't so much about sisterhood after all. (para. 40)

It should be noted that even though this chapter does not specifically deal with the ongoing problem of hazing among Greek organizations on college campuses, it is important to recognize that this practice can have a deleterious effect on the mental and emotional health of fraternity and sorority members, as noted by Apgar and Szabo (n.d.). They point out that many students are aware of the physical risks or the legal ramifications of hazing, but most are oblivious to the mental harm hazing can cause. Hazing activities can trigger mental health problems in a short time span, leading to a relapse of a mental disorder for some or causing a breakdown that could take years to recover from, if ever.

As alluded to previously, the anecdotal evidence is mixed regarding the impact belonging to a fraternity or sorority can have on an individual student. Although Osby (2015) obviously had a bad experience, other students such as Moore (2017) seem to have a more optimistic assessment of what involvement in Greek organizations has to offer:

> I know it's hard. Coming out and telling people about my depression has
> been one of the hardest things I have ever done, however, I found out I was
> not alone, and that helped more than anyone could ever know. I had sisters
> that let me stay with them when my world felt like it was falling apart. I had
> other sisters who told me about their struggle with mental illness. I also had
> some girls send me an encouraging text, just to make me smile. (para. 8)

In line with Moore's experience, oftentimes social supports and other relationships can be helpful in promoting positive emotional support for individuals (Phi Delta Theta, 2018). Participating in Greek-letter organizations can help students build new friendships and connections as well as assist with their feelings of acceptance (Taylor, 2010) and provide other benefits such as greater self-efficacy (Wilder, Hoyt, Surbeck, Wilder, & Carney, 1986), increased self-esteem (Bohnert, Aikins, & Edidin, 2007), increased confidence (Robbins, 2004), and developed leadership skills (Hughes & Winston, 1987). However, Greek life can also be associated with risky behaviors and health issues, such as more alcohol use, cigarette smoking, sexual partners, and sex under the influence of drugs or alcohol than the average college student, which can potentially lead to increased stress (Scott-Sheldon & Carey, 2008).

In addition, Greek-life membership includes a major commitment for college students accompanied by social and financial obligations. For example, in sorority life, Robbins (2004) noted that belonging to the group and the urge to fit in can be exhausting and terrifying, leading some new girls to go to great lengths to conform and blend in as quickly and flawlessly as possible while maneuvering in an atmosphere of conformity, intolerance, a a heavy reliance on men for social validation, time, and financial commitments. These factors can also lead to stress, eating disorders, and anxiety. The author asserted, "for every girl who emerges from a sorority with improved self-esteem, there are numerous others whose confidence has been crushed" (Robbins, 2004, p. 320).

Moreover, those who assume leadership roles within Greek organizations are also subject to additional stressors that can lead to mental and emotional health challenges. College students who participate in leadership activities and take on a leadership role in an organization demonstrate higher gains and growth in decision-making skills and conflict resolution skills than students not involved; increased ability to deal with complexity, uncertainty, ambiguity, and growth in goal setting and civic responsibility; and a dedication to developing leadership skills for others around them (Cress, Astin, Zimmerman-Oster, & Burkhardt, 2001); however, some members of Greek Life may be faced with stressors at times (i.e., financial cost for dues and required events; time commitment for activities, events, and meetings; expectation to uphold minimum or high GPAs; and community involvement). Although a certain level of stress is necessary and results in optimal performance (Yerkes & Dodson, 1908), too much stress can lead to health problems, and stressors can influence mood, sense of well-being, behavior, and health (Schneiderman, Ironson, & Siegel, 2005). Anxiety is a way an individual reacts to stress which can affect them behaviorally, cognitively, and physiologically (Kazdin, 2000), often experienced, for example, via panic attacks, increased sleep problems, or increased blood pressure (Schneiderman, Ironson, & Siegel, 2005) that interfere with students' daily life and possibly relationships.

An additional consideration when investigating the mental and emotional health of the Greek community involves intervening characteristics that may confound the research. For example, being a member of the LGBTQIA community can be a factor in how stress manifests itself. Within the Division of Student Affairs and Enrollment Services at the University of Houston (2017), Lambda10 is a resource that advises members how to come out to their brothers or sisters and provides information on how to express acceptance to their brothers and sisters. In addition, on campus is Gamma Rho Lambda, "a national sorority for women, trans-women, and non-binary students of any race, culture, or sexual orientation" (para. 9).

Chartoff and Bundy (2017) explained that social support, that is, one of the principal reasons students are drawn to fraternities and sororities (Capone, Wood, Borsari, & Laird, 2007), tends to have a positive effect on college students' mental and emotional health and well-being and suggest that "joining social groups might be a resource for battling mental health issues in college" (p. 63). More specifically, Szabo (2014) offers three reasons that the Greek community is ideally situated to offer support for college students who are experiencing mental and emotional challenges:

1. Support. Members of fraternities and sororities have built-in support. There is someone to check in on members, encourage them to attend classes, and help them work through difficulties. Each chapter also has an adult advisor who can develop a protocol to follow if a member shows signs of distress.
2. Connection. Greek life provides an opportunity for its members to serve and volunteer in their communities. Connecting to something larger than themselves can be helpful for members dealing with mental health challenges.
3. Shared Values. Because members join a Greek organization since they like what that chapter offers and have shared interests and perspectives with their brothers and sisters, caring about fellow members with mental health challenges should be a natural extension and enhance their emotional development.

Peer support can be seen as a first-line defense against the debilitating mental and emotional health challenges that can negatively affect fraternity and sorority members. Even so, brothers and sisters should use active listening and attending behaviors when speaking with a distressed member; let them tell their story, accepting it as their truth; get clarification while not asking questions that seem judgmental or making comments that are critical; commend them for their honesty and for seeking support; make referrals if necessary to professional helpers; and understand the reasonable support they can offer while focusing on their self-care and emotional well-being (Burke et al., 2017).

While not trained as professional counselors, student affairs professionals can also support Greek life students who are dealing with distress. Actually, student affairs professionals often report frequently addressing a variety of mental health concerns among their students. In a study of student affairs practitioners, issues such as stress management, anxiety, transitioning to college, health and wellness, interpersonal conflicts, and depression were cited as among the most common student concerns (Reynolds, 2013). Using Cooper (2009) and Burke et al. (2017) as a framework, the following recommendations are offered for student affairs professionals helping students in the Greek community who are dealing with mental and emotional issues, especially if the conditions have the potential to escalate into substance abuse and even suicide:

- If helping a student, assess personal attitude toward psychological disorders, including suicide.
- Use active listening skills when speaking directly with the student, letting them know there is concern and sincerity.
- Encourage students to seek professional help, especially if their safety becomes a concern. Appropriately, familiarity with campus and community mental health resources and those agencies' referral procedures is a must. Further, the purpose of the referral should be made clear to the student, noting it is in their best interest. If the student is receptive, pick up the phone at that time to contact the professional counselor, and if willing and able, accompany the student to the agency.
- Avoid chastising or criticizing a student who does not follow through or who has a setback.
- Student affairs professionals who work with the Greek community should learn to spot signs of depression, possible suicidal tendencies, and substance abuse in students. Greek brothers and sisters should also be educated about the signs for concern and empowered to help within their limits. Consideration should be given to inviting a counseling professional to meet with chapter advisors and officers to instruct them to spot signs of mental health distress including depression, suicidal tendencies, and substance abuse.

If a commitment to student welfare is embedded in student affairs professionals' actions, those most effective are willing to invest time and energy, connect with students, understand their needs, aspire to impact students, enjoy relating to them, and are able to respond to their unique situations (Schreiner, Noel, Anderson, & Cantwell, 2011).

Respectful communication, relationship building, reassurance, and support are also critical in helping students in mental distress (Martin & Oswin, 2010).

Further, there should be knowledge and an understanding of the needs of the student who is experiencing emotional and mental distress. Therefore, educational preparation and coaching (e.g., workshops and symposiums) can produce more positive attitudes and increased confidence to help students (Becker, Martin, Wajeeh, Ward, & Shern, 2002). For example, shortly after the shooting at Virginia Tech, Fallahi, Austad, Fallon, and Leishman (2009) found that although faculty and staff indicated they should be alert to students' behavior and provide support and referrals when a student is in need, they realized a need for better training on issues of mental illness and school safety as well as more resources for referral. Schwartz and Kay (2009) also divulged a need to be well-versed in the laws pertaining to college students (i.e., the Family Educational Rights and Privacy Act and the Americans with Disabilities Act) but stressed that student affairs professionals primarily should act in the "best interest of the student" when making decisions in complex cases, not dictating case management in crisis situations.

Considering college students do experience mental and emotional distress and agreeing that institutions of higher education, as well as Greek organizations, should provide some level of service for those students, initiatives should be instituted to respond to and support students in distress. For example, Jones (2018) outlined a recent trend in how Greek organizations are responding to the evolving mental and emotional needs of their members through virtual counseling. To address an increase in depression and suicide among college students and support the health and wellness of the local chapters, fraternities and sororities at the national level partnered with the New York City-based company TalkSpace to offer virtual counseling for its members nationwide, potentially reaching hundreds of thousands of students. Virtual counseling is an attractive alternative to students who may feel more comfortable with a virtual encounter through a digital app rather than seeking help in person.

Another development in responding to the mental and emotional needs of the Greek community involves the creation of "Mental Health Chairs," as Dotson (2018) reports. This approach was recently initiated at the University of Michigan within Interfraternity Council (IFC) organizations and offers proactive, positive strategies and awareness surrounding mental health. The purpose of the Mental Health Chair is "to provide brothers with an outlet for other members to come to when they are in need, as well as being someone who is knowledgeable on the various resources on campus so that they can direct brothers to those resources" (para. 3). Members across organizations participate in comprehensive training that includes various topics such as Question, Persuade, and Refer training for Suicide Intervention and Prevention (QPR), dialogue facilitation sessions hosted by the institution's Counseling and Psychological Services, as well as restorative justice sessions. As Espiritu (2015) astutely observes, just talking about mental health is taking a step forward that will help break down the stigmas associated with the term, and it is important for institutions to bolster their mental health infrastructure within Greek organizations to help students in need.

In conclusion, when considering the mental and emotional health of fraternity and sorority members, it is important to recognize that this is a multifaceted issue and concern. Whereas the Greek community can precipitate considerable stress among college students who choose to join these organizations (Estes, 2012), the support that members receive can also have a profoundly therapeutic impact on many students, as David-Luc Graap (2016) acknowledges when describing his personal experience of receiving compassion, encouragement, and support from his fraternal brothers and how it saved him. He discloses,

> Since then, I've slowly crawled from my abyss. Yes, there are still bad days where I battle my depression, but I know I have an entire chapter supporting me. A chapter that doesn't judge me for a chemical imbalance that is out of my control. A chapter that accepts me for who I am, no matter my faults. (para. 15)

When it comes to the challenge of mental and emotional health among members of the Greek community on campus, perhaps Moore (2017) has the best perspective, alluding, "If we as a Greek community could just come together and support one another, no matter what organization you belong to, we could truly make an impact on the way mental illness is viewed" (para. 10). Mental health issues can have a profound impact on students in need as well as others; therefore, addressing mental health issues should become an organizational responsibility and priority for the Greek-life community.

References

American College Health Association. (2018, Spring). *American College Health Association—National College Health Assessment II: Reference Group Executive Summary Spring 2018*. Silver Spring, MD: Author. Retrieved from https://www.acha.org/documents/ncha/NCHA-II_Spring_2018_Reference_Group_Executive_Summary.pdf

Apgar, T., & Szabo, R. (n.d.). *What we don't know can hurt us most: The hidden harm of hazing*. Retrieved from https://deanofstudents.arizona.edu/sites/deanofstudents.arizona.edu/files/Hidden_Harm_of_Hazing_article.pdf

Arroyo, A. (2015, April). *Mental health within Greek life* [Prezi]. Retrieved from https://prezi.com/59kd1bvmchqu/mental-health-within-greek-life/

Becker, M., Martin, L., Wajeeh, E., Ward, J., & Shern, D. (2002). Students with mental illnesses in a university setting: Faculty and student attitudes, beliefs, knowledge, and experiences. *Psychiatric Rehabilitation Journal, 25*(4), 359–368.

Bohnert, A. M., Aikins J. W., & Edidin, J. (2007). The role of organized activities in facilitating social adaptation across the transition to college. *Journal of Adolescent Research, 22,* 189–208.

Burke, M. G., Sauerheber, J. D., Hughey, A. W., & Laves, K. (2017). *Helping skills for working with college students: Applying counseling theory to student affairs practice.* New York, NY: Routledge.

Capone, C., Wood, M. D., Borsari, B., & Laird, R. D. (2007). Fraternity and sorority involvement, social influences, and alcohol use among college students: A prospective examination. *Psychology of Addictive Behaviors, 21*(3), 316–327.

Chartoff, B., & Bundy, M. B. (2017). Does social support diminish depression in students? Evidence from athletes and Greek life. *Kentucky Journal of Undergraduate Scholarship, 1*(1), 63–73.

Cooper, A. (2009, April). *Helping fraternity and sorority members with mental health issues that lead to substance abuse.* Retrieved from https://documents.kenyon.edu/odadas/HelpingFraternityandSorority.pdf

Cress, C. M., Astin, H. S., Zimmerman-Oster, K., and Burkhardt, J. C. (2001). Developmental outcomes of college students' involvement in leadership activities. *Journal of College Student Development, 42,* 15–27.

Dotson, C. (2018). *Mental health chairs implemented in IFC chapters.* Retrieved from the University of Michigan Fraternity and Sorority Life website: https://fsl.umich.edu/article/mental-health-chairs-implemented-ifc-chapters

Espiritu, G. (2015, April). Depression in Greek life at Longwood University. Retrieved from https://medium.com/@espiritugn/depression-in-greek-life-at-longwood-university-e28837e09a47

Estes, A. (2012, July). Sorority recruitment is worth the stress and work involved. *The Red & Black.* Retrieved from https://www.redandblack.com/opinion/sorority-recruitment-is-worth-the-stress-and-work-involved/article_83c649ca-d5d4-11e1-be09-0019bb30f31a.html

Fallahi, C. R., Austad, C. S., Fallon, M., & Leishman, L. (2009). A survey of the perceptions of the Virginia Tech tragedy. *Journal of School Violence, 8*(2), 120–135. doi:10.1080/15388220802074017

Galderisi, S., Heinz, A., Kastrup, M., Beezhold, J., & Sartorius, N. (2015). Toward a new definition of mental health. *World Psychiatry: Official Journal of the World Psychiatric Association (WPA), 14*(2), 231–233.

Graap, D-L. (2016). How my fraternity saved my life: A battle with depression. Retrieved from https://www.theodysseyonline.com/how-my-fraternity-saved-my-life

Hughes, M. J., & Winston, R. B., Jr. (1987). Effects of fraternity membership on interpersonal values. *Journal of College Student Personnel, 28,* 405–411.

Jones, L. (2018, August 24). New semester, old challenges for fraternities, sororities. *Diverse Issues in Higher Education.* Retrieved from https://diverseeducation.com/article/124158/

Kazdin, A. E. (Ed.). (2000). *Encyclopedia of psychology: 8 volume set.* American Psychological Association. New York, NY: Oxford University Press.

Martin, J., & Oswin, F. (2010). Mental health, access, and equity in higher education. *Advances in Social Work, 11*(1), 48–66.

McNamara, K. J. (2016). Sorority and self-esteem: You are not alone [Blog post]. Retrieved from http://blog.phiredup.com/sorority-and-self-esteem-you-are-not-alone/

Moore, J. (2017). Why being in a sorority was the best thing for my mental illness. Retrieved from https://www.theodysseyonline.com/mental-illness-greek-life

National Council on Disability. (2017, July). *Mental health on college campuses: Investments, accommodations needed to address student needs.* Retrieved from https://diversity.ucsf.edu/sites/diversity.ucsf.edu/files/NCD_Mental_Health_Report_508.pdf

Osby, J. C. (2015). I got PTSD from pledging to a Black Greek-letter organization. *MadameNoire*. Retrieved from https://madamenoire.com/582992/my-experience-with-ptsd-after-pledging-a-black-greek-letter-organization/

Phi Delta Theta. (2018). Member resources: Health and safety resources. Retrieved from https://www.phideltatheta.org/members/resources/health-safety-resources/

Reifman, Alan. (2011, September). How fraternities and sororities impact students (or do they?) [Blog post]. Retrieved from https://www.psychologytoday.com/us/blog/the-campus/201109/how-fraternities-and-sororities-impact-students-or-do-they

Reynolds, A. L. (2013). College student concerns: Perceptions of student affairs practitioners. *Journal of College Student Development, 54*(1), 98–104.

Robbins, A. (2004). *Pledged: The secret life of sororities*. New York, NY: Hatchette Books.

Rudavsky, S. (2018, August 16). With college counselors in short supply, Greek organizations find alternative. *Indianapolis Star*. Retrieved from https://www.indystar.com/story/news/2018/08/16/sorority-offers-members-new-option-hard-get-counseling/996147002/

Schneiderman, N., Ironson, G., & Siegel, S. D. (2005). Stress and health: psychological, behavioral, and biological determinants. *Annual Review of Clinical Psychology, 1*, 607–628.

Schreiner, L., Noel, P., Anderson, E., & Cantwell, L. (2011). The impact of faculty and staff on high-risk college student persistence. *Journal of College Student Development, 52*(3), 321–338.

Schwartz, V., & Kay, J. (2009). The crisis in college and university mental health. *Psychiatric Times, 26*(10), 30–32, 34.

Scott-Sheldon, L. A., Carey, K. B., & Carey, M. P. (2007). Health behavior and college students: does Greek affiliation matter? *Journal of Behavioral Medicine, 31*(1), 61–70.

Stephens, T., Dulberg, C., & Joubert, N. (1999). Mental health of the Canadian population: A comprehensive analysis. *Chronic Diseases in Canada, 20*(3), 118–126.

Szabo, R. (2014, September 17). Three reasons Greek life is a great place to address mental health. *Huffington Post*. Retrieved from https://www.huffingtonpost.com/ross-szabo/3-reasons-greek-life-is-a_b_5833408.html

Szabo, R. (2018). Hugging it out: Mental health in fraternities. Retrieved from https://www.deltau.org/hugging-it-out-mental-health-in-fraternities

Szabo, R., & Hall, M. (2018). Sigma Nu launches new mental health education program. Retrieved from https://www.sigmanu.org/the-delta/latest-news/sigma-nu-launches-mental-health-education-program

Taylor, G. (2010). An analysis of leadership programming sponsored by member organizations of the National Panhellenic Conference. *Research Journal of the Association of Fraternity/Sorority Advisors, 5*, 22–33.

University of Houston's Division of Student Affairs and Enrollment Services. (2017). What is Greek life? Retrieved from https://www.uh.edu/caps/resources/greek_life.html

University of Michigan. (n.d.). The Greek community addresses the topic of mental health. Retrieved from https://fsl.umich.edu/article/greek-community-addresses-topic-mental-health

Wilder, D. H., Hoyt, A. E., Surbeck, B. S., Wilder, J. C., & Carney, P. I. (1986). Greek affiliation and attitude change in college students. *Journal of College Student Personnel, 27*, 510–519.

Yerkes, R. M., & Dodson, J. D. (1908). The relation of strength of stimulus of rapidity of habit-formation. *Journal of Comparative and Neurological Psychology, 18*, 459–482.

CHAPTER 4

Substance Abuse Among Fraternity and Sorority Members: Causes, Consequences, and Countermeasures

Aaron W. Hughey

> *Fraternity and sorority members make up some of the highest-risk college students in the nation when it comes to continued and excessive substance abuse.*
>
> —ADDICTION CENTER (2018)

ALCOHOL AND SUBSTANCE abuse on college campuses have long been associated with Greek letter organizations. As Ensor (2014) found:

> Analyses of drinking and drug abuse patterns of 4,299 young adults who were surveyed first as high school seniors and then during college confirm that members of fraternities and sororities engage in significantly higher rates of substance abuse than their college peers . . . Data show that fraternity and sorority members had elevated rates of substance abuse while they were in high school and higher levels of binge drinking, annual marijuana use, and current cigarette smoking during the college years than nonmembers. (paras. 1–2)

Participating in Greek organizations obviously has many benefits, many of which are explained in other chapters of this book. At the same time, it is important to acknowledge that the Greek population is also much more likely to engage in many activities and be-haviors—either individually or collectively—that can be self-defeating and ultimately harmful (Bailey & Hughey, 2013). Chief among these behaviors is the propensity to abuse alcohol or other drugs (Capone, Wood, Borsari, & Laird, 2007). The reasons for this are often complex and interrelated, and involve social as well as physiological factors (Kanazawa, 2010). Consider the following:

> Members of both fraternities and sororities are at a higher risk for binge drinking and drug use than the rest of the college population. However, re-search suggests young men are more likely to drink excessively than young women are. Men are also more likely than their female counterparts to en-gage in risky or dangerous activities or feel pressured by male competition.
>
> Because of this, fraternity members (specifically those who are white and under 25) comprise the group of college students at the highest risk of devel-oping a substance abuse problem or facing severe consequences for drinking or drug use. (Addiction Center, 2018, paras. 8–9).

The negative effects of alcohol and substance abuse have been well-documented; the detrimental impacts on personal health, safety, and academics are often severe (Brad-ford Health Services, 2018). Ensor (2014) found that, compared with their non-fraternity or non-sorority peers, over half of the students associated with Greek organizations re-ported performing poorly on a test or project, missing classes, and engaging in significant interpersonal conflict. Moreover, these consequences seem to be disproportionately distributed among the leaders of Greek organizations:

> The leaders of fraternities and sororities suffer even greater consequences than other members. One study found that:
>
> - 26.9 percent of fraternity leaders have an alcohol-related injury.
> - 82.4 percent of fraternity leaders and 78.7 percent of sorority leaders had had a hangover.
> - 71.3 percent of fraternity leaders and 66.2 percent of sorority leaders be-came nauseated or vomited.
> - 53.3 percent of fraternity leaders and 45.6 percent of sorority leaders re-ported having alcohol-related memory loss. (Ensor, 2014, para. 7)

The reality is that fraternity and sorority members do tend to brag (or at least make jokes about) their drinking and substance abuse habits (Summit Behavioral Health, 2018). In recent years, however, headlines about student deaths, hospitalizations, haz-ing, sexual assault, and death have put Greek organizations under the microscope and called into question the efficacy of fraternities and sororities, at least among the general population (Lohse, 2015).

Causes

The motivations college students often state for their alcohol and drug use seem to revolve around connecting with others and coping with stress and anxiety (Drug Wise, 2017). Sixty percent of the full-time, traditional-age (18–22 years old) college students who responded to the 2014 National Survey on Drug Use and Health (NSDUH) indicated that they had consumed alcohol within the past month, while 38% reported that they had engaged in binge drinking (Campus Answers, 2016). Moreover, when college students were asked about their reasons for drinking alcohol, they reported the following:

- Breaks the ice: 74.4%
- Enhances social activity: 74.4%
- Gives people something to do: 71.7%
- Gives people something to talk about: 66.6%
- Allows people to have more fun: 63.1%
- Facilitates male bonding: 60.1%
- Facilitates a connection with peers: 61.7%
- Facilitates sexual opportunities: 53.0%
- Facilitates female bonding: 28.8%
- Makes women sexier: 28.8%
- Makes food taste better: 22.7%
- Makes me sexier: 20.4%
- Makes men sexier: 19.9% (Campus Answers, 2016, para. 4)

Any discussion of alcohol and substance abuse among members of Greek organizations must include how the individuals associated with fraternities and sororities are depicted in the media. Indeed, both television shows and especially movies regularly portray the Greek community as leaders in alcohol and substance abuse on campus (Friedman, 2015). This fascination has served to reinforce and extend stereotypes and is suggestive of the need for a culture change regarding how Greek organizations are represented in entertainment projects (Oliveira, 2016). The following description is fairly typical:

There are quite a few movies that link Greek life and substance abuse. In May 2016, the film *Neighbors 2: Sorority Rising* hit movie theatres. This movie is a sequel to the 2014 movie *Neighbors*. Both movies feature college students making questionable choices, including using illegal drugs. The *Neighbors* movies aren't the only movies featuring such behavior by college students, of course. There's a long tradition of such college movies. In *National Lampoon's Animal House* (1978), several characters drink a great deal of alcohol, while characters in *Revenge of the Nerds* (1984) smoke marijuana joints. The movies show how these substances change the behavior of the characters who are using them. (Willow Springs Recovery, 2018, paras. 2–3)

A substantial number of studies have investigated the disproportionate prevalence of alcohol and drug abuse among fraternity and sorority members. Several factors have been identified that seem to explain the elevated use of these substances among the Greek community, including self-selection, socialization, distorted social norms, and unrealistic expectations (Summit Behavioral Health, 2018). Regarding self-selection, those who tend to abuse alcohol and drugs have a well-documented propensity to seek out and align themselves with those who share their counterproductive attitudes and behaviors (Melton, 2017). Students who want to drink or use drugs are more likely to join Greek organizations, which may, in turn, reinforce their drinking or substance abuse (Thompson, 2017). Similarly, students who have a predisposition to abuse alcohol and drugs often attempt to promote these behaviors in others; in many instances pledges are encouraged to drink alcohol to excess in order to gain approval (Bruni, 2017). With respect to social norms, Greek housing can evolve into an enabling environment that actually promotes and rewards alcohol and drug use (Flanagan, 2014). In this situation, students tend to be more involved in behaviors they perceive their peers to be engaged in, so it becomes a means of gaining approval. Finally, many in the Greek community have bought into the myth that use of alcohol and drugs enhances social skills (Essays, UK, 2018).

It is also important to understand that the consequences of alcohol and substance abuse during the college years can have implications for decades beyond the time period when the student was involved in Greek life. For example, in a longitudinal study that followed almost 16,000 high school students (10% of both the men and the women in the study eventually joined fraternities or sororities) from ages 18 through 35, McCabe, Veliz, and Schulenberg (2018) found that:

> Male fraternity members who lived in fraternity houses during college had the highest levels of binge drinking and marijuana use relative to non-members and non-students in young adulthood that continued through age 35, controlling for adolescent sociodemographic and other characteristics. At age 35, 45% of the residential fraternity members reported alcohol use disorder (AUD) symptoms reflecting mild to severe AUDs; their adjusted odds of experiencing AUD symptoms at age 35 were higher than all other college and noncollege groups except non-residential fraternity members.

> Residential sorority members had higher odds of AUD symptoms at age 35 when compared with their noncollege female peers. (McCabe, Veliz, & Schulenberg, 2018, p. S35)

The researchers concluded that binge drinking and marijuana use was significantly elevated among male residential fraternity members as compared to their non-affiliated and non-college student counterparts (McCabe, Veliz, & Schulenberg, 2018). Further, they found that "the increased risk of substance-related consequences associated with fraternity involvement was not developmentally limited to college and is associated with higher levels of long-term AUD symptoms during early midlife" (p. S35).

Specifically, researchers found that males who live in a fraternity house for only one semester exhibit significantly higher rates of binge drinking both during and after college than their college peers who were not Greek-affiliated as well as students of comparable age who did not attend college (National Institute on Drug Abuse, 2018). With reference to marijuana use, it was found that fraternity and sorority members who lived in Greek housing had a significantly higher prevalence of marijuana use into their mid-30s compared to other college students and non-college youth. Interestingly, however, their adult cannabis use did not differ significantly from their non-Greek counterparts; only about 6% of those in both categories reported two or more symptoms of cannabis use disorder (CUD) at age 35 (National Institute on Drug Abuse, 2018).

With respect to addictive behaviors in general, Greek-affiliated college students were also found to be at higher risk in a number of categories (Zen College Life, 2018). Consider hookah tobacco smoking, for instance. Using data from the National College Health Assessment, which involved responses from over 82,000 students, Sidani, Shensa, and Primack (2013) concluded that:

> Compared to non-Greeks, Greek resident members had nearly double the odds for current use of hookah tobacco and three times the odds for alcohol bingeing. Similar to other substances, hookah tobacco smoking is highest among Greek resident members, compared with both Greeks living outside Greek housing and non-Greeks. It is valuable for substance use surveillance and intervention to focus on Greek resident members. (p. 238)

Consequences

Alcohol and substance abuse among college students has serious implications. For example, about 25% of students indicate that engaging in these behaviors has adversely affected their academic experience, including missing class, falling behind in coursework, not doing well on exams or papers, and/or receiving lower grades than expected

(Campus Answers, 2106). In fact, according to the National Institute on Alcohol Abuse and Alcoholism:

- About 1,825 college students between the ages of 18 and 24 die from alcohol-related unintentional injuries, including motor-vehicle crashes.
- About 696,000 students between the ages of 18 and 24 are assaulted by another student who has been drinking.
- About 97,000 students between the ages of 18 and 24 report experiencing alcohol-related sexual assault or date rape (Campus Answers, 2016, para. 3).

Unfortunately, this story, which appeared in the Miami Herald in January of 2018, has become an all-too-common news item in recent years:

The University of Florida becomes the latest school to suspend a fraternity for alleged incidents involving alcohol and drug use.

In December, Heather White, UF's interim dean of students, sent the university's chapter of Tau Epsilon Phi a three-page letter recommending a four-year suspension from Dec. 7 to Dec. 17, 2021.

The chapter was accused of violating five student conduct codes, including serving alcohol to minors, illicit drug possession and use and an incident in which several intoxicated people were sent to the hospital. Also, the letter cited the fraternity for causing more than $3,000 in damages to a hotel while on a weekend trip to New Orleans in September. (Cohen, 2018, paras. 1–3)

Similarly, the following scenario has been playing out in Greek organizations throughout the country for the last several decades (Thompson, 2017):

My fraternity had a drug problem. The problem was two-fold. First, about half of the brothers started using drugs occasionally. While drug use should not be condoned, the recreational use by most of these brothers never interfered with their standing in fraternity. Drug use was not condoned on fraternity property, and the brotherhood respected that rule.

The bigger problem was the divide it caused. Brothers often worried that these were signs of a real problem and not just recreational use. Many of the brothers who didn't use drugs stopped going to the house. While the use was not on the property, it was happening just across the street. The use also seemed to encourage unsavory characters to be around the house, another turn-off for a lot of brothers. (The Fraternity Advisor, 2018, paras. 1–2)

Membership in a Greek organization (fraternity or sorority) is associated with a significantly heightened risk for experiencing alcohol or drug-related consequences (Soule, Barnett, & Moorhouse, 2013). Clercq (2014) reinforces this conclusion:

> Research consistently shows that Greek life involvement leads to a heightened risk of alcohol and drug abuse, to the point that 25 percent of colleges in two recently researched states have had to outright bar participants from imbibing to keep them academically on track. (para. 1)

As Turrisi, Mallett, and Mastroleo (2006) have observed, "Problem drinking and related consequences are a major social issue plaguing college campuses across the United States. Each year, alcohol is responsible for fatalities, assaults, serious injuries, and arrests that occur among college students" (p. 401). In their landmark study, the researchers identified and described the risk factors, drinking patterns, and consequences associated with membership in a Greek organization. Their findings corroborate those articulated by professionals at the University of Pennsylvania (2018) who outlined the following consequences of alcohol and substance abuse:

> Common negative consequences experienced by college students include, but are not limited to, the following:

- Hangovers.
- Being late for class or missing class as a result of being hungover.
- Getting sick or vomiting from too much drinking or drug use.
- Being hurt or injured as a result of being too intoxicated or high.
- Being hospitalized for alcohol and/or other drug use.
- Blacking out or browning out.
- Getting into verbal arguments or fights that you would not have participated in if you were sober.
- Getting into physical fights due to alcohol or other drug use.
- Damaging property while under the influence.
- Having unprotected sex while under the influence.
- Experiencing unwanted or unanticipated sexual encounters (touching, intercourse, etc.).
- Taking advantage of someone else sexually.
- Finding yourself in threatening or unsafe situations as a result of poor judgement while under the influence. (para. 1)

Similarly, Capone, Wood, Borsari, and Laird (2007) examined the role gender and Greek affiliation plays in the consumption of alcohol and the ensuing problems it precipitates during the first two years of the college experience. The model they developed sorts challenges into one of three distinct categories: selection, socialization, or reciprocal influence processes:

> Three social influences (alcohol offers, social modeling, and perceived norms) were examined as potential mediators of these effects. Undergraduate participants (N = 388) completed self-report measures prior to enrollment and in the spring of their freshmen and sophomore years. Male gender and involvement in the Greek system were associated with greater alcohol use and problems prior to college. Both gender and Greek involvement significantly predicted increases in alcohol use and problems over the first 2 years of college. Cross-domain analyses provided strong support for a mediational role of each of the social influence constructs on alcohol use and problems prior to matriculation, and prematriculation social modeling and alcohol offers mediated relations between Greek involvement and changes in alcohol use over time. Findings suggest that students, particularly men, who affiliate with Greek organizations constitute an at-risk group prior to entering college, suggesting the need for selected interventions with this population, which should take place before or during the pledging process (p. 316)

Finally, Thompson (2017) identified the connection to hazing and a potential precursor to criminal behavior as being two of the most high-profile and detrimental consequences associated with alcohol and substance abuse among fraternity and sorority members:

> Drinking is sometimes a part of fraternity hazing rituals. Pledges may be encouraged to drink large quantities of alcohol to gain membership in a fraternity. At Cornell University in 2013, for example, eight fraternities were investigated for hazing and alcohol abuse incidents, with some of these incidents combining alcohol and hazing.

> The alcohol-fueled party environment at some fraternities can contribute to criminal behavior, particularly rape . . . alcohol commonly played a role in on-campus date rapes and . . . members of Greek organizations were more likely to be involved in these incidents than students who were not members of fraternities or sororities. The Robert Wood Johnson Foundation's Center for College Health and Safety reports that drinking, particularly

among members of fraternities, can also play a role in on-campus vandalism
(paras. 3–4)

Clearly, alcohol and substance abuse within the Greek community on campus has
many deleterious consequences for individuals and their families, fraternities and sororities, the institutions in which they are situated, the general student population, the
surrounding community, and society in general. It is imperative that the challenges
the use of these substances precipitates be met with evidence-based strategies that are
conscientiously developed and implemented.

Countermeasures

Dealing with the problem of alcohol and substance abuse among members of the
Greek community on campus is complicated. Negative media reports and ongoing concerns about student safety have led to sanctions by national chapters, yet what happens
in fraternity and sorority houses once the doors close often remains problematic to
discern and even more difficult to change (Summit Behavioral Health, 2018). Complex
problems require complex solutions. As is usually the case, and although awareness does
not necessarily lead to action (Hamm, 2012), education typically constitutes the first
line of defense in any attempt to ameliorate the negative consequences precipitated by
alcohol and substance abuse among fraternity and sorority members. As such, most institutions have adopted policy statements that include language similar to the following:

> The social aspect of fraternity and sorority life is one of the many reasons
> that students get involved in the community, however, alcohol and sub-
> stance abuse is not tolerated. All chapters are expected to uphold city,
> county, state, and federal laws, as well as the University of Nevada, Reno's
> policies regarding alcohol and substance use.
>
> All fraternities and sororities have strict policies that address alcohol and
> substance use at chapter-sponsored events. These risk management guide-
> lines are established by each organization's local and/or inter/national
> governing body and must adhere to the University of Nevada, Reno's poli-
> cies. Additionally, alcohol and other substances are often addressed through
> educational programs offered to chapters and individual members, often
> times through a partnership with the Office of Student Conduct on campus
> (University of Nevada, 2018, paras. 10–11)

Many institutions are exploring the integration of protective behavioral strategies
into their professional development initiatives as a means of combating alcohol and

substance abuse among fraternity and sorority members (LaBrie, Kenney, Lac, Garcia, & Ferraiolo, 2009). In a general sense, protective behavioral strategies are the procedures that individuals use to keep others from engaging in negative behavior (Learnet, 2018). Barry, Madson, Moorer, and Christman (2016) found that members of the Greek community used protective behavioral strategies significantly less than non-Greeks and reported significantly higher levels of alcohol-related problems than the general student population. The utility of protective behavioral strategies, however, has not been consistently established, as noted by Prince, Carey, and Maisto (2013):

> Protective behavioral strategies (PBS) have been conceptualized as skills used by drinkers to moderate their drinking and/or resulting consequences. The correlational evidence for the relationships among PBS, alcohol use, and related problems has been mixed. Experimental research reveals inconsistent relationships among intervention condition, PBS use, and alcohol outcomes. There is currently insufficient evidence to support the claim that PBS function as a mechanism of behavior change for college drinkers. (p. 2343)

Soule, Barnett, and Moorhouse (2013) mirrored the findings of Prince, Carey, and Maisto (2013) in their study, which analyzed the responses of 18,354 college students between the ages of 18 and 25 who participated in the Fall 2010 National College Health Assessment II survey. Using an adjusted logistic regression model, they found that:

> Compared to non-fraternity/sorority members, fraternity/sorority members were more likely to report using all but two PBS examined in the study. Additionally, fraternity/sorority members were more likely to report binge drinking, driving after drinking, and experiencing negative consequences of alcohol use. These findings indicate PBS alone may be insufficient for preventing negative outcomes associated with drinking in high-risk groups. Future research should examine if PBS combined with other alcohol use intervention strategies among fraternity/sorority members are more effective at preventing negative outcomes (p. 16)

Hamm (2012) examined the efficacy of the Alcohol Skills Training Program (ASTP) on college fraternity members' drinking behaviors in an effort to determine which aspects of the program are most effective. The ASTP "is an alcohol abuse prevention program designed for anyone who drinks alcohol. It was developed to promote harm reduction by teaching the knowledge and skills necessary to drink with less risk. It is based on a review of scientific evidence and focuses on alcohol's effects on the body, as well as its more subtle effects on feelings and thinking" (Florida Atlantic University, 2017, para. 1). The study also explored the influence of chapter culture on efforts to modify the drinking behaviors of members of the Greek community. The conclusions of the investigation were mixed:

> The researcher in this study did not find evidence to support ASTP as an effective alcohol education program for reducing high-risk drinking and its associated negative consequences among fraternity members. However, the researcher did identify certain elements of the ASTP program which do seem to be viewed as useful by members of college fraternities and that facilitator style was viewed as very important by participants. The findings from this study enabled the researcher to make several recommendations regarding alcohol education within the fraternity and sorority community. (Hamm, 2012, p. 1)

Scott-Sheldon, Carey, Kaiser, Knight, and Carey (2016) conducted a systematic review and meta-analysis of alcohol interventions with fraternity and sorority members over the course of 27 years (1987–2014). Their primary conclusions, which clearly indicate that successful interventions must entail a multifaceted approach, were summarized by Summit Behavioral Health (2018):

- The efficacy of interventions in Greek housing would be moderated by population subgroup (e.g., fraternity or sorority), residential environment (in Greek housing or otherwise), and intervention level (individual or chapter). Specifically, they thought that interventions delivered to chapter houses vs. individuals would be effective in reducing alcohol use and other alcohol-related problems. They made this prediction based on the higher incidence of drinking in these environments, leaving more room for improvement.
- Prior alcohol use will affect intervention efficacy. For example, students who report more baseline alcohol use will benefit more from intervention. Previous studies suggest that heavy drinkers benefit more from current intervention styles.
- Interventions that included personalized feedback about alcohol consumption and challenged established alcohol expectancies would prove more effective in reducing overall alcohol consumption, compared to interventions that did not include these strategies.
- Multifaceted interventions (i.e., those with goal setting and moderation strategies) and those of longer duration would prove more successful, as compared to those using a single alcohol-reduction strategy. (para. 25)

In the final analysis, the only effective strategy for overcoming the devastating effects of alcohol and drug abuse among fraternity and sorority members seems to be one that seeks to change the culture present in these organizations (Corbin, 2018). Perhaps Fraternity Advisor (2018) sums it up best: "A fraternity that wants to avoid a drug problem needs to develop an anti-drug culture" (para. 9). After the death of Timothy Piazza, a 19-year-old sophomore who died after a hazing ritual involving the overconsumption of alcohol, officials at Penn State implemented several policy changes designed to alter the Greek culture:

> Citing the self-governance model of Greek life as failing to address pervasive issues of excessive drinking, hazing, and sexual assault, Penn State described the new policies as 'an unprecedented transfer of responsibility to the University for disciplinary matters.'

> The changes include:

> - University — rather than Greek organization — control over misconduct and adjudication process
> - Hazing that involves alcohol or physical or mental abuse will result in swift permanent revocation of recognition for the chapter involved
> - Monitoring of social events by University staff members
> - A social and behavioral contract signed by students
> - Report cards with information about every Greek organization on campus
> - Organizations will be charged an additional fee to fund increased police services and monitors. (Jackson, 2017, paras. 4–5).

As noted previously, alcohol and substance abuse among fraternity and sorority members presents a formidable challenge for everyone associated with the Greek system. Its causes are myriad and complex, its consequences are potentially devastating, and effective countermeasures are anything but straightforward. At the same time, the advantages of being involved in Greek life on campus—both while in college and for the decades that follow—are significant and do make a difference in the lives of the students who choose to affiliate with these organizations (Tyler, 2012). It's imperative that efforts to move the Greek culture in a more positive direction continue with resolve and enthusiasm.

References

Addiction Center. (2018). Drinking and drug abuse in Greek Life. Retrieved from https://www.addictioncenter.com/college/drinking-drug-abuse-greek-life/

Bailey, H. E., & Hughey, A.W. (2013, January). A realistic, pro-active approach to eradicating hazing for Greek organizations. *Diverse Issues in Higher Education*. Retrieved from http://diverseeducation.com/article/50714/

Barry, A., Madson, M., Moorer, K., & Christman, K. (2016, June). Predicting use of protective behavioral strategies: Does fraternity/sorority affiliation matter? *Journal of Student Affairs Research and Practice, 53*(3), 1–11.

Bradford Health Services. (2018). The consequences of drug and alcohol abuse. Retrieved from https://bradfordhealth.com/consequences-drug-alcohol-abuse/

Bruni, F. (2017, November). Their pledges die. So should fraternities. *The New York Times*. Retrieved from https://www.nytimes.com/2017/11/17/opinion/pledges-fraternities-violence-deaths.html

Campus Answers. (2016, April). Why do college students drink so often? Retrieved from http://www.campusanswers.com/why-college-students-drink/

Capone, C., Wood, M. D., Borsari, B., & Laird, R. D. (2007). Fraternity and sorority involvement, social influences, and alcohol use among college students: A prospective examination. *Psychology of Addictive Behaviors, 21*(3), 316–327.

Clercq, B. D. (2014). *Alcohol and drug abuse in Greek-letter organizations* [Prezi]. Retrieved from https://prezi.com/ojana78vbpat/alcohol-and-drug-abuse-in-greek-letter-organizations/

Cohen, H. (2018, January). UF suspends fraternity for four years over alleged alcohol and drug abuse. *Miami Herald*. Retrieved from http://www.miamiherald.com/news/local/education/article194020969.html

Corbin, C. (2018, January). Florida student's drinking death renews calls for aggressive "culture change" in fraternities. *Fox News*. Retrieved from http://www.foxnews.com/us/2018/01/18/drinking-death-florida-student-renews-call-for-aggressive-culture-change-within-u-s-fraternities.html

Drug Wise. (2017, January). Why do young people take drugs? Retrieved from http://www.drugwise.org.uk/why-do-young-people-take-drugs/

Ensor, L. (2014, September). Fraternities and sororities: Alcohol and drug use. *Addiction Hope*. Retrieved from https://www.addictionhope.com/blog/fraternities-and-sororities-alcohol-and-drug-use/

Essays, UK. (2018, November). Alcoholism from a social learning theory perspective. Retrieved from https://www.ukessays.com/essays/psychology/alcoholism-from-a-social-learning-theory-perspective-psychology-essay.php?vref=1

Flanagan, C. (2014, March). The dark power of fraternities. *The Atlantic*. Retrieved from https://www.theatlantic.com/magazine/archive/2014/03/the-dark-power-of-fraternities/357580/

Florida Atlantic University. (2017, December). Alcohol Skills Training Program. Retrieved from https://calendar.fau.edu/event/alcohol_skills_training_program_astp_8963#.WqShGedG3IU

Fraternity Advisor. (2018). Fraternity drug problem. Retrieved from http://thefraternityadvisor.com/fraternity-drug-problem/

Friedman, J. (2015, November). Should colleges ban fraternities and sororities? *Greek Life on Campus (CQ Researcher), 25*(42). Retrieved from http://library.cqpress.com/cqresearcher/document.php?id=cqresrre2015112000

Jackson, A. (2017, June). Penn State issues sweeping changes to its Greek system after horrifying death of fraternity pledge. *Business Insider*. Retrieved from http://www.businessinsider.com/penn-state-fraternity-pledge-hazing-death-2017-6

Hamm, K. J. (2012). Impact of Alcohol Skills Training Program on college fraternity members' drinking behaviors. *Electronic Theses and Dissertations*, 397. Retrieved from https://
digitalcommons.georgiasouthern.edu/cgi/viewcontent.cgi?article=1397&context=etd

Kanazawa, S. (2010, November). Why intelligent people use more drugs. *Psychology Today*. Retrieved
from https://www.psychologytoday.com/blog/the-scientific-fundamentalist/201011/why-
intelligent-people-use-more-drugs

LaBrie, J., Kenney, S. R., Lac, A., Garcia, J. A., & Ferraiolo, P. (2009, January/February). Mental and social health impacts the use of protective behavioral strategies in reducing risky
drinking and alcohol consequences. *Journal of College Student Development, 50*(1), 35–49.

Learnet. (2018). Mini-tutorial: Behavior management prevention strategies. Retrieved from http://
www.projectlearnet.org/tutorials/behavior_management_prevention_strat.html

Lohse, A. (2015, March). Why fraternities need to be abolished. *MSNBC*. Retrieved from
http://www.msnbc.com/msnbc/why-fraternities-need-be-abolished

McCabe, S. E., Veliz, P., & Schulenberg, J. E. (2018, March). How collegiate fraternity and
sorority involvement relates to substance use during young adulthood and substance
use disorders in early midlife: A national longitudinal study. *Journal of Adolescent Health,
62*(3), S35–S43).

Melton, W. (2017, August). Characteristics of substance abuse. *Livestrong.com*. Retrieved from
https://www.livestrong.com/article/148188-characteristics-of-heroin-addicts/

National Institute on Drug Abuse. (2018, February). Greek life membership associated with
binge drinking and marijuana use in later life. Retrieved from https://www.drugabuse.
gov/news-events/news-releases/2018/02/greek-life-membership-associated-binge-
drinking-marijuana-use-in-later-life

Oliveira, P. D. (2016, May). Second take: Hollywood films inaccurately portray Greek life, reinforce stereotypes. *The Daily Bruin*. Retrieved from http://dailybruin.com/2016/05/23/
second-take-hollywood-films-inaccurately-portray-greek-life-reinforce-stereotypes/

Prince, M. A., Carey, K. B., & Maisto, S. A. (2013, July). Protective behavioral strategies for
reducing alcohol involvement: A review of the methodological issues. *Addictive Behaviors, 38*(7), 2343–2351.

Scott-Sheldon, L. A., Carey, K. B., Kaiser, T. S., Knight, J. M., & Carey, M. P. (2016). Alcohol
interventions for Greek letter organizations: A systematic review and meta-analysis,
1987 to 2014. *Health Psychology, 35*(7) 670–684.

Sidani, J. E., Shensa, A., & Primack, B. A. (2013, April). Substance and hookah use and living
arrangement among fraternity and sorority members at US colleges and universities.
Journal of Community Health, 38(2), 238–245.

Soule, E. K., Barnett, T. E., & Moorhouse, M. D. (2013, October). Protective behavioral
strategies and negative alcohol-related consequences among US college fraternity and
sorority members. *Journal of Substance Abuse, 20*(1), 16–21.

Summit Behavioral Health (2018). Fraternity members unaffected by alcohol intervention
programs, study suggests. Retrieved from https://www.summitbehavioralhealth.com/
blog/fraternity-members-alcohol-intervention-programs/

Thompson, V. (2017, September). Information on drinking and drug use in fraternities. *Classroom*.
Retrieved from https://classroom.synonym.com/information-drinking-drug-use-
fraternities-15327.html

Turrisi, R., Mallett, K. A., & Mastroleo, N. R. (2006, October). Heavy drinking in college
students: Who is at risk and what is being done about it? *Journal of General Psychology,
133*(4): 401–420.

Tyler, A. (2012, October). Fifteen revealing stats on the current state of Greek life. *Elite Daily*. Retrieved from https://www.elitedaily.com/news/world/15-revealing-stats-current-state-greek-life

University of Nevada, Reno. (2018). Office of Fraternity and Sorority Life: Information for parents. Retrieved from https://www.unr.edu/fraternity-and-sorority-life/about-fraternity-and-sorority-life/fraternity-and-sorority-life-for-parents

University of Pennsylvania. (2018). Negative consequences of alcohol and other drug use can mean different things to different people. *Alcohol and Other Drug Program Initiatives*. Retrieved from https://www.vpul.upenn.edu/alcohol/negativeconsequences.php

Willow Springs Recovery. (2018). Fraternities, sororities, and substance abuse in the movies. Retrieved from http://www.willowspringsrecovery.com/alcohol-abuse/fraternities-sororities-substance-abuse-movies/2105

Zen College Life. (2018). Fifteen frightening facts about sororities and fraternities. Retrieved from http://www.zencollegelife.com/15-frightening-facts-about-sororities-and-fraternities/

PART TWO:

CHAPTER ADVISING

CHAPTER 5

Advising Local Fraternal Organizations

Wendi Kinney and Allison Swick-Duttine

Historical Context

Local fraternities and sororities are organizations that either only exist on one campus or who may have a few chapters regionally that operate independently. Local fraternities and sororities trace their roots back to the founding of fraternal organizations. In the early to mid-1800s the first Greek-lettered organizations were founded—the first fraternities at Union College and the first sororities at Wesleyan College. In 1831, Sigma Phi was the first fraternity to open a chapter at a second institution (Anson & Marchesani, 1991, pp. 1-11), and in 1868, I.C. Sororsis (later named Pi Beta Phi) became the first women's organization to open a second chapter (Pi Beta Phi Sorority, n.d.). Prior to that, the Greek-letter organizations and their precursors, the literary societies, existed at singular institutions and were, in essence, what we now call local fraternal organizations.

While many organizations strove to expand to other campuses, some chose to maintain their local roots. A study by Phired Up (2013) indicated that 40% (140 of the 352 responding campuses) reported having at least one local organization. Among them are institutions who still host fraternal organizations founded in the 1800s (Table 5.1).

Also included in these local organizations are those groups who have been inter/national at one point and have either had their inter/national charter revoked or voluntarily withdrew their charter from the organization. Throughout the history of fraternal life, the reasons this occurred have varied. In some instances the campus chapter's conduct or operations no longer met the inter/national's standards, resulting in the revocation of their national charter. For others, the opposite is true and the local chapter believed that it no longer wished to support the values or operational decisions of its parent group. A recent example is the former Sigma Phi Epsilon chapter at Tufts University. Citing "divergent values acknowledged by both the chapter and the national organization," the membership voted to withdraw from the national organization in 2015 with the support of the university (Karasin, 2015).

The State University of New York (SUNY) system banned all inter/national organizations on October 8, 1953, in response to discriminatory membership practices that denied membership to students based upon their race or religion ("State U. Bans," 1953). Several organizations challenged that the policy was unconstitutional, but the United States District Court upheld the policy, which stated:

> Resolved that no social organization shall be permitted in any state-oper-
> ated unit of the State University which has any direct or indirect affiliation
> or connection with any national or other organization outside the particular
> unit; and be it further
>
> Resolved that no such social organization, in policy or practice, shall oper-
> ate under any rule which bars students on account of race, color, religion,
> creed, national origin or other artificial criteria; and be it further
>
> Resolved that the President be, and hereby is, authorized to take such steps
> as he may deem appropriate to implement this policy, including the deter-
> mination of which student organizations are social as distinguished from
> scholastic or religious, and his decision shall be final. (*Webb v. State of New
> York*, 1954)

The ban on inter/national organizations at SUNY remained in effect until 1977 (Buffalo State, n.d.). By then, chapters that had dropped their inter/national affiliation in order to continue to operate had adopted new names, new traditions, and a 24-year history that made them unlikely to want to re-affiliate. In many, practices had developed that were not ideal for the inter/national organizations to want to bring them back into the fold. For many SUNY campuses, this has created unique fraternity/sorority communities comprised of locals who began as literary societies, locals who were once national, and inter/national organizations.

There also exist local organizations that have been created to serve niche populations for which no inter/national organization of its type exists. This was particularly common in the 1990s and early 2000s when organizations were founded to serve diverse popu-lations such as Armenian, Asian-American, Latino, LGBTQA+, multicultural, Muslim,

Native American, Persian, and South Asian Cultural interest fraternities and sororities. While many of these organizations went on to expand to other institutions, there remain those with a presence on only one campus.

Research about the history and evolution of local organizations proves challenging to find as there is relatively little documentation related to their collective history and continued existence. The nature of these groups makes it difficult to collect and maintain accurate information about which groups exist and where, and there is no clearinghouse for this information. In recent years, with the availability of the Internet and social media to connect campuses and organizations, websites such as Wikipedia and Greekpages as well as Facebook groups help to provide some record of local organizations across the United States.

Just as there is little historical documentation regarding local organizations, there are few publications offering advice on advising them or suggesting best practices for local organizations to follow. The authors attempt to provide some practical guidance related to working with local organizations drawn from their combined three decades of advising local fraternities and sororities at two public institutions in New York.

Advantages and Disadvantages

When one hears the word "local" to refer to a fraternity or sorority, there can be a variety of reactions. For those whose own membership experience is in a local, there is a great sense of pride in their organization's heritage and ability to sustain itself independently. For those who work on a college campus or for an inter/national organization, there is often great skepticism of the organization's ability to make a positive impact and an assumption that they are inherently high-risk organizations. Just as their inter/national counterparts, there are advantages and disadvantages that come with local organizations.

One of the most obvious disadvantages is the lack of oversight from, or accountability to, any governance board or staff. While some local groups have alumni boards, day-to-day chapter operations, as well as internal controls and membership standards practices, are often left to the undergraduates. The alumni board (if one exists) and undergraduate chapter are often disconnected from larger industry trends as they lack regular exposure to the types of strategic discussions happening within and among inter/national organizations and their umbrella organizations. As a result, local chapters can be labor intensive for the host institution to advise.

Another disadvantage is that local chapters often lack the financial resources to engage in activities that are considered an industry standard. The purchasing of group liability insurance, for example, can cost upward of $6,000–$10,000 annually per chapter, regardless of chapter size or claim history. Attendance at regional and national leadership experiences such as Association of Fraternal Leadership and Values or Northeast

Greek Leadership Association conferences, Leadershape, or the Undergraduate Inter-fraternity Institute can cost several thousand dollars for a small group of student leaders. Even a keynote speaker or fraternal consultant can cost $5,000 or more. An organization who operates only on local membership dues does not typically have the purchasing power that an inter/national organization would to contract with or provide these types of programs and services. As a result, members of local organizations may not have access to these developmental leadership experiences.

For those organizations that were once a chapter of an inter/national organization, another disadvantage is their tendency to hold on to the practices, policies, and operations they adhered to as a national chapter. While this may be effective in the short-term after disaffiliation from the inter/national organization, it becomes highly ineffective for a chapter to adhere to outdated practices and to use resources and officer handbooks that can be decades old. Because they lack the human and fiscal resources, as mentioned previously, chapter members are unaware that their practices have become stagnated and antiquated.

For as many disadvantages that are often cited about local fraternal organizations, there may be just as many advantages. Though local chapters often lack exposure to industry trends, they remain fairly nimble and responsive to the need for progressive change. Alterations to standard operating procedures, whether introduced by the chapter or by the campus, do not require authorization from an inter/national office/ volunteer to adopt. The ability to make swift changes to risk management policies, adopt culturally competent and inclusive membership policies, reframe their governance structure, or alter their election cycle are a few examples of how a local chapter can be responsive to a campus's and students' needs with few roadblocks.

An additional advantage is that the chapter has the freedom to establish membership selection criteria, continuing membership expectations, and operational practices that meet the unique needs of the students on their campus. The timing and term cycle of officer positions, for example, can better align with the academic calendar and requirements of a campus with trimesters or co-op programs. The minimum academic requirements for membership and holding office can be adjusted to fit the academic profile of the student population. The financial commitment of local chapter membership is also advantageous, since all dues collected are retained by the local chapter. The chapter only needs to collect what it deems necessary to meet operational expenses, and this often means there are no separate new member/candidate and initiate fees, no lifelong membership fee, and no alumni membership fee or dues.

As mentioned previously, there exist local organizations that were once a chapter of a inter/national organization. The decision to permit a university-registered inter/national fraternity/sorority to remain registered as a local organization should be given careful consideration. Institutional policies related to expansion and registration should indicate whether local organizations are permitted and, if so, under what circumstances. Some questions to consider include:

- Can a new local organization apply for and receive recognition?
- Can a registered inter/national fraternity/sorority lose its affiliation with its inter/national body and remain recognized by the institution?
- Can the chapter voluntarily relinquish its charter with their inter/national body and remain recognized by the institution?
- Will a currently registered local fraternity/sorority be permitted to return to the campus should they close due to conduct action or to low membership numbers?

The advantages and disadvantages discussed here, along with consideration of campus and fraternity/sorority community history, federal and state regulations related to college and community associations, and student needs, should weigh into the policy formation discussion.

Advising Strategies

As indicated previously, providing advisement to local organizations can be resource (human and financial) intensive. The campus-based professional may need to provide a different level of service and resources to the local chapter(s) on their campus. One recommended approach is to envision the fraternity/sorority life office as the inter/national organization. The fraternity/sorority life office should maintain accurate membership rosters and work with the institution's alumni relations office to maintain alumni membership records. The advisor can collaborate with the institution's library or archivist to assist in documenting and preserving organizational documents and artifacts, such as composites, meeting minutes, and memorabilia. The office staff should also provide a range of training and educational programs and information about what a high-functioning chapter looks like, which includes access to materials on current industry trends (e.g., policies, handbooks, changes in terminology).

Providing additional advising support outside of the fraternity/sorority life office can also be helpful to local organizations. Requiring an advisor who is also a faculty/staff member can be useful in helping these student leaders navigate campus dynamics and to provide access to academic coaching. While some local organizations may not have regular alumni contact, others have consistent interaction with those who have graduated, and it can be helpful to intentionally enhance that relationship. Assisting local chapters with forming alumni advisory boards is a recommended practice. The advisory board should be comprised of several geographically close alumni who can maintain ongoing supervision and guidance to the organization. Advisory boards may also consist of campus employees, business persons, or area residents who may not be affiliated with the organization, but who can offer support to the development of the organization. These individuals can offer resources related to community and civic engagement, financial advice, and harm reduction, and provide the type of guidance and direction an inter/national organization might receive from their network of content area experts who serve on staff or as volunteers.

Beyond alumni advisory boards, the fraternity/sorority life staff should make a concerted effort toward building relationships with alumni and undergraduate members. Particularly on campuses comprised of both local and inter/national organizations, or where the organization has severed its ties with the inter/national affiliate, there can be issues of mistrust between the organization and the institution. By maintaining open communication with these groups' members and including them in decisions and discussions, when possible and appropriate, regarding policy changes and implementation, conduct concerns, and trends, the advising staff can help to build trust and ameliorate concerns that the institution is seeking to eliminate or unfairly treat local organizations. The trust built with the organization and its alumni can be vital should conduct issues need to be addressed.

Some campuses have communities that consist only of local organizations, while some recognize both local and inter/national organizations. It can be beneficial to both types of organizations if they are given the opportunity to be part of a common governance unit. For example, SUNY Plattsburgh has an Inter-Sorority Association for all sororities and an Interfraternity Council for all fraternities, while SUNY Geneseo has an Inter-Greek Council for all fraternal organizations.

A common governance experience has many benefits, including allowing local and inter/national organizations to set common community expectations, permitting these organizations to work together for the long-term health and well-being of the fraternal community, and providing both types of organizations the opportunity to learn from one another's experiences and perspectives. Separating organizations into separate councils by type can lead to division and unnecessary competition between organizations.

By adopting a chapter services type model and incorporating local organizations into a governance model that includes any inter/national organizations present, the fraternity/sorority life staff can ensure that the local organization's essential needs are being met in a manner that is consistent with those of the inter/national organizations. This also can help the staff in identifying other people and resources that can assist the local chapter, thus broadening the scope of services provided in a cost-effective manner.

Risk and Harm Reduction

Local organizations are not any more inherently risky than inter/national groups. The amount of risk a local organization assumes is largely based on campus culture. If the inter/national groups on campus have adopted high-risk practices which have been unchecked, then the local organizations will likely mirror that behavior.

A few tips for managing risk in local organizations include:

- Hold all organizations on the campus to the same risk management policies; allowing different expectations for different types of organizations can cause confusion about campus expectations and norms. Though inactive as of 2016-2018, using industry recognized standards like the Fraternal Information and Programming Group (FIPG) policy can provide a blueprint for expectations about risk management in the areas of alcohol, drugs, hazing, and sexual abuse/harassment, and fire, health, and safety for all campus fraternal organizations.
- Require local organizations to maintain liability insurance. The cost of insurance can be cost-prohibitive for many local groups. However, some insurance companies will offer umbrella policies that cover all local organizations under one policy, which can be overseen administratively by the college/university. It is important to ensure that the members understand that a claim against the umbrella policy due to the actions/behaviors of one group will affect the coverage and costs for all local groups.
- In addition to providing harm reduction training, connect local organizations to campus resources that can help them learn more about risk management and harm reduction practices. Professionals that work in the areas of university police/campus safety, Title IX/sexual assault prevention, alcohol/drug prevention, and emergency management can help students develop stronger policies and practices.
- Provide sample crisis management or emergency response protocols that include steps for the president to take in the event of an emergency, a practical checklist of information to collect to assist in an emergency situation, and a guide for cooperating with outsiders (e.g., emergency response officials, college officials, the media, etc.).

Conduct Matters and Closing Organizations

One of the most difficult challenges in advising a local organization may be when they are involved in student conduct issues. With the lack of an inter/national entity, it is up to the institution to investigate, adjudicate, and sanction these organizations.

As mentioned, institutions should have a policy in place related to the registration, closure, and re-registration of local organizations. Both Geneseo and Plattsburgh have policies that when a local organization is closed for disciplinary reasons or folds for organizational troubles, then it will not have the opportunity to re-register at a later time. In addition, both institutions no longer allow for the formation of new local organizations. The rationale behind this decision is because (a) there is not a system in place outside of the institution to support these groups through the formative phases of their development; (b) there is a strong likelihood that upon closure for disciplinary reasons, a local organization may attempt to operate unchecked as an unrecognized group until they are permitted to re-apply for recognition; and (c) limited financial and human resources at the university level can make it difficult to effectively support local organizations so that they are providing positive, enriching experiences for members.

When local organizations must be sanctioned for violating college policy, there are a few key points to keep in mind. Without the support of a inter/national staff member or trained volunteer to help coach them through the change process, the onus of this responsibility falls on the campus fraternity/sorority life professional. It is important to understand that helping students understand why the behavior was problematic and how to redirect the negative behavior is a good investment of time. This can be resource-intensive, but some suggestions include:

- Challenge the organization to do a self-assessment that includes an exploration of the behavior they were disciplined for, why that behavior was problematic, what outcome they were trying to achieve with the behavior, and what alternate solutions may help them achieve a similar outcome without breaking policy. They may not be able to develop a complete solution on their own, but allowing them to wrestle as a group with the process can be enlightening to them and help to get more organizational buy-in for change.
- Engage influential alumni who understand why the behavior is problematic in helping to coach the organization toward positive changes. These alumni can also be ambassadors to other alumni and help them to understand why the changes are necessary.
- Utilize an outside consultant/professional to help the organization develop new practices that will accomplish their desired outcomes in a healthier way. Oftentimes, consultants will meet with multiple groups over the course of a campus visit, which can allow the local organization to split the cost with another group or with the fraternity/sorority life office. For example, if a local group is disciplined for violating the campus alcohol policy, a risk management consultant may also agree to provide a community-wide risk management training or one-on-one organization consultations, in addition to his or her work with the local organization during their visit.

Unfortunately, not all sanctions are effective and sometimes it is necessary to close the organization. Closing a local organization should not be taken lightly, especially for those organizations who have rich histories on a campus. However, it may be the only option when multiple attempts to correct dysfunctional behavior have not been successful or when the behavior is so egregious that it likely cannot be reformed.

Steps must be taken to notify alumni of the reasons behind the closure and to allow them to determine how to memorialize the organization and store any historical artifacts. Particular attention should be paid by the institution to insure that the organization does not attempt to continue to operate as an unrecognized group, including understanding the legal perspectives, getting student buy-in, and taking proactive measures to end underground activity (Crane, Stollman, & Swick-Duttine, 2007).

Conclusion

Although advising local fraternal organizations may provide a unique set of challenges, they need not be viewed as entirely different from their inter/national counterparts. From a day-to-day operational perspective, local and inter/national organizations are indistinguishable. Both are built on a foundation of guiding principles; honor their founders and rituals; recruit, educate, and develop their members; engage in community service and philanthropy; and provide a social and familial connection for students. Locals should not be viewed as, or assumed to be, inherently risky or unruly. Instead, these organizations can offer a campus an opportunity to foster a tradition that is uniquely their own. With some focused attention on establishing office practices and institutional and governance council policies that aim to provide locals with fair and equitable resources, services, and expectations, these groups can contribute meaningfully to the fraternity/sorority community and the campus as a whole.

Table 5.1 Sample Listing of Early Local Organizations Still in Existence in 2018

Organization	University	Year	Fraternity/Sorority
Lambda Iota	University of Vermont	1836	Fraternity
Kappa Kappa Kappa	Dartmouth College	1842	Fraternity
Delta Psi	University of Virginia	1850	Fraternity
Excelsior Men's Society	Heidelberg University	1851	Fraternity
Rensselaer Society of Engineers	Rensselaer Polytechnic Institute	1866	Fraternity
Delta Kappa Tau	SUNY Geneseo	1871	Fraternity
Delta Kappa Pi	Doane University	1883	Fraternity
Pi Beta Sigma	Otterbein University	1908	Fraternity
Phi Chi Epsilon	University of Wisconsin - Whitewater	1921	Fraternity
Zeta Sigma	Alma College	1887	Fraternity
Chi Heorot	Dartmouth College	1897	Fraternity
Nu Sigma Alpha	Heidelberg University	1859	Sorority
Alpha Clionian (Phi Kappa Pi)	SUNY Geneseo	1872	Sorority

Organization	University	Year	Fraternity/Sorority
Agonian Society (Alpha Kappa Phi)	SUNY Geneseo	1885	Sorority
Arethusa (Sigma Gamma Phi)	SUNY Geneseo	1892	Sorority
Sigma Psi	Case Western Reserve University	1897	Sorority
Alpha Delta Epsilon	SUNY Geneseo	1901	Sorority
Sigma Alpha Tau	Otterbein University	1910	Sorority
Epsilon Kappa Tau	Otterbein University	1917	Sorority
Phi Nu	MacMurray College	1853	Sorority
Willard Sorority	Nebraska Wesleyan University	1889	Sorority
Alpha Sigma	University of Wisconsin - Whitewater	1898	Sorority
Sigma Beta Sigma	Young Harris College	1892	Sorority

References

Anson, J. L., & Marchesani, R. F., Jr. (Eds.). (1991). *Baird's manual of American college fraternities* (20th ed.). Indianapolis, IN: Baird's Manual Foundation.

Buffalo State, The State University of New York. (n.d.). History 1950–1959. Retrieved from http://suny.buffalostate.edu/19501959

Crane, M., Stollman, D., & Swick-Duttine, A. (Spring 2007). Exterminating unrecognized groups. *Association of Fraternity/Sorority Advisors Perspectives*, 12–14.

Cultural interest fraternities and sororities. (n.d.). In *Wikipedia*. Retrieved from https://en.wikipedia.org/wiki/Cultural_interest_fraternities_and_sororities

Karasin, R. (2015, November 18). Tufts' Sigma Phi Epsilon chapter disaffiliates from national organization. *The Tufts Daily*. Retrieved from https://tuftsdaily.com/news/2015/11/18/tufts-sigma-phi-epsilon-chapter-disaffiliates-national-organization/

Phired Up. (2013). Campus growth survey. Retrieved from http://phiredup.com/Websites/phiredup/images/2013_CAMPUS_GROWTH_SURVEY_RESULTS_-_FINAL_12.2.2013_942.pdf

Pi Beta Phi. (n.d.). Timeline. Retrieved from https://www.pibetaphi.org/pibetaphi/About_Us/History/Timeline/

State U. bans social societies on bias count. (1953, October 9). *Cornell Daily Sun*. Retrieved from https://cdsun.library.cornell.edu/cgi-bin/cornell?a=d&d=CDS19531009.2.8&

Webb v. State of New York, 125 F.Supp. 910 (1954).

CHAPTER 6

The Role of the Campus Professional

Kelly Jo Karnes Hendricks and Carolyn E. Whittier, PhD

Introduction

Advisor. Educator. Administrator. Manager. Advocate. Leader. These elements are universal to the role of the campus based professional; however, the manner in which each of these elements is executed may differ significantly. The campus philosophy and relationship with fraternities and sororities will be a fundamental element that defines the role of the campus based fraternity and sorority advisor, and it cannot be ignored when working to understand the role from campus to campus.

At the foundation, the campus based fraternity and sorority professional should serve as an educator. Using their foundation as an educator, the skill set then expands to understanding the specific needs of the fraternity and sorority population on the campus, and advocating for the healthiest possible experience. Knowing the best practices in fraternity and sorority advising, having access to resources, and participating in continuous professional development are elements that will aid in gaining a stronger understanding and implementation of the fraternity and sorority professional role.

"It is the responsibility of those who work with these organizations to apply practices that enable success at both the student and organizational level" (Council for the Advancement of Standards, 2014, pg. 4). This should be universal regardless of campus approach or relationship with individual fraternities and sororities, governing councils, alumni, or other related entities.

Being the Face of Fraternity and Sorority Life on Campus

Campus based fraternity and sorority professionals are often expected to be a campus expert on all things that relate to fraternities and sororities, including housing, student conduct, member development, recruitment, retention, advisor training, networking, and so on. Therefore, the campus professional can find themselves being the public face of the experience to all other entities on campus, including faculty, administrators, coaches, parents, prospective students, and alumni.

Being the face of the fraternity and sorority experience will require that the campus professional is well versed on the statistical facts of the community, including but not limited to: number of chapters, number of members, percentage of campus population, academic standing, graduation rates, community service hours, philanthropy dollars, and other critical statistics. It is also imperative that the campus based fraternity and sorority professional is up to date on the events impacting the fraternity and sorority industry around the country.

Another part of being the face of the experience is to challenge and support students to create a relevant fraternity and sorority experience for today's college student. Not accepting the status quo is imperative, and continuing to evaluate the experience to ensure relevance of activities, events, and programs will be critical.

Finally, the campus based professional must determine the balance between all of the different areas of responsibility that are part of the position. How much time should you spend advising councils versus individual chapters and chapter officers? What time should be dedicated to the training and development of chapter and faculty advisors? How will you balance programmatic responsibilities with evaluation and assessment of the programs being offered? And, how will your time be spent when a crisis or major incident occurs?

Serving as the public face of the fraternity and sorority experience can be an engaging opportunity when meeting with prospective students and parents, faculty and staff members, and alumni. Campus professionals need to work with their supervisor to gain understanding about the manner in which the fraternity and sorority advisor is the face, and when there are better opportunities for the student leaders to be the face of their own experience.

The Role of the Campus Professional in Advising Councils

One of the primary roles that any fraternity and sorority advisor (FSA) will assume with their position is that of working with the various governing councils on their campus. These governing councils are the umbrella organizations to similar typed groups. They may include interfraternity councils, Panhellenic councils, National Pan-Hellenic Councils (NPHC) and united or multicultural Greek councils. The names may vary from campus to campus, but the councils' mission generally remains the same: to serve as the information-disseminating bodies to the chapters and participate as the programming team for the member organizations within their council.

The governing councils on our campuses are seen, for some, as the next level of leadership opportunities for a student within the fraternity and sorority community. Not only are these council officers asked to think more globally about the larger fraternity and sorority experience versus focusing on the needs and successes of their own chapter, but they have tremendous access to a variety of university administrators.

Often the council leaders are most visible and active when working with the fraternity and sorority advisor on campus. At times, the energy the FSA puts into the council-level students can come at a cost to the greater fraternity and sorority community. "With a focus on system-level activity, [the FSA] meets most often with system-level student leaders, such as Order of Omega, Interfraternity Council, Panhellenic, and All-Greek Council leaders, and have less routine contact with other student leaders, non-officer chapter members, or volunteer advisors of individual chapters. Unfortunately, their interactions with chapters are more often reactive to a particular issue or problem rather than proactive in terms of group or member development" (Hogan, Koepsell, & Eberly, 2011).

While the councils serve an important role in the governance of the communities to insure they are following both university and national policies, they can at times present larger challenges for the fraternity and sorority advisor, and can distract from opportunities of time better spent with chapter-level leadership. We offer just a few common pitfalls at the council level, as well as a few suggestions on how FSAs might work with their teams to overcome the following:

1. **A growing number of young leaders assuming council-level positions.** We often see men and women running for a council leadership role having only been a member of their own organizations for one (1) semester, or maybe one (1) year. These students are still learning the business of being a member of a fraternity or sorority, yet they are yearning for the titles and experiences that will help them after graduation. This misplaced confidence can be an issue when a younger leader has not yet graduated to the "what's best for the community" mentality.

Suggestion: Try working with your councils to establish guidelines for officer requirements. While most bylaws may include GPA requirements, consider working with leaders to add minimum years of membership requirements and previous leadership roles within a chapter executive board as a qualification to run for a position.

2. **Councils that manage significantly large bank accounts.** It is not unheard of on some campuses for councils to have thousands, if not hundreds of thousands of dollars in various accounts, both on campus and off. As councils collect chapter dues, fees for potential new members to participate in experiences such as recruitment, step show revenues, as well as the execution of various fundraising and philanthropy events, it is not surprising that council officers between 19 and 21 years old are left to oversee and manage large budgets of these organizations.

    Suggestion: Make sure safety nets are in place for both on-campus and off-campus accounts that include multiple checks and balances with how money is spent. The FSA should never be the sole signer on an account but should also be a part of a two-step process for writing checks and spending council funds. Councils that continue to collect and build up large sums of money should really consider working with the university foundation office to create and endow scholarships for members. FSAs should work with councils to properly invest back into the leadership experiences, academic achievements, and community service endeavors of outstanding members within the community.

3. **Holding peers accountable to achieve "self-governance" within the council.** Accountability at any age is never easy, but add in the peer pressure of college life, and it becomes even more difficult. Councils often want to have a role in the governance of their chapters when mistakes and wrongdoings occur, yet when these opportunities are not taken seriously, the university will revoke this privilege and resort to conduct hearings and judicial panels through the Dean of Students office.

    Suggestion: Councils should work hand in hand with the university conduct office to be trained on how to self-govern their member organizations, providing due process when hearing cases and understanding what appropriate sanctions might include. The fraternity and sorority advisor should insure that a clear understanding of judicial processes and procedures are used for each hearing, with the same "script" followed, as to offer no room for deviation or self-interpretation by the students. The FSA should be there to listen and answer questions during the hearing process but should not be making the decisions for the students.

Ultimately, working with council officers can be a very rewarding experience for fraternity and sorority advisors. The best role that an FSA can take with each council is that of an individualized approach to advising. You may not have the same new member paperwork with the Panhellenic council as you would with the NPHC. Remember that processes and experiences for member organizations within the different councils are unique, and there should not be a blanket advising approach to all. Understanding each organizational culture and how to best work with each council comes with time and by asking questions and educating yourself.

Ozaki and Johnston (2008) offer a few suggestions to advisors when supporting a wide variety of students, which include understanding how your own identity may be perceived by students and keeping in mind the potential and important impact you can have on the development of organizations and their members. These thoughts offer a good road map to assist campus professionals as they define their work with student leaders of various councils.

The Role of the Campus Professional in Advising Chapters

An additional primary role for the fraternity and sorority advisor is working with the individual chapters on the campus. There are multiple ways in which chapter advising responsibilities are managed based on the number of professional and graduate staff members working with fraternities and sororities. On some campuses, the chapter advising assignments correlate with the council advising assignments; that is, the NPHC advisor then advises all of the chapters with membership in the NPHC council. On other campuses, the office holds a selection process to have different staff members working with a wider variety of chapters both inside and outside of their council advising responsibilities.

When working with individual chapters and chapter officers, it is important to know and understand what role the current chapter advisor and advisory board members are playing. The fraternity and sorority advisor should be working in cooperation with the other advisors that have been asked to serve in the chapter advisory roles. It is not the FSA's job to serve as the primary chapter advisor to each of the organizations, and when there is no primary chapter advisor present, the FSA should be working with the inter/national organization to recruit, select, and train someone to serve in that role.

The primary purpose of working with the individual chapters is to assist in their focus on chapter goals within the context of the larger fraternity and sorority experience. Meeting with chapter presidents and other primary chapter officers to provide guidance and resources that will aid the chapter in providing a healthier experience for their members should be paramount. The campus based fraternity and sorority advisor will also play a vital role with individual chapters in time of crisis and risk management.

When chapter members make poor choices, it is often the responsibility of the fraternity and sorority advisor to make the initial outreach to the chapter leadership to review the details of the situation and create a plan of action moving forward. The FSA will also be responsible for working with the chapter advisors as well as the inter/national organization staff and volunteers on the cooperative response to the undergraduate students.

Often during the response to a chapter behavioral situation is when the lines of fraternity and sorority advocate and fraternity and sorority accountability get blurred. Campus based fraternity and sorority advisors must understand that working to hold chapters accountable for their behavior choices *is* being an advocate for the experience. Often, the relationship between the FSA and the individual chapter is tested during these types of situations, and the FSA must remain diligent in their efforts to help the chapter learn and grow rather than being worried about the chapter liking them personally.

When working with individual chapters, there can be wonderful accomplishments and relationships developed, and there can also be a number of pitfalls that campus based professionals walk into. Here, we make a few suggestions on how to work through these situations:

1. **Serving as a surrogate chapter advisor:** In the absence of a chapter advisor, or when there is one in name only, it is natural for the FSA to want to step in to help. The assistance of the FSA is wonderful and often welcomed by the individual chapter. It is critical that the fraternity and sorority advisor know and understand the limits by which they should be involved in chapter operations.
    Suggestion: Assisting chapter officers in areas such as member development, new member education, public relations, risk management, and scholarship are all well within the appropriate areas of advising for a university professional. When the FSA begins to get involved with chapter finances, chapter member accountability, and ritual is when the advising relationship may have crossed a boundary that is not desired. If the chapter is in need of assistance with things such as finance, internal member accountability, and ritual, the FSA should defer to the inter/national organization professional staff and volunteers to engage with the undergraduate student leaders.

2. **Be their advisor and not their friend:** When working with individual student leaders in chapters, strong interpersonal relationships will be formed, and that is natural. "A grey area, however, is balancing the line between friendship with the students we interact with and maintaining our role as advisor" (Sassman, 2011, pg. 17). The FSA will serve as a role model and guide for many within the fraternity and sorority community. When those relationships turn into friendships

that no longer follow professional boundaries, that is when challenges can occur.

Suggestion: When working to establish strong working relationships with individual chapter officers, make sure that you are always meeting in a professional location and not in personal spaces (homes, student rooms, etc.). Meeting for coffee on campus is a great way to be in a more casual setting for your conversations and meetings, or you could go for a walk on campus if there is a desire to get out of your office. We do not recommend socializing with students or spending time with them in their personal spaces as to ensure that the advisor–student boundary is clear and understood by all.

3. **Know when to back away:** Following a critical incident or a chapter crisis, the campus based professional may have spent a great deal of time with the undergraduate members and leaders in a specific chapter, and that may have been needed during that time. As the chapter operations begin to return to normal, it is important to know when to back away and allow the chapter to operate on their own with the support of their chapter advisors and advisory board. This step will not devalue the role you played during the critical issue, but will allow the chapter to learn to self-govern again and not be so reliant on the time you have been giving them to assist during a very challenging time.

Advising chapters is a wonderful part of the campus based fraternity and sorority advisor responsibilities. Supporting students through the challenges of leading their peers, the interpersonal relationship management of serving as a chapter leader, and the realities of responding to chapter member behavior is filled with opportunities to help students learn and grow. Campus based fraternity and sorority professionals must maintain professional boundaries and know the limitations when it comes to engaging with specific chapter operations.

The Role of the Campus Professional in Working with Alumni and Corporation Boards

Within any campus fraternity and sorority community, there are a variety of stakeholders inside and outside of the institution. Stakeholders include students, alumni, inter/national fraternity/sorority staff, volunteer governing bodies of these organizations (e.g., the National Panhellenic Conference), parents, police and fire officials, and community members, among others (Mamarchev, Sina, & Heida, 2003). Many would argue that our most successful chapters, as defined by chapter size, high academic standards, and ability to follow both campus and inter/national policies, can be traced to a high functioning and robust alumni board. The opportunities for a campus based fraternity and sorority advisor to invest time and energy into these chapter "coaches" can be extremely valuable not only for the individual chapters, but for the entire community.

Unfortunately, we know that often chapters may have one or maybe two active alumni advisors with their organization who are tasked with overseeing all of the aspects of chapter business. "Individuals serving in these intersecting advising roles often have common personal experiences in a fraternity or sorority, limited professional experience in student and/or organizational development, and little or no training" (Hogan, Koepsell, & Eberly, 2011).

As an FSA on a college campus, do not underestimate the power that these stakeholders have with your chapters, and your ability to collaborate and invest time with these boards will provide long-standing effects on the success of the chapters. Some best practices for ways to invest with advisors might include the following:

1. **Define the Roles:** It is important that the chapter's on-campus or off-campus advisor or a housing corporation board member understand what their intended role should be with assisting the chapter. Often chapter advisors may take on not only the specific role (i.e., Recruitment Advisor, New Member Advisor, House Corporation Board President, etc.), but also undefined roles, such as mentor, team builder, conflict mediator, educator, motivator, or policy interpreter. A chapter advisor may assume numerous roles, but the key idea to convey to them is that they are the *advisor*, not the leader (ACPA Commission for Student Involvement, Advisor Manual, 2006).

2. **Provide advisors the tools to succeed:** The FSA should provide chapter advisors copies of campus/council policies, contact information for frequently used resources, training manuals for online tools used by the fraternity and sorority community, and regular consistent communication about upcoming events, programs, and trainings within the community. Err on the side of providing more information to insure advisors feel included and informed.

3. **Model a "team approach" in working with the chapter:** Each person has a role to play in the success of working with a chapter and its members. "Volunteer advisors attend chapter meetings at which they can ostensibly influence the entire group and better understand the entire organization's health. FSAs support inter-fraternal or governance bodies that provide a consistent message and offer systemic solutions to persistent problems" (Hogan, Koepsell, & Eberly, 2011). In addition, for chapters with housing structures, the House Corporation Board insures that the physical building is properly maintained and serves as

the property owner to the contracted renters within the chapter. Each person has a responsibility to the success of the various aspects of the chapter.

Ultimately, fraternity and sorority chapters are small businesses that not only provide social outlets, leadership skills, and academic support for students, but in some cases provide members their living and learning community outside of campus life. Strong advisors can be the one consistent factor as each new academic year cycles in another group of student leaders and members. Investing time into training and providing the tools necessary for these chapter coaches will guarantee long-term success for our organizations.

The Role of the Campus Professional as a Partner

One of the most important relationships for the campus based professional is the one with the Director of Chapter Services (or similar title) at each of the inter/national organizations that host a chapter on the campus. Making contact with each of these headquarters based professionals or volunteers should be one of the very first actions a new campus professional makes as they get established on campus. Creating an effective working relationship with the inter/national organization will aid in working through both positive and challenging times for the chapter.

There has often been a reference of an "us vs. them" mentality when thinking about campus based and headquarters based fraternity and sorority professionals, and this is absolutely the wrong approach. Both sets of professionals need to work together as a team to ensure that the collegiate chapter is providing a healthy experience for the undergraduate members.

While the approach is as a team, each entity plays a different role in the success of the undergraduate chapter, and here are a few things to consider when establishing a strong working relationship with individual inter/national organization staff and volunteers.

1. **Understanding Role Differences:** The role of the campus based professional is to be the content expert on campus culture, student climate, and institutional rules, regulations, and policies. The inter/national organization staff and volunteers are to be the content experts on their fraternity/sorority, organizational culture, expectations of chapters and members, and policies. The campus based professional should work diligently to learn as much as they can about the individual organizations and read the materials that are sent to help inform the fraternity and sorority advisor about the expectations for a specific chapter. However, when you do not know the answer, don't guess.

Campus professionals should pick up the phone and ask how a specific inter/national organization expects the chapter to engage in certain areas of chapter operation. While many things are similar among all fraternities and sororities, there is very little that is universal among all individual groups. Seeking guidance from the inter/national organization when advising their chapter on your campus is a must, and it is not a step that can be skipped along the way.

2. **Business model vs. educational model:** Both the inter/national organization and the college/university desire a healthy and vibrant experience for undergraduate students, and both will work cooperatively to make that happen. Tension can enter into the relationship when working through a response to a chapter behavioral issue. For the campus based professional, the educational outcomes are paramount. The inter/national organization is also focused on the educational outcomes, but it must also give consideration to other areas such as organizational procedures, financial implications, and investment in the chapter. When there is a recommendation to close a chapter, the campus based professional would be wise to ask questions about the financial implications of that decision, such as the future dispensation of a chapter facility (if there is one), any debt that the chapter is currently carrying, the impact of alumni donations to either the university or the organization, and other areas. None of these should be used as a deciding factor in the decision to not close a chapter; however, they all need to be reviewed and discussed prior to a final decision to ensure proper communication and planning has taken place.

3. **Freedom of Information inquiries:** Campus based fraternity and sorority advisors need to learn how Freedom of Information inquiries are processed at their college or university. Understanding of the law and how the institution responds to those requests is a must for all fraternity and sorority advisors. Given that information, the campus based professional will better understand if and when the inter/national organization may not be willing to share certain documents or other communication items. Inter/national fraternities and sororities are private membership organizations and have the right to protect information; therefore, the campus based professional should not assume that the inter/national organization is a bad partner or hiding something.

Spending time developing a strong working relationship with each of the inter/national organizations that host a chapter on your campus is a critical element for success.

Failing to communicate, share, and build that relationship will not serve the undergraduate students well, and will cause more challenges moving forward.

Other Duties as Assigned for a Fraternity & Sorority Advisor

As with many jobs within Student Affairs, the ominous line in our position descrip-
tions that states "other duties as assigned" can truly take on a whole other meaning for
those working with fraternity and sorority communities. There are tangible tasks that
many of us may not have factored into our jobs, but there are also numerous intangible
responsibilities that may be coupled with working with fraternity and sorority students
on a college campus. The following is not an exhaustive list, but it will give those supervising or considering work as an FSA an accurate glimpse at the other roles campus
advisors take on.

1. **Unofficial Landlord/House Inspector/Housing Authority:** For
    campuses with either university owned housing, privately owned fa-
    cilities (owned by a chapter House Corporation Board), or "unofficial"
    housing, the FSA is often looked to as the person to reassure parents,
    students, university officials, or city officials that living conditions are
    maintained and humane for anyone in the spaces. It is not unheard
    of for FSAs to do a start and end of the year walk-through of proper-
    ties with university or city officials, nor to be the receiver of calls and
    requests from neighborhood associations or neighbors if properties
    become unsightly or unkempt.
2. **Chaperone/Crowd Control/Security:** Serving as an FSA, there is
    often an expectation that any event occurring on or off campus that
    includes a chapter or council will have a staff member present for part of
    the event, if not the full duration. The thought of having a "responsible"
    university staff member at the event is to insure that there are no issues.
    Other duties might include serving as crowd control for large events,
    social monitoring for tailgating and other athletic events, or even in
    some cases being security for programs such as late night dances, con-
    certs, comedians, and so forth.
3. **Expert of all topics that could be related to fraternities and sorori-
    ties:** The title of Fraternity and Sorority Advisor also comes with the
    responsibility of now being the campus expert for topics including:
    hazing, alcohol abuse and use, mental health, academic excellence,
    event planning, risk management, recruitment of new members, re-
    lationships (with parent, students, alumni, house corporation boards,
    neighborhood association, etc.), and so forth. Others on campus call

you because of your ample experience with waiver forms, liability insurance, bystander intervention, ability to have critical conversations,
and serving as a mediator between individuals and groups. Most FSAs
do not receive comprehensive training on all of these topics, yet we
rely on sessions at the Association of Fraternity/Sorority Advisors
Annual Meeting, virtual training sessions, or conferences such as the
National Association of Student Personnel Administrators (NASPA)
or the American College Personnel Association (ACPA) to help with
tips and tricks to at least act the role until, after a while, they truly are
the expert.

"Advising undergraduate fraternity and sorority organizations is a multifaceted
function within student affairs" (Council for the Advancement of Standards, 2014, p.
2). Managing the multiple relationships, policies, and best practices can be exciting and
overwhelming. Staying focused on the educational outcomes of the fraternity and sorority experience will always prove to be an outstanding foundation from which to work.

References

ACPA Commission for Student Involvement. (2006). Advisor manual.
Council for the Advancement of Standards. (2014). Fraternity and sorority advising programs.
Hogan, T., Koepsell, M., & Eberly, C. (2011). Rethinking fraternity and sorority advising: The
    role of coaching and technology. *Leadership Exchange, 9*(3), 12–15.
Mamarchev, H. L., Sina, J. A., & Heida, D. E. (2003). Creating and managing a campus
    oversight plan: Do they work? What are the alternatives? In D. E. Gregory (Ed.), *The
    administration of fraternal organizations on North American campuses.* Asheville, NC:
    College Administration Publications.
Ozaki, C. C., & Johnston, M. (2008). The space between: Issues for multiracial student orga-
    nizations and advising. *New Directions for Student Services, 123,* 53–61.
Sassman, S. (Summer 2011). Should I befriend the students I advise? *Perspectives,* 17.

CHAPTER 7

The Impact of Short-Term Visits: Consultant Perceptions on Organizational Development

Jamie Workman and Gary Ballinger

Introduction

Research about the fraternity and sorority experience and the impact it has on student behavior and development is plentiful. A smaller portion of research examines fraternity and sorority member leadership and the impact of organizational development (Biddix & Underwood, 2010; Taylor, 2010). These studies, however, focus on individual chapters and not the larger functions of their parent organizations. Undergraduate chapters are part of a larger entity, and many report to an inter/national headquarters or central office. Some headquarters are staffed entirely by paid professionals, some by volunteers, and some use a combination of the two. One common responsibility of headquarters staff is to focus on chapter growth and development. While each organization classifies this position differently, the term "consultant" is commonly used. For the purpose of this chapter, we define this term as a professional or volunteer who provides a variety of services to chapters including operational support, organizational development, and programming, among others.

This chapter addresses the role of fraternity and sorority short-term consultant visits. Current and former consultants, both professional and volunteer, were interviewed regarding their perceived level of effectiveness. The chapter provides a history on chapter visits and the consultant program creation and purpose. It continues with current common practices of short-term visits including chapter leadership training, advisement, and assessment. This chapter assesses the impact of current practices and concludes with a discussion on recommendations for change to better support the needs of the fraternity and sorority community.

Literature Review

Research on the modern-day fraternity and sorority experience dates back to 1930 (Brailey, 1951). A significant portion of the literature relates to behavioral topics such as alcohol use (Asel, Seifert, & Pascarella, 2009; Caudill et al., 2006; Pascarella & Terenzini, 2005; Perkins, Zimmerman, & Janosik, 2011) and hazing (McCreary, Strategies, Bray, & Thoma, 2016; Owen, Burke, & Vichesky, 2008; Sweet, 1999). Each of these research topics highlights negative behaviors and stigmatizes the fraternity and sorority experience. Another area of research relates to the diversity, or lack of diversity, in organizational membership (Pascarella & Terenzini, 2005) and members' interactions with diverse others (Asel, Seifert, & Pascarella, 2009). Conversely, Hughey and Parks (2011) and Moreno and Banuelos (2013) noted the importance of Greek-letter organizations that historically support underrepresented populations, particularly within the African American and Latinx communities (Hughey & Parks, 2011; Moreno & Banuelos, 2013), as key factors in student success.

Additional research explores members' leadership development. Havel, Martin, and Pascarella (2014) examined the impact membership in a Greek-letter organization has on the development of socially responsible leadership, an element of the Social Change Model (SCM), a widely used model of college student leadership development developed by the Higher Education Research Institute (HERI). Based on the SCM, students demonstrate socially responsible leadership by meeting goals related to self (consciousness of self, congruence, commitment), group process (collaboration, common purpose, controversy with civility), and community values (citizenship and change) (HERI, 1996). Their initial research of academic year 2012–2013 first-year students found positive significant differences in three of the eight measured areas: common purpose, citizenship, and change. In a follow-up study conducted with the same population four years later, the team found no statistical significance in any area. Based on those results, the team determined that fraternity or sorority membership did not promote the development of socially responsible leadership (Havel, Martin, & Pascarella, 2014).

Research has also been conducted on the impact central office programming has on member leadership development. Biddix and Underwood (2010) conducted a 10-year study of a leadership program sponsored by a fraternity national office. Their study included over 2,000 undergraduate men who were members of the organization. The study found that participants who attended the program attained leadership positions in chapters, volunteered to serve in advisory capacities, and made financial contributions to the organization. Similarly, Taylor (2010) examined leadership programs by National Panhellenic Council (NPC) headquarters. In her study, Taylor surveyed 26 NPC organizations and found their headquarters offered a variety of leadership programs to its members, including leadership institutes, workshops, conferences, and consultant presentations. Taylor found these programs developed women in a variety of ways but lacked a connection to women's leadership theory. Further, Wright (2011) conducted a four-year evaluation and strategic assessment plan of a similar central office leadership program. Wright's research focused on group outcomes such as Grade Point Average (GPA), recruitment class and initiate class sizes, risk management violations, and chapter recognition. Significant correlations were found between leadership program participation and both recruitment rates and chapter recognition. GPA, initiation rates, and risk management violations varied from year to year and did not yield a correlation to program participation.

Organization and Governance

Prior to the Civil War, existing fraternities were not fully developed. Chapters were united only by relative geography, their common name, and their common principles. Baird described organization as "independent to the verge of anarchy" (1963, p. 14) and inter-chapter communication as "inadequate and not used" (p. 14). He noted practices such as organizations established at colleges without prior approval from other chapters, and in some cases no communication to the institution where it was established. This lack of communication, both between chapters and with institutions, often resulted in groups dissolving before they truly became part of the larger organization.

During the post-Civil War era, fraternities began to make progress toward an organized government. "Grand" chapters, either the alpha or another early chapter, were created to serve as a resource to other entities and act as the governing body of the organization. These chapters took direction from the assembly of delegates during conventions, which were established to maintain administration of the organization as a whole (Baird, 1963).

From this, a new governance began to form. While convention delegates maintained legislative authority, the executive, administrative and, when necessary, judicial functions of the organization began to shift to alumni. Alumni representatives were elected based on location or connection to a specific chapter. According to Baird they "resembled in dignity and complexion the board of trustees of a college" (p. 15). Titled an "executive council" or similar name, alumni boards began to oversee the governance, administrative and, when needed, judicial aspects of the organization.

Fraternities began efforts to visit chapters and provide additional support early on in the establishment of the early fraternal movement. The topic of traveling secretaries was discussed at early meetings of the Inter-Fraternity Conference dating back to the early 1900s. In notes from those meetings, many fraternities discussed their plan to provide volunteer or professional support to undergraduate chapters. Theta Delta Chi was recognized as being an early adopter of chapter support, as it noted that the national president made an effort to visit each chapter every year beginning as early as 1861. The goal of the visits was to create uniformity in ritual and initiation ceremonies and examine chapter records (Hulley, 1912; Syrett, 2009). Other organizations would begin to adapt this visitation model, and the program was expanded steadily with the addition of professional staff, often beginning as a solitary individual to serve as what was called a traveling secretary. With the rapid expansion of organizations in the 1950s and 1960s, the need for a central office became necessary. Central offices were created to provide governance, expand organization, and further engage alumni.

Today's central offices vary in structure, ranging from a body of volunteer alumni to multiple full-time staff supporting the organization as a whole. Derived from the role of traveling secretaries, a current common practice among central office staff or volunteers is to provide chapter visitations. Some fraternities and sororities employ leadership consultants to serve in this role. Beta Theta Pi, for example, defines a leadership consultant as someone who:

> Fosters strong relationships with chapters, volunteers, and universities within a region while providing coaching on operations, organizational development and general Fraternity initiatives. This person assists members and communities in the form of operational support, leadership development, expansion and education through the promotional principles and obligations of [the] fraternity. (Beta Theta Pi, 2017, para. 1)

Other organizations rely on alumni volunteers to serve in this role. Many National Pan-Hellenic Council (NPHC), National Association of Latino Fraternal Organizations (NALFO), and National Asian Pacific Islander Desi American Panhellenic Association (NAPA) organizations are heavily driven by volunteers. These volunteers often provide support to their organizations on top of other full-time employment, and often without financial and other resources that organizations with full-time staff can provide. Early in the 1990s Kappa Alpha Psi (an NPHC organization) led the way in the NPHC community by creating consultants similar to North-American Interfraternity Conference (NIC) and NPC organizations, but the program was not continued (Kimbrough, 2003).

Short-Term Visit Common Practices

As part of a larger study, individuals who have served as consultants, either professionally or in volunteer capacities, were interviewed to discuss their experiences. From this, several common practices were determined. Participants were assigned approximately 25 chapters per year, with some requiring multiple visitations. The typical length of a visit is two to three days, with some being slightly longer, depending on the needs of the chapter. Consultants performed a wide variety of services during their visits, including but not limited to meeting with executive officers, committee chairs, chapter members, campus fraternity and sorority professionals, and chapter advisors. They conducted various presentations on recruitment strategies and risk management protocol. A number of activities included the engagement of students through goal setting and mission, vision, and values development. Additionally, consultants worked with chapters to address any conduct or behavioral issues, and assisted chapters who struggled with low membership, lack of engagement, or other organizational challenges.

When asked about their impact on the organizations during short-term visits, the consultants consistently said it was minimal. A common concern was that a two- to three-day visit was not enough time to build genuine relationships with the members, which was a high priority. Christopher, a former consultant of an NIC organization, stated:

> Those two- to three-day visits were definitely not enough time to build those relationships in order to have a real impactful and honest conversation about those issues.

> It turns into someone else in the national office telling me about risk management stuff.

> As a consultant you can't not bring it up but if you didn't have time to build that relationship then that conversation is not going to be very effective.

Addison, a former consultant of an NPC organization and current fraternity and sorority campus professional, elaborated on how she believed she needed more time to make an impact on organizations:

> there's some [chapters] where it was just a check in and ask the questions I needed to and left. I think the ones that I had longer visits with and spend more time with I was able to build stronger relationships with the women in the chapter and help them figure out if there were issues in the chapter what they needed to do.

While some large organizations have the ability to utilize a paid professional staff, a number of organizations rely on an intricate body of volunteers to assist in the day-to-day operation of undergraduate chapters. Darren, a regional volunteer for a National Pan-Hellenic Council fraternity noted:

> I have responsibility for several different entities in my area and work with nearly fifty undergraduate and graduate chapters in the region. The process can take a lot of time and effort to coordinate and communicate with all volunteers and undergraduate students, but I enjoy it. It is a challenge to connect with each organization and I have to rely on local advisors to support the daily operations.

Jillian, a volunteer and member of the National Association of Latino Fraternal Organizations, believed that it is imperative for headquarters and alumni volunteers to have regular face-to-face interaction with chapters:

> The best time that I am able to connect with students and chapters I work with is during regional drive-ins or workshops. My organization hosts these events on an annual basis at least. Chapters that do not attend the meetings often times have substantial fines that they will take on as attendance at the regionals is mandatory.

Jon, a member of a multicultural interest fraternity, reiterated the importance of regular contact but noted that as a volunteer it was difficult to connect without the use of current technology:

> I may not get to physically visit a chapter each year, but we are able to utilize technology with skype or conference calls to help fill in the gaps when necessary. My fraternity also conducts regular national conference calls where undergraduate brothers call in to receive updates from the national board on various initiatives and expectations. It has been an effective communication tool for us.

Regardless of the type of organization the consultants served, based on their experiences and perspectives, the current practice of short-term visits is not the only model of support that should be offered for today's fraternities and sororities.

Recommendations for Change

As we consider the current practice of short-term visits, particularly when coupled with the tenets of the SCM, several recommendations for change are suggested in order to best support undergraduate members of Greek-letter organizations. As noted previously, a short-term, two- to three-day visit is not enough time to truly engage with students. When trying to develop students in the SCM areas of congruence, commitment, and common purpose, for example, consultants can only have minimal impact during a short-term visit. Multiple professional consultants noted that those organizations which incorporate longer visitation programs, particularly for new or struggling chapters, were much more effective. It is therefore imperative that national bodies consider programs or a staffing model that accounts for the need to develop deep and meaningful relationships between staff and students. A modified model of support may include a very strong commitment of local and regional volunteers with additional expert level support from the national organization and staff.

Additionally, several consultants noted the typical length of employment and age at which many take on the positions as a concern. Those in NIC or NPC organizations typically served as consultants for one to two years and were employed immediately after completing their undergraduate degrees. In multiple cases, former consultants noted they had difficulty establishing authority with chapter leadership, as they were often seen as a peer. The length of service for any NIC or NPC member that served as a consultant was two years, with one year being more common. It was noted that a longer duration of employment would aid in a consistent consultant working with a particular chapter. Consistency could be key to develop organizational culture, establish rapport, and build a sense of commitment and institutional memory.

While many fraternities and sororities have developed support systems utilizing precise geographic regions related to chapter management, it may be valuable to develop smaller chapter groupings of 10 or fewer chapters. Regional associations are often expansive, and some chapters travel hundreds of miles to attend regular workshops or events. Developing regions that put minimal stress and impact on undergraduate students could help alleviate financial stress, time management, and risk management issues concerning travel. Organizations may want to reconsider establishing chapters where there is not a strong alumni volunteer network for support. Geographically isolated chapters result in disconnect from the inter/national organization and is antithetical to the purpose of what are supposed to be close associations of like-minded people with shared values.

Many former staff members stressed the importance of a strong group of local alumni as a method of support. We would encourage the expansion of the volunteer "alumni" support system and supplement it with a strong volunteer training and advisory network of members and non-members alike. While fraternities and sororities have their own private rituals, traditions, and values, there are a number of commonalities that translate from one organization to another. Training and recruiting volunteers that are dedicated to the fraternal movement and student development as a whole can provide sustained supplemental support for undergraduate chapters. Membership in a particular organization should not be a barrier for someone who can be a dedicated passionate volunteer.

A final recommendation for the chapter support program would be the development of a thorough assessment system that will allow organizations to track the impact of the inter/national organization support and the development of student leaders. In an era where the value of fraternity and sorority membership is constantly doubted, having empirical data to show the impact on personal development can be key to sustaining growth of fraternal organizations. Inter/national organizations need to measure the growth of their leaders and all of the programs and services that they offer. They must constantly adapt to the changing times and needs of college students as the needs of each generation changes. A leadership development model should be selected and become a heavy influence on the programmatic pieces offered by the organization. Utilizing a program developed around the Social Change Model would allow an organization to identify both personal and chapter growth.

Summary and Conclusion

Fraternities and sororities have existed on college campuses since the formation of Phi Beta Kappa in 1776 and have evolved over time to meet the changing demographics and needs of student members and alumni. The chapter support model that many organizations currently have in place is based upon a dated model that no longer fits the needs of today's fraternity or sorority member. Based upon data gathered as part of a larger body of research, this chapter explored the perceptions of current and former consultants from a variety of Greek-letter organizations. The recommendations are based on participants' perspectives. While further research could provide additional recommendations, those noted previously, coupled with the tenets of the SCM, can better serve today's fraternity and sorority leader.

References

Asel, A. M., Seifert, T. A., & Pascarella, E. T. (2009). The effects of fraternity/sorority membership on college experiences and outcomes: A portrait of complexity. *Oracle: The Research Journal of the Association of Fraternity Advisors, 4*(2), 1–15.

Baird, W. R. (1963). *Baird's manual of American college fraternities.* J. Robson (Ed.). New York, NY: The Alcolm Company. (Original work published 1905)

Beta Theta Pi. (2017). Leadership consultants. Retrieved from http://beta.org/about/traveling-staff/

Biddix, J. P., & Underwood, R. (2010). A ten-year study of individual outcomes from a fraternity center office leadership program. *Oracle: The Research Journal of the Association of Fraternity/Sorority Advisors, 5*(2), 1–21.

Brailey, L. (1951). Fraternity literature, 1930–50. *Banta's Greek Exchange, (39)*2, 58–61.

Caudill, B. D., Crosse, S. B., Campbell, B., Howard, J., Luckey, B., & Blane, H. T. (2006). High-risk drinking among college fraternity members: A national perspective. *Journal of American Health, 55*(3), 141–155.

Hevel, M. S., Martin, G. L., & Pascarella, E. T. (2014). Do fraternities and sororities still enhance socially responsible leadership? Evidence from the fourth year of college. *Journal of Student Affairs Research and Practice, 51*(3), 233–245.

Higher Education Research Institute. (1996). *A social change model of leadership development: Guidebook version III.* College Park, MD: National Clearinghouse for Leadership Programs.

Hughey, M. W., & Parks, G. S. (2011). *Black Greek-letter organizations 2.0: New directions in the study of African American fraternities and sororities.* Jackson, MS: University Press of Mississippi.

Hulley, E. B. (Ed.). (1912). *The Phi Gamma Delta of the ΦΓΔ Fraternity.* Pittsburgh, PA: Phi Gamma Delta.

Kimbrough, W. M. (2003). *Black Greek 101: The culture, customs, and challenges of Black fraternities and sororities.* Cranbury, NJ: Associated University Presses.

McCreary, G., Strategies, D., Bray, N., & Thoma, S. (2016). Bad apples or bad barrels? Moral disengagement, social influence, and the perpetuation of hazing in the college fraternity. *Oracle: The Research Journal of the Association of Fraternity/Sorority Advisors, 11*(2), 1–15.

Moreno, D. R., & Banuelos, S. S. (2013). The Influence of Latina/o Greek sorority and fraternity involvement on Latina/o college student transition and success. *Journal of Latino-Latin American Studies (JOLLAS), 5*(2), 113–125.

Owen, S. S., Burke, T. W., & Vichesky, D. (2008). Hazing in student organizations: Prevalence, attitudes, and solutions. *Oracle: The Research Journal of the Association of Fraternity/Sorority Advisors, 3*(1), 40–58.

Pascarella, E. T., & Terenzini, P. T. (2005). *How college affects students: A third decade of research.* San Francisco, CA: Jossey-Bass.

Perkins, A. B., Zimmerman, J. D., & Janosik, S. M. (2011). Changing trends in the undergraduate fraternity/sorority experience: An evaluative and analytical literature review. *Oracle: The Research Journal of the Association of Fraternity/Sorority Advisors, 6*(1), 57–73.

Sweet, S. (1999). Understanding fraternity hazing: Insights from symbolic interactionist theory. *Journal of College Student Development, 40*(4), 355–363.

Syrett, N. (2009). *The company he keeps.* Chapel Hill, NC: The University of North Carolina Press.

Taylor, G. E. (2010). An analysis of leadership programing sponsored by member organizations of the National Panhellenic Conference. *Oracle: The Research Journal of the Association of Fraternity/Sorority Advisors, 5*(2), 22–33.

Wright, J. T. (2011). *Leadership programming offered by a fraternity central office from 2003-2007: A multi-year evaluation and strategic assessment plan* (Unpublished doctoral dissertation). Valdosta State University, Valdosta, GA.

CHAPTER 8

(Re)Establishing a Fraternal Community

Eric M. Norman and J. Patrick Biddix

FRATERNITY AND SORORITY chapters and communities largely operated on a self-governance model throughout the 20th century. The Dean of Men and Dean of Women would address behavior, but the daily administration was left largely alone until lawsuits changed the liability landscape (Jelke, 2001; Zacker, 2001). Research on fraternity and sorority involvement further demonstrated the need to consider the behavior and future of the campus fraternal community as a whole. As a result, higher education institutions increased administration of chapters through the implementation of university employed fraternity and sorority advisors, mandated reporting, training, assessment programs, campus judicial procedures, and relationship statements.

While these changes have brought forth significant organization, accountability, and policies, there has been an increased need to further address members, chapters, communities, and their problematic behaviors. Increased visibility and severity of incidents has led to community bans across the country (Krone, 2017). For example, in 2017 Ohio State University suspended activities for all 37 fraternities following multiple alcohol and hazing infractions (Jackson, 2017). University administrators at Penn State, Louisiana State, Florida State, Texas State, Indiana University at Bloomington, and the University of Idaho also have suspended fraternity activities, while they examine means with which to change the environment. However, as Allen (2017) mentioned, "if a school were to purge a fraternity for years, until the problem members cycle out, a new crop of students would eventually find their way back to the traditions" (p. 15).

This relatively newer development of wholesale community bans or suspensions has led to greater questions about the sustainability of fraternal communities. Ideas for reform emerging from deliberations and task forces historically have led to incremental changes and developments, but there is some reluctance on the viability of these approaches (Allen, 2017). Some institutions have considered a blank slate approach. This chapter considers the design, operation, function, and implementation of a new fraternal community, built on the framework of a century of lessons from research, policy, practice, and experience.

This chapter posits that the fraternal community today has a significant role and need in higher education. However, administration of this community can be accomplished more effectively though a comprehensive approach that includes the following:

- Identifying Guidance and Supervision
- Understanding Risk Management
- Ensuring Clear and Consistent Expectations
- The Case for Deferred Recruitment
- Standardizing Education and Training
- Assessing Community Service Outcomes
- Reconsidering Chapter Housing
- Planning for Expansion

This chapter reviews of each of these considerations and includes recommendations for practice and implementation. Many of these proposals directly parallel and enhance the 1990 American Council of Education recommendations to enhance fraternity and sorority life.

Identifying Guidance and Supervision

Campus administrators have continuously developed, updated, and implemented policies and practices to support and supervise student organizations. Properly guiding and managing a fraternal community takes resources. There are developmental, personal, and professional gains if the experience is shepherded effectively and sufficiently (Schaffer & Kuh, 1983; Zacker, 2001). Unfortunately, staffing and financial resource limitations can result in negative, tragic, and potentially irreversible adverse effects. Staff who can establish and nurture connections to national offices, alumni, student leaders, university faculty and staff, and campus stakeholders must be provided, trained, and invested in a successful experience.

University operations tend to focus on weekday 9–5 operations, whereas student meetings and activities are more often after these hours and on weekends. This means that the individuals involved in advising groups must be available outside of traditional university business hours (Jelke, 2001; Maholchic-Nelson, 2010; Peress, 1998; Zacker, 2001). Specifically, there should be a university or paid professional advisory presence at all chapter events, including social activities. These staff need to attend executive council, All Fraternity Council, chapter meetings, and advisor meetings. Advisory representation needs to be fully present regularly to have a positive impact. Executive council and All Greek Councils need to be properly mentored to guide members and to withstand pressures to move toward poor decision-making.

This practice is a far departure from present operations where complete self-governance is the responsibility of each chapter, and specifically to the undergraduate members (Maholchic-Nelson, 2010). In one study Maholchic found that less that 24% of advisors were present at the majority of chapter activities and events. Staff or advisors need to be at the chapter to build greater partnerships and understanding for student success. This model has been pressed with significant success in residence life through resident assistants and complex coordinators (Blackburn & Janosik, 2009). As Biddix, Matney, Norman, and Martin (2014) stated, "Appropriately coaching students within these organizations can yield greater learning in these locations across the campus" (p. 112).

Effectively, fraternity and sorority housing is an enhanced form of special interest housing. Institutions, such as Virginia Tech, have used this model for the Oak Lane Community (Virginia Tech, 2018). Faculty in Residence can further assist in connecting the curricular and cocurricular foci, while assisting the persistence and graduation rates. If live-in opportunities are not feasible, utilizing programs such as Purdue's Faculty Fellows Program (Purdue, 2018) to create connections and faculty interactions can be added and facilitated. Current academic advising within the chapter has traditionally resided with an undergraduate student leader. While peer mentoring is effective (Maholchic-Nelson, 2010), thoroughly understanding and navigating the academic blueprints may be more effective with professional guidance. Returning the focus on college and the academic mission may yield enhanced academic success.

While chapters are similar to other registered student organizations, there are enough differences that warrant a dedicated staff. These personnel may be funded through student and chapter fees, corporate sponsorship, and fundraising initiatives. Working in tandem with the university office of advancement, a fraternity community can secure grants and donations. An area of opportunity is the naming rights, such as the Cliff Alexander Office of Fraternity and Sorority Life (Miami of Ohio, 2018). In addition, students serve as paraprofessionals and supplemental staff on some campuses, and they may receive federal work study. Capitalizing on this resource will provide additional learning opportunities and peer influence (Elam-Geuting, 2016).

Understanding Risk Management

From 1987 until approximately 2018, the Fraternity Insurance Purchasing Group (FIPG, 2013) convened to provide comprehensive risk management guidance. FIPG authored a risk management guide and other resources as a means of changing fraternity culture on campus. However, FIPG was phased out in 2016 and a clarifying announcement was made in 2019 by AFA to reinforce its inactive status of FIPG. While FIPG Risk Management Policy was adopted by numerous campuses and national organizations, the policy exists only in recommendations and not mandates (Krone, 2017). The institution, which gives recognition to chapters, must codify these policies and provide the resources to manage them effectively. Penn State has recently moved to heightened monitoring as a result of the Timothy Piazza death (Rossman, 2017). Other institutions, such as the University of Michigan, are conducting chapter assessments, a practice which has been in place since 1997 at the University of Delaware (Norman, 2003). West Virginia University has purchased card scanners for events and has banned the use of chapter funds for the purchase of alcohol (Zamudio-Suarez, 2017). Clemson University has required fraternities to follow the FIPG policies, including the hiring of security guards to monitor student IDs, limited alcohol consumption, and more staff oversight (Zamudio-Suarez, 2017). Uniform standardized risk management policies and procedures must be established across all councils and chapters. However, using the FIPG Risk Management Policy as a guide may positively improve the environment and clarify conflicting or vague policies. Eliminating bulk quantities and common sources of alcohol, utilizing third party providers, and limiting consumption through tracking may help reduce conduct incidents, while recognizing that students may still work around control systems.

Ensuring Clear and Consistent Expectations

Fraternal bylaws and university policies and procedures are documented in standardized operation manuals and national training guides. Potential new members typically become aware of these only after they have gone through the formal or informal recruitment process, which may have greater focus on social integration activities. Students need to have a better understanding of all that is involved at the onset of interest and recruitment, similar to a well-designed course syllabus. Ritual and founding values need to be emphasized as a priority and not as an afterthought (Callais, 2002; Eberly, 1967; Liza, 2017). In addition, while the learning objectives and outcomes may be spelled out clearly, the delivery can be haphazard based on who is providing the information. Normed online delivery with nationally consistent facilitation can assist when paired with institutional representation on non-ritual topics.

Expectations for all members should be introduced, emphasized, and (re)established at the onset through an institutional relationship statement paired with a standardized assessment program (Norman, 2003; Shaffer & Kuh, 1983). This relationship statement and assessment program should identify objectively (rather than philosophically) the specific obligations and expectations of members, advisors, university staff, national office representatives, and other stakeholders. Students and other stakeholders should be provided time to discuss and reflect on these expectations each semester to facilitate an understanding of the purpose, functions, and responsibilities of membership in relation to the institution. While a relationship statement should be codified through a university process, its development should be conducted with representation of all councils and chapters to ensure a uniform application, similar to the NIC position statement on Relationship Statements (2014).

The Case for Deferred Recruitment

Across the higher education landscape, there are a variety of fraternity recruitment models. The timing, means, and method can vary based on campus, council, and organization. While NPHC and NALFO organizations primarily recruit upper-class students, NIC chapters tend to recruit first semester males. NPC chapters have formal recruitment prior to fall classes, during fall semester, and in the spring, with a concentration on freshman students. While the fraternal support of first semester students is beneficial, a number of factors might influence the deferment of recruitment to the second semester of freshman year.

First, contemporary college students are the most diverse population ever entering higher education. Their academic and social needs are less homogenous than prior entering students. Many need to successfully acclimate to the academic rigor of the institution and the environment prior to dedicating additional time to a fraternal experience (Nelson, Halperin, Wasserman, Smith, & Graham, 2006). Chapters benefit by being able to ascertain how potential new members fit with respect to major, GPA, and interests. Considering the large number of students who change their major (Lederman, 2017; Straumsheim, 2016) and who find new interests as a result of being exposed to new opportunities, this model could help to better serve a broader population of students. Debard, Lake, and Binder (2006), as well as Debard and Sacks (2010) found that students who joined during their second semester earned a higher GPA compared to their predicted GPA and they completed more credit hours.

Second, a deferred recruitment period allows students to remain more fully engaged during their undergraduate experience. This is the approach that George Washington University implemented as a result of their Recruitment Evaluation Committee in 2016 (Witkowicki, 2016). The off cycle encourages students to stay involved over a longer period of time, thereby addressing the senior melt that some chapters experience. Some institutions, such as Princeton, defer recruitment until the sophomore year (Krone, 2017). Kovac (1995) recommended this approach based on the premise that after a full academic year, a student should have a very complete picture of the obligations, and it further solidifies their level of fit and may increase dedication and participation.

Third, and most critically, a student may only join one chapter in their lifetime. This is a significant difference between fraternities/sororities and other student organizations. The additional time allows for a more complete exploration of the chapters, members, inter/national organizations, expectations, and lifelong commitment. Providing this extra time to fully research and engage in the decision will enhance ownership, understanding, and appreciation that is difficult to facilitate in an accelerated recruitment process first semester of the freshman year. This approach was also recommended by the American Council on Education (1990).

Standardizing Education and Training

Fraternity and sorority members are initiated into their organizations though ritual standardized at the inter/national level. Additional leadership and values-based education and training for executive members, advisors, faculty advisers, general members, and alumni also exists for members. The degree to which members are integrated into the fraternal community, in a uniform, evidence-based program, varies considerably based on university, chapter, advisors, professional staff members, and national officers. A standardized national curriculum, similar to the NCAA myPlaybook: The Freshman Experience (NCAA, 2018), could help to reduce the potential for conflicting (or absent) information.

Education and training needs to be continuous and involve peers in the presentation and facilitation (Elam-Geutig, 2016). It should cover alcohol and other drug use/abuse (and appropriate/healthy drinking behaviors, and with the opioid epidemic, prescription drug use cycles), harassment/sexual violence prevention, academic resources, and psychological and physical health. The training should be expanded to include legal liability, bystander intervention training, understanding and valuing diversity and inclusion, conflict resolution/mediation, personal finance, mentoring, and other programs to address the 10 dimensions of wellness (Institute for Wellness Education, 2018). An expanded educational program consistent with the vision and missions of fraternal organizations would be a focus on personal identity development and leadership-based topics (Corey, 2011). This also would allow for continued education on the concept of fraternalism, so members comprehend the connectivity across chapters and governing counsels. While policies and codes address conduct, and standards documents address choices, the education and training need to focus on learning and well-being throughout the life span.

Professional and personal development topics need to be infused, which is critical as the current generation of students enrolling has a heightened focus on obtaining a successful career post-graduation. Many students neglect to consider their behavior in social settings when making personal choices in the moment when less positive directions are available. Pairing behavior with values discussions will aid in this change.

It would be advisable to have a standardized for-credit program that orients and facilitates a deep discussion on being a member of a chapter. A credit-based curriculum has been found to positively address fraternity men (Isacco, Warnnecke, Ampuero, Donofrio, & Davis, 2013). Expanding this type of program across the fraternal community could have significant impacts in guiding the chapter members to live their rituals and reinforce supplemental programming.

While online training provides a standardized approach and a means in which to track completion, these programs need to be conducted in small groups where deep discussions can be had in a safe sharing environment that has a cross section of members and chapters. FIJI's (Phi Gamma Delta). Tell Me Something I Don't Know successfully utilizes this model (Phi Gamma Delta, 2018). A posttest sent upon completion and at a 30-day interval can be used to measure learning and retention.

Universities have reduced new member education periods to 8-, 6-, and 4-week programs, while some headquarters have discontinued the new member education completely (The Fraternity Adviser, 2018; Kimbrough, 2003). A holistic education and training course could be used to replace the existing new member education program. Moving to an educational process for all members would provide a means to connect seasoned members to new members without segregating the chapter. It would also allow for effective role modeling and leadership development. Having topics cycle around in a guided discussion format would allow for deeper connections and meaning to occur throughout the chapter in this model. Several existing programs follow a similar model, such as Balanced Man, Beta Theta Pi Men of Principle, and the Delta Zeta Being More! Program (Delta Zeta, 2018). Work on this endeavor is currently underway through the NIC 2.0 initiative (North-American Fraternity Conference, 2018). This effort will be expanded nationally through "Focus Campuses." While this initiative covers the NIC affiliated fraternities, it could have an expanded footprint across all chapters and councils.

Assessing Community Service Outcomes

While social activities gather a large degree of programming attention, extensive volunteering, and community service should be embedded into the fraternal experience. Engaging in community service increases connectivity, lowers depression, and has been found to help clarify one's values and beliefs (Wassel, 2017). Everhart, Elliott, and Pelco (2016) found that service learning enhances empathy. Infusing a variety of service projects within and between chapters will enhance the experience and increase understanding across the community. This is especially pertinent to incorporate cross council projects, which may improve multicultural competencies (Krauth, 2011).

Despite this focus on community service and philanthropic efforts, very few chapters, universities that host them, or inter/national offices maintain accurate records beyond hours of service or dollars raised. Many fraternal organization efforts are already aligned with the contemporary increased emphasis on community service and civic engagement in postsecondary education. Yet, very few make the connection from hours and dollars to learning outcomes. For example, Matney et al. (2016) found that fraternity members were exposed to developmental opportunities through service, leadership, and involvement, but few were able to translate their experiences in relation to civic values. Learning outcomes assessment should be a key component to fraternal activity to understand and enhance a potentially rich, but undocumented, learning environment.

Reconsidering Chapter Housing

Chapter houses were built to hold members at a time when higher education institutions had insufficient beds to support the increasing enrollment. As the landscape of higher education changed, so did on-campus housing. Residence halls were built and expanded, providing additional options. This led to mandatory on-campus living requirements. In many cases, housing contracts that restricted activities in residence halls often led to fraternity chapter houses becoming hosting venues for large social events, particularly with alcohol, resulting in a high-risk environment (De Los Reyes & Rich, 2003). Researchers have found that members who live in fraternity houses specifically have both higher drinking rates and higher problematic drinking rates (e.g., binge drinking) than non-residents (Park, Sher, & Krull, 2009; Wechsler et al., 2000; Zakletskaia, Wilson, & Flemming, 2010). A preferred model is to host chapter houses on campus with alcohol-free facilities.

Having university employees residing in the halls provides additional supervision and the ability to consistently enforce policies regardless of which members are also residents. With chapters ranging in size, building units that are smaller and flexible in room quantity and composition may aid in the economic vitality. A smaller number of rooms per chapter may increase the ability for smaller chapters to create a parallel environment to large chapters. If a chapter should see a decrease or increase in membership and rental desires, adjusting hall composition can be accomplished through lock access on hallways. By clustering chapters in the same proximity (or even hall), cohesion and engagement across the fraternal community can be facilitated. Chapters can reside in the same building in different halls while sharing some of the larger spaces, increasing utilization and fraternalism while reducing duplication of space. Joint programming can also be offered with this model, thereby reducing the need for academic classrooms or other on-campus space.

Using a Residential Learning Community (RLC) model provides additional opportunities for chapters and potential new members (Blackburn, 2009; Zunick, 2017).

Sigma Phi Epsilon has developed and launched this model at Rutgers; however, it is administered by chapter alumni, and one study did not demonstrate statistical significance between RLC and non-RLC members (Zunick, 2017). If a deferred recruitment model is used, new students who have an interest in joining a chapter can reside in the same community through a unique Special Interest Housing community. An introduction to fraternity and sorority membership class also could be conducted in the hall, along with more advanced for-credit leadership and academic-based classes.

Planning for Expansion

In the creation of a new fraternal community, sufficient time needs to be dedicated in the establishment of each respective chapter. Rate of expansion needs to be determined based on institutional resources. If a larger staff is available, it is more feasible to expand more rapidly. If the supervisory responsibilities are part of a broad portfolio for a campus administrator, it may be more advisable to add chapters at a more progressive frequency. The quantity of chapters will be determined by membership composition. The number of members should parallel what is required by other registered student organizations. If continued interest exists, measured expansion should continue, paying particular attention to the diversity of national organizations.

Rather than organically having organizations charter, intentional efforts should be made to invite those that parallel the mission of the institution and environment. Establishing chapters also provides an effective means in which to recruit a diverse student body. Efforts should be made to examine what populations may be more interested in attending if the correct social network were established. It is advised to have a dedicated consultant from the national organization stay with the chapter, preferably for a year. Starting an organization from the beginning correctly takes a significant amount of time and resources. Establishing, recruiting, and educating as a standardized process is aided by having the same individual throughout the colonization process.

Conclusion

While fraternal membership offers developmental benefits throughout an individual's life span, the undergraduate experience has the ability to be most impactful (Pike, 2003). Further, a well-designed and facilitated experience can greatly benefit persistence, graduation, and satisfaction at an institution. Many of the suggestions in this chapter directly parallel the 1990 American Council on Education's recommendations to improve their fraternal systems. Even though the recommendations were circulated extensively, many institutions of higher education can benefit from suggestions to properly support, guide, and elevate the fraternal experience.

References

Allen, R. (2017, December 11). Hazing expert Walter Kimbrough: 2017 one of deadliest years for campus fraternity deaths. *The Advocate*. Retrieved from http://theadvocate.com/baton-rouge/news/education/article_fec19898-deaa-11e7-b582-473f747ba4ee.html

American Council on Education. (1990). Greek organizations on the college campus. Self-regulation initiatives: Guidelines for institutional action. 10. Retrieved from https://www.scribd.com/document/356875221/self-regulation-as-applied-to-fraternities-and-sororities

Biddix, J. P., Matney, M., Norman, E. M., & Martin, G. L. (2014). The influence of fraternity and sorority involvement: A critical analysis of research (1996–2013). *ASHE Higher Education Report, 39(6)*.

Blackburn, S.S., & Janosik, S.M. (2009). Learning communities in fraternity/sorority housing. *Oracle: The Research Journal of the Association of Fraternity/Sorority Advisors, 4(2)*, 56–70.

Corey, A. J. (2011). *The influence of fraternity or sorority membership on the leadership identity development of college student leaders* (Doctoral dissertation). Retrieved from ProQuest dissertations & thesis global. (3460368)

Debard, R., Lake, T., & Binder, R. S. (2006). Greeks and grades. *NASPA Journal, 43(1)*, 56–68.

Debard, R., & Sacks, C. (2010). Fraternity/Sorority membership: Good news about first-year impact. *Oracle: The Research Journal of the Association of Fraternity/Sorority Advisors, 5(1)*, 12–23.

De Los Reyes, G., & Rich, P. (2003). Housing students: Fraternities and residential colleges. *The Annals of the American Academy of Political and Social Science, 585(1)*, 118–123.

Delta Zeta. (2018). Being more! program. Retrieved from http://www.deltazeta.org/lifelong-learners/being-more-program/

Eberly, C. G. (1967). The influence of the fraternity ritual. *College Student Survey, 9–10*.

Elam-Geuting, K. (2016). *Peer educators in National Panhellenic Conference (NPC) sororities.* (Unpublished master's thesis). University of Tennessee, Knoxville.

Everhart, R., Elliott, K., & Pelco, L. E. (2016). Empathy Activators: Teaching tools for enhancing empathy development in service-learning. *VCU Scholars Compass*. Retrieved from http://scholarcompass.vcu.edu/community_resources/42

FIPG, Inc. (2013). *FIPG risk management manual*. Indianapolis, IN: Author.

The Fraternity Advisor. (2018). SAE eliminates pledging – Our questions answered. *The Fraternity Advisor*. Retrieved from http://thefraternityadvisor.com/sae-eliminates-pledging-our-questions-answered/

Institute for Wellness Education. (2018). *The 10 dimensions of wellness*. Retrieved from https://www.instituteforwellness.com/10-dimensions-of-wellness/

Isacco, A., Warnecke, A., Ampuero, M., Donofrio, L., & Davies, J. A. (2013). Evaluation of a leadership program for fraternity men. *The Journal of Men's Studies, 21(3)*, 217–235.

Jackson, A. (2017, November 17). Ohio State University suspended 37 fraternities on campus – the most aggressive move yet on the rush for colleges to crack down on hazing. *Business Insider*. Retrieved from http://www.businessinsider.com/ohio-state-university-suspends-fraternities-2017-11

Jelke, T. B. (2001). A cross-case analysis of Greek systems perceived to be high performing (Doctorial dissertation, Indiana University, 2001). *Dissertation Abstracts International*, AAT 3024170.

Kimbrough, W. M. (2003). *Black Greek 101: The culture, customs, and challenges of Black fraternities and sororities*. Madison, NJ: Fairleigh Dickenson University Press.

Kovac, D. C. (1995). *Failure by virtue: A case study of the transmission of fraternity values* (Doctoral dissertation). Retrieved from Dissertation abstracts international. (DAI-A 56/05, p. 1677)

Krauth, S. A. (2011). *Service participation as a predictor of multicultural competency in college graduates: A comparative study of sectarian and nonsectarian institutions* (Doctoral dissertation). Retrieved from ProQuest dissertations & thesis global. (3494169)

Krone, C. J. (2017). *The nature of inclusivity and exclusivity of social Greek-letter organizations on college campuses: A case study* (Doctoral Dissertation). Retrieved from ProQuest dissertations & thesis global. (10618952)

Lederman, D. (2017, December 8). Who changes majors? (Not who you think). *Inside Higher Ed.* Retrieved from https://www.insidehighered.com/news/2017/12/08/nearly-third-students-change-major-within-three-years-math-majors-most

Liza, J. P. (2017). *A qualitative case study of the congruence between fraternal organizations' and members' values, principles, and standards* (Doctoral dissertation). Retrieved from ProQuest dissertations & thesis global. (10262403)

Maholchic-Nelson, S. (2010). *High- and low-achieving fraternity environments at a selective institution: Their influence on members binge drinking and gpa* (Doctoral dissertation). Retrieved from ProQuest dissertations & thesis global. (3429063)

Matney, M. M., Biddix, J. P., Arsenoff, S., Keller, T., Dusendang, J., & Martin, D. (2016). Fraternity member reflections on civic learning and social responsibility. *Journal of College and Character, 17*(4), 1–18.

Miami of Ohio. (2018). History of Greek Life at Miami. Retrieved from https://miamioh.edu/student-life/fraternity-sorority-life/about/miamis-greek-history/index.html

NCAA. (2018). *myPlaybook: The freshman experience.* Retrieved from http://www.ncaa.org/sport-science-institute/myplaybook-freshman-experience

Nelson, S., Halperin, S., Wasserman, T. H., Smith, C., & Graham, P. (2006). Effects of fraternity/sorority membership and recruitment semester on GPA and retention. *Oracle: The Research Journal of the Association of Fraternity/Sorority Advisors, 2*(1).

NIC. (2014). *Position statement on relationship statements.* Retrieved from http://nicindy.org/wp-content/uploads/2016/07/Position-Statement-Relationship-Statements.pdf

Norman, E. M. (2003). *Analysis of the Greek five-star chapter evaluation program* (Doctoral dissertation). Retrieved from ProQuest dissertations & thesis global. (DAI-A 64/08)

North-American Interfraternity Conference. (2018). *NIC2.0: The future of fraternities.* Retrieved from https://nicfraternity.org/fraternity-growth-accelerator/

Park, A., Sher, K., & Krull, J. (2009). Selection and socialization of risky drinking during the college transition: The importance of microenvironments associated with specific living units. *Psychology of Addictive Behaviors, 12*(3), 404–414.

Peress, K. (1998). *Factors which distinguish successful and marginal fraternities at three small private colleges* (Doctoral dissertation). Retrieved from Dissertations abstracts international. (DAI-A 59/06, p. 1941)

Phi Gamma Delta (2018). Tell me something I don't know. Retrieved from https://www.phigam.org/tmsidk

Pike, G. R. (2003). Membership in a fraternity or sorority, student engagement, and educational outcomes at AAU public research universities. *Journal of College Student Development, 44*(3), 369–382.

Purdue. (2018). Purdue fellows. Retrieved from https://www.housing.purdue.edu/residentiallife/FacultyFellows/index.html

Rossman, S. (2017, November 22). Greek Life suspensions keep coming up on college campuses. Here's all of them from 2017. *USA Today*. Retrieved from https://www.usatoday.com/story/news/nation-now/2017/11/22/greek-life-suspensions-keep-coming-college-campuses-heres-all-them-2017/875699001/

Shaffer, R. H., & Kuh, G. D. (1983). Evaluation in decision making. In W.A. Bryan & R. A. Schwartz (Eds.), *The Eighties: Challenges for fraternities and sororities* (p. 31–48). Carbondale, IL: American College Personnel Administrators.

Straumsheim, C. (2016, August 24). Decision time. *Inside Higher Ed*. Retrieved from https://www.insidehighered.com/news/2016/08/24/study-finds-students-benefit-waiting-declare-major

Virginia Tech. (2018). Oak Lane community guide. Retrieved from https://fsl.vt.edu/housing_information/Oak_Lane_Community_Guide.html

Wassel, B. (2017). *Demographic differences in community service engagement among undergraduate college students* (Doctoral dissertation). Retrieved from ProQuest dissertations & thesis global. (10270359)

Wechsler, H., Kuo, M., Lee, H., & Dowdall, G. W. (2000). Environmental correlates of underage alcohol use and related problems of college students. *American Journal of Preventative Medicine, 19*(10), 24–29.

Witkowski, C. (2016, April 7). Op-ed: Deferred recruitment will benefit the Greek community. *The GW Hatchet*. Retrieved from https://www.gwhatchet.com/2016/04/07/op-ed-deferred-recruitment-will-benefit-the-greek-community/

Zacker, T. Y. (2001). *An exploratory study of the institutional factors relating to the quality of social Greek letter societies* (Doctoral dissertation). Retrieved from Dissertation Abstracts International. (DAI-A 62/12, p. 4095, June 2002)

Zakletskaia, L., Wilson, E., & Flemming, M. F. (2010). Alcohol use in students seeking primary core treatment at university health services. *Journal of American College Health, 59*(3), 217–223.

Zamudio-Suarez, F. (2017, November 7). What happened after 3 universities suspended Greek life. *The Chronicle of Higher Education*. Retrieved from https://www.chronicle.com/article/What-Happened-After-3/241699

Zunick, T. (2017). *Assessing academic and personal outcomes for men engaged in the Sigma Phi Epsilon residential learning community* (Doctoral dissertation). Retrieved from ProQuest dissertations & thesis global. (10629232)

PART THREE:

PROGRAMMING ISSUES

CHAPTER 9

Issues and Challenges:
Leadership Development

Sarah Schoper, Todd Rotgers, and Kristen Wagner

THE MACHINE MODEL of running an organization was created and broadly implemented in the United States as the creation of Taylorism came about in the early 1900s (Morgan, 2006). This assembly line form of running an organization values efficiency and task completion without much regard to relationship building. Yet, people comprise organizations, and therefore relationships can be what deters an organization from running as efficiently and productively as a well-oiled machine. This consideration applies to fraternity and sorority communities at each level, governing organizations to inter/national individual organizations, and all the way down to individual chapters and executive boards on various campuses.

One only needs to peruse the vast amount of "how to" manuals for running meetings or other such tasks to gather an idea of how infiltrated the machine model is within the fraternity and sorority community. This strong focus naturally leads to a value of positional leadership too. Those voted into positions such as president, vice president, standards chair, or others are identified as the leaders of their respective organizations almost without much regard to their leadership abilities. Leadership development thus becomes reduced to a variety of skills that members need to acquire in order to fulfill their responsibilities. One can similarly scan various workshops provided to chapters on individual campuses by their inter/national organizations to explore their adherence to the machine model. Such and such officer is encouraged to enact such and such program on, say, active listening during a chapter meeting for all members and—voilà!—the

chapter members become knowledgeable in that skill. Occasionally, there are requirements such as serving in past leadership positions in order to become qualified for
various other positions, which again reinforces the assumption that leadership skills
develop by simply serving in a position.

Outside of programs provided by various inter/national offices, campus community
offices also work to fill the gap of leadership development by providing parallel opportunities for the recognized chapters and larger governing community to participate in
through sponsorship or attendance. An example of this parallel behavior is encouraging
students to attend the large regional conferences. The assumption is that leadership development occurs via attendance at a variety of workshops spread throughout a few days.
Yet, during those few days students often feel stressed by continually being reminded
that they represent their Fraternity and Sorority Life (FSL) communities, and/or may
feel anxiety about experiencing their first conference, interacting with new people, or
missing their courses while in a new environment. Stress and anxiety can inhibit deep
learning, which includes leadership development.

The positional, machine method approach to leadership development also focuses
on *what* students need to know and lacks an intentional focus on *how* students come to
know it. It results in FSL communities continually spinning their wheels to develop leaders and attributing their need to do so to the ever-changing groups of students gaining
membership within their organizations. Concurrently, the need to develop leadership
skills is often identified as necessary because processes "have always been" enacted in
certain ways, and thus students claim that any lag in leadership abilities is attributed to
culture change lag time. Both justifications fail to consider that perhaps it is futile to continually aim to develop students in regard to what they need to know about leadership
without simultaneously aiming to develop how they make meaning of leadership. For
example, it seems unfair to ask students to enact active listening skills in their interactions with others after engaging them in a program that highlights the ins and outs of
active listening by requiring them to quickly memorize and regurgitate the five steps
for active listening when the environments and conditions in which they need to enact
their skills are much more complex.

Certainly, it can be argued that the programs are "not that simple" and "we are doing
our best with the resources that we have"; and, yet, perhaps there are ways in which
more can be done. This is not to say that ignoring the areas in which students need help
developing their leadership skills is the solution. Rather, it is to argue for incorporating
more fully how students within fraternities and sororities make meaning as a means to
promote leadership development. That important issue is explored more fully throughout this chapter. In other words, a more holistic approach to leadership development
can be taken, which can potentially assist institutions in achieving their missions while,
at the same time, allowing the wide variety of chapters to adhere to their own purposes.

Indeed, a more holistic approach to development has been a purpose of higher education for quite some time (American Council on Education, 1937, 1949; Keeling, 2004,

2006), and yet, as institutions grow more specialized, they separate out various aspects of students' experiences. Classrooms are the location where learning takes place, and outside the classroom is the location of life skills development. However, perhaps within fraternity and sorority life, out of all places on campus, it is appropriate and necessary to step back from further perpetuating the segregation of various aspects of the student experience and enact a more holistic approach. After all, "Life skill development is a learning process that is supported by brain development" (Fried & Troiano, 2016, p. 27), and students bring all of who they are into all of their environments.

As previously stated, beyond examining the student experience holistically, this chapter examines connections between how individuals make meaning and their individual leadership development. It also explores the overall development of FSL chapters, as it is perhaps unsurprising that how the individual chapter members make meaning of leadership influences how the chapter itself, and even in some cases the community, makes meaning of its experiences. Finally, this chapter focuses on intentionally shaping various environments to promote holistic leadership development for chapters and individuals and will identify practical strategies for promoting leadership development among members at all levels.

Meaning-Making Process

Researchers such as John Dewey (1925), Maria Montessori (1948), and Jean Piaget (1974) all explored the process of how meaning is made while focusing their research primarily on children. In fact, the meaning making of adults was not considered until researchers, including Robert Kegan and Marcia Baxter Magolda in the 1980s and 1990s, began exploring the topic. For the purposes of this chapter, how meaning is made is considered in regard to holistic development and transformative learning, thereby drawing attention to *how* development is happening and expanding the potential ways and environments in which members and chapters can grow leadership. This section further explores the meaning-making process of each individual chapter member, as well as the chapter organization as a whole.

How Meaning Is Made

Robert Kegan's (1994) research on the evolution of the meaning-making process involves a holistic structure, thereby making it important to consider. The holistic structure is comprised of three intertwined dimensions of development—cognitive, interpersonal, and intrapersonal—which influence how someone makes sense of information, how they sees themselves in relation to others, and their internal value and belief systems, respectively. In Kegan's meaning-making structure, the three intertwined dimensions are continually used to take in information, make sense of experiences, and evolve toward greater complexity as individuals encounter diverse experiences. This evolution of the meaning-making systems involves the processing of one's assumptions, values, and beliefs through a subject–object balance and allows for more complex meaning to be made.

According to Kegan, what is subject are "those elements of our knowing or organizing that we are identified with, tied to, fused with or embedded in," and what is object are "those elements of our knowing or organizing that we can reflect on, handle, look at, be responsible for, relate to each other, take control of, internalize, assimilate, or otherwise operate upon" (p. 32). For example, if I live around others who have my same social class, it is easy for me to unconsciously assume that they approach money, as well as other components of social class, from my same perspective. In this case, social class would be subject to me, as I am not aware that I am making such an assumption; and I proceed to use that assumption to determine how I understand the world, including leadership. If, however, I can see that my social class is leading me to such assumptions, it becomes object for me. It does not mean that social class is no longer a part of me, but rather it means that I can determine more how my own understanding of social class influences the meaning I make. This example illustrates how the evolution process might work for one identity and what it means for how meaning is made. Here social class was used as an example, but it could easily be replaced with other identities and information, all of which, over time, move from subject to object repeatedly and continually. Eventually, my ability to make choices about the influence of my social class will allow me to consciously set aside my own personal values and beliefs about social class and make a decision for the betterment of my chapter membership and indirectly myself.

Thus, transformation in how I make meaning occurs by moving what is subject to that which is object and, through this transformation, how I make meaning becomes more complex. Eventually, individuals more consciously interact with what is object in their thinking, as well as begin to see how items that are object are connected to each other. Such raised consciousness allows individuals to consider multiple perspectives, notice systems at work, and navigate and allocate resources responsibly; in other words, enact leadership.

Experiential and Transformative Learning

Other researchers who discuss the development of greater complexity within how meaning is made include James Zull (2002) and Jack Mezirow (2000), whose findings are connected to Kegan's. Zull (2002) speaks specifically about the biological and transformational changes to the brain that deep learning brings as he addresses connections between the physical brain and Kolb's (1984) experiential learning cycle. Specifically, Zull (2002) addresses the importance of engaging the whole learning cycle, a process that includes active testing, concrete experiences, reflective observation, and abstract hypothesis. Engaging the whole learning cycle leads to physical transformation within the brain's neuronal structure, and such physical transformations are what Mezirow (2000) defines as transformative learning.

Transformative learning is, according to Mezirow (2009), "learning that transforms problematic frames of reference to make them more inclusive, discriminating, reflective, open, and emotionally able to change"; in other words, transformative learning leads to complex thinking (p. 22). Similar to Zull (2002) noting the importance of reflective observation, Mezirow (2000) notes that reflection is necessary for learning to be transformative: "We can think about our experience—muse, review, and so on—but to reflect critically, we must also examine the underlying beliefs and assumptions that affect how we make sense of the experience" (Merriam, Caffarella, & Baumgartner, 2007, p. 145). Both Zull (2002) and Mezirow (2000, 2009) identify diverse experiences, epistemological reflection, and participation as methods for developing greater complexity in meaning making.

All of the aforementioned authors note that the more complexly individuals see and understand their world, the greater the amount they can notice, consider, question, and engage in their experiences. This means that, instead of going along with what has always been done or doing to others what was done to them when in a leadership position, a chapter member in a more complex place might make a different choice for the betterment of the chapter—even if it is not congruent with her own experiences and even if it is unpopular. Additionally, such a chapter member might propose a new idea or learn a new skill for the betterment of the chapter. The key is to develop an increased ability to complexly engage in the environment in order to enact leadership, and it makes promoting complex meaning making an imperative for those seeking to develop leadership within chapter members.

Organizational Meaning Making

This same process of developing meaning making with individuals can also be extrapolated to how an organization, such as an FSL chapter, makes meaning. Each organization has assumptions it is making that it is subject to, that those who comprise it cannot see, as well as items that are object to it that the members can see and therefore have choices over. It is through the surfacing of what is subject that progress can be made in such a way that an organization can make a choice different from in the past. For example, assuming that alcohol consumption is the reason for alcohol-related problems might result in creating a policy against its use. If, however, alcohol consumption is made object, an organization might start to understand that alcohol consumption is not only connected to alcohol-related problems, but also to athletic events, the script of masculinity, White culture, and the entire campus culture, among other reasons. [1] Thus, it makes sense that a dry policy does not end alcohol-related problems, and it explains why it is so challenging to adhere to it.

Moving an assumption treated as truth by an organization from subject to object assists in "the expansion of ideas about the significance of new information in a variety of contexts" (Fried & Troiano, 2016, p. 26). In other words, more complex thinking can evolve about the issue for all involved. Such complexity is necessary for success, given that "human beings learn their way through life by engaging with the environment and the challenges it presents" (p. 26). Indeed, if FSL chapters are to become leaders among organizations within a campus community, transformative learning must be promoted consistently and constantly in order to inhibit the development of groupthink and to move both the chapters and their members toward complexity in how meaning is made of complex and diverse experiences. In fact, Kegan and Lahey (2016) provide evidence that the ongoing development of those within organizations contributes to the ongoing development and standard measures of success of the organization in a multitude of ways.

Promoting Development of Meaning Making

If complex meaning making is an imperative for developing leadership within chapter members that will then positively influence the entire chapter and eventually the greater campus community, promotion of movement toward complexity needs to be executed. Indeed, any approach needs to be incorporated into the environment by those working within offices across the campus community, as well as by alumni advisors serving as volunteer advisors to chapter members. In other words, it does no good to encourage strategies for promoting complex development of how meaning is made if those working with chapter members cannot incorporate it into their everyday interactions. This does not mean that doing so will always go smoothly or be easy, but rather that the process requires embracing obstacles and valuing challenges.

Additionally, another consideration regarding any strategies offered involves the manner in which they are enacted. Research demonstrates the importance of co-constructing learning with the learner if one desires the learning to be used in various contexts (Fried & Troiano, 2016). Co-construction does not mean that "anything goes," but rather it means a movement away from simple memorization or regurgitation, away from an approach to learning that emphasizes telling learners what to do without helping them apply it to their lived experiences. It means completing the entire learning cycle as noted by Zull (2002), and it means embracing transformative learning as a method for promoting holistic development toward complexity in how meaning is made (Kegan, 1994; Mezirow, 2000, 2009). Thus, the practical steps advanced in this chapter need to be implemented in a co-constructed manner.

Furthermore, students must holistically participate in what they are learning for it to become a part of how they make meaning; and doing so necessitates involving all of who they are within the learning environment. This means no longer separating out emotions from thinking (Zull, 2002). In fact, it is impossible to think of a cognitive task, such as doing mathematics, without involving feelings. Moreover, if what is being learned matters, it can be challenging for feelings to not overtake thinking (Zull, 2002). Given this, "we must find some way to encourage our learners to want to use their reason" (p. 76). One way in which we can embrace students' feelings, so that they can move beyond them, is to engage them in mindfulness activities such as two minutes of deep breathing exercises. Mindfulness has been found to lead to "looking, listening, and remembering," which are connected to self-management behaviors (Barbezat & Bush, 2014, p. 103). Ultimately, leadership development is about self-management in that it requires students to "become aware of their reactions, and consider the consequences before they speak or act" (Fried & Trioano, 2016, p. 99). Such learned action has the potential to create a ripple effect in other areas of students' lives, including entire chapters and communities.

Reflection

The first practical behavior offered is to incorporate reflection. Reflection is a part of any experiential learning process, and according to Kolb (1984) involves four areas: having an experience, reflecting on that experience, conceptualizing why the experience happened, and taking action based on what was conceptualized. More recent research on the neuroscience of learning blurs the distinctions between the various areas Kolb identified. It establishes that without engaging in the complete process, the neuronal connections are weakened; and weak neuronal connections prevent learning from sticking with the learner (Brown, Roediger, & McDaniel, 2014; Zull, 2002, 2011). Stated differently, in order for students to use their leadership skills in various contexts, it is essential that reflection be incorporated. By incorporating reflection, students are asked to consider how they have come to know what they have come to know, as well as what they think of the process they used to make meaning individually and as an organization.

Using reflection as a part of the learning process, for example, means changing the practice of telling chapter members the steps to take to no longer be a bystander and quizzing them on it during a chapter meeting. Instead, chapter members are potentially asked at the beginning of the program how they would define and describe what it means to be a bystander; during the program how they are experiencing the topic; and then again at the end of the program being posed questions such as, how they would use what they learned about bystander intervention in their roles within their chapter? This approach provides an opportunity for the learner to consider applying the topic to their role, even when their role is that of chapter member. In interacting with individual chapter members, incorporating reflection might look like starting out the conversation by asking them what steps they know they need to take or asking them to consider how intervening as a bystander could have realistically been enacted in whatever context is being discussed. These examples are designed to get students involved in the learning process rather than remaining passive recipients.

Dissonance

Next, we should work to value dissonance within all interactions. Dissonance can be described as welcoming into the environment unique challenge and support—unique in the sense that it engages the learner in just the right way. If too much support is offered, none of the chapter members, or the chapter as a whole, will consider their experiences in such a way that they reflect on them. We should eschew a level of support that leads to dependency upon advisors and groupthink at the organizational level, and which can plateau any advancement toward complex meaning making. Thus, too much support can hinder the leadership development of chapter members and the organization.

Providing too much support might look like chapter advisors or campus community members are taking away the responsibility to deeply consider how a chapter member or the chapter found themselves or itself in a situation. It implicitly tells them what they should have done instead. Most likely, providing such answers is done in good faith because the chapter members claim to not know how they got themselves into a situation, and it can be challenging to sit with the students in silence for longer than a minute. Alternatively, the chapter member or members might state that it is "too hard" for them to have to "think about" what led up to the situation, and thus an answer is provided as a way to remove the uncomfortableness the students are experiencing. Yet, by removing the challenge of considering the issue without effort, the chapter members are prevented from engaging in deep processing, which is what leads to learning that sticks and thus can be used in other situations (Brown, Roediger, & McDaniel, 2014). Ultimately, it comes down to not using support so that the chapter members have challenges removed from their lived experiences; it is reasonable for students to sit and struggle when learning.

Earlier, the importance of reflection was noted as assisting in completing the learning cycle. The incorporation of reflection is often what it takes to welcome dissonance into the environment. Similar to providing too much support in an environment, it is possible to provide too much challenge. Providing too much challenge may lead to students choosing to no longer engage with the topic, and/or only doing what is minimally necessary for a responsibility to be fulfilled. For example, if the chapter members are to create their own program on bystander intervention for their chapter, as well as evaluate the experience once the program is completed, the task might seem too hard to them. Yet, this challenge of too much work does not mean that it cannot be done. Quite often in such situations a program is provided to the chapter members to bring into their chapter that is diluted from making a lasting impression because it needs to apply to a wide variety of situations and individuals. This lowered threshold of challenge is not ideal for an advancement toward complex meaning making of leadership, as apathy can lead to disengagement and stalled development. Instead, what is needed is the incorporation of, "an ingenious blend" of challenge and support (Kegan, 1994, p. 42). This, again, may mean allowing chapter members to experience discomfort so that they fully consider the ways bystander intervention can realistically be brought into a situation, while simultaneously letting them know that you believe they are the experts of the environments they create and therefore they know best how to bring in successful interventions.

Start with What Is Known

Finally, it is imperative that those seeking to advance the development of leadership within students by encouraging them to become more complex thinkers need to work from wherever the students are at in their current understanding of the issue. This can be challenging to do, as it might mean starting at a place of discomfort because of misinformation or because of emotions, which were addressed earlier. Yet, it is the interactions of the neurons in the brain that both create and store information. Therefore, it is necessary to start with what is known because, "any change in knowledge must come from some change in neuronal networks" (Zull, 2002, p. 92). Furthermore, it is important to realize that whatever is known is fact to the learner in the sense that there is a biological connection within the brain to that information, persistent in terms of the neural connections that were built and are being followed, and that what is known only changes through effort and interest. In other words, there is no unlearning: "no one can understand anything if it isn't connected in some way to something they already know" (p. 94). Therefore, a useful approach is to build on the existing neuronal networks.

This can be done by asking students how they are making sense of whatever issue one wants them to know, and it must be done without judgment. For example, if a chapter is in trouble for hazing, it is important to find out how it came to understand hazing as the desired behavior. Perhaps the chapter members will share that it helps them to bond the group and has been done for years. Perhaps they will share the ins and outs of all of the hazing, some of which was known and some that was not. This quite often occurs if a trusting relationship has been built with students. The chapter members can then be asked to consider if they can think of other ways that group bonding can be achieved that is a step away from the hazing culture that has been created. Whatever realistic response they give is the place to start from, and if the group tries out a new activity, we can follow up to see how it went and validate that the step they took was huge and important. Validating is a significant part of the process even if the step does not seem huge, because they should not have been engaging in the behavior. Remember that learning something new and doing it at both the individual and organizational level, no matter how small, can feel like a big step—as well as be exhausting—when it is being learned in such a way that it is ingrained. Alternatively, perhaps what you will discover is that the subjects are wanting to move away from what they are doing because they see the danger in it and they cannot think of another method for reaching their goal. At that point, you can brainstorm ideas with them. The key is connecting what they are learning to their understanding of themselves, their organization's purpose, and what they already know (Zull, 2002).

Conclusion

Leadership development is often approached from a machine model perspective, which leads to focusing primarily on *what* students need to learn. Similar to an assembly line having a prescribed order of steps, focusing on only *what* students need to learn entails a set order of steps that must be memorized or passed down. The transformative learning perspective advocated for in this chapter incorporates *how* students learn into the process as well. Through reflection, dissonance, and starting with what students know, the meaning that students make of their experiences can be used to help promote more complex thinking. More complex thinking can lead to better incorporation of leadership throughout all levels of the FSL communities. It takes them from specific skills needed in whatever position to learning that sticks—leadership development that aids them beyond the college experience.

Note

1. See Brown-Rice & Furr, 2015, for statistics regarding who in the FSL community consumes the most alcohol.

References

American Council on Education. (1937). *The student personnel point of view. (American Council on Education Studies, series 1, no. 3)*. Washington, DC: Author.

American Council on Education. (1949). *The student personnel point of view*. Retrieved from http://www.myacpa.org/student-personnel-point-view-1937

Barbezat, D., & Bush, M. (2014). *Contemplative practices in higher education*. San Francisco, CA: Jossey-Bass.

Baxter Magolda, M. B. (2000). *Creating contexts for learning and self-authorship: Constructive-developmental pedagogy*. Nashville, TN: Vanderbilt University Press.

Brown, P. C., Roediger, H. L., & McDaniel, M. A. (2014). *Make it stick: The science of successful learning*. Cambridge, MA: The Belknap Press of Harvard University Press.

Brown-Rice, K., & Furr, S. (2015). Differences in college Greek members' binge drinking behaviors: A dry/wet house comparison. *The Professional Counselor, 5*(3), 354–564. doi:10.15241/kbr.5.3.354

Dewey, J. (1925). *Experience and nature.* Peru, IL: Carus Publishing Company.

Fried, J., & Troiano, P. (2016). *Of education, fishbowls, and rabbit holes: Rethinking teaching and liberal education for an interconnected world.* Sterling, VA: Stylus.

Keeling, R. (2004). *Learning reconsidered.* Washington, DC: American College Personnel Association & National Association of Student Personnel Administrators.

Keeling, R. P. (Ed.). (2006). *Learning reconsidered 2: A practical guide to implementing a campus-wide focus on the student experience.* Washington, DC: ACPA, ACUHO-I, ACUI, NACADA, NACA, NASPA, & NIRSA.

Kegan, R. (1994). *In over our heads: The mental demands of modern life.* Cambridge, MA: Harvard University Press.

Kegan, R., & Lahey, L. L. (2016). *An everyone culture: Becoming a deliberately developmental organization.* Cambridge, MA: Harvard Business Review Press.

Kolb, D. (1984). *Experiential learning as the science of learning and development.* Englewood, NJ: Prentice Hall.

Merriam, S. B., Caffarella, R. S., & Baumgartner, L. M. (2007). *Learning in adulthood: A comprehensive guide.* San Francisco, CA: Jossey-Bass.

Mezirow, J. (2000). Learning to think like an adult: Core concepts of transformation theory. In J. Mezirow & Associates (Eds.), *Learning as transformation: Critical perspectives on a theory in progress* (pp. 3–34). San Francisco, CA: Jossey-Bass.

Mezirow, J. (2009). Transformative learning theory. In J. Mezirow, E. W. Taylor, & Associates (Eds.), *Transformative learning in practice: Insights from community, workplace, and higher education* (pp. 18–32). San Francisco, CA: Jossey-Bass.

Morgan, G. (2006). *Images of organizations.* Thousand Oaks, CA: Sage Publications.

Montessori, Maria. (1948). *The discovery of the child.* Madras: Kalkshetra Publications Press.

Piaget, J. (1974). *Origins of intelligence in children* (2nd Ed.) International Universities Press.

Zull, J. E. (2002). *The art of changing the brain.* Sterling, VA: Stylus Publishing.

Zull, J. E. (2011). *From brain to mind: Using neuroscience to guide change in education.* Sterling, VA: Stylus.

CHAPTER 10

Service, Philanthropy, and the Fraternity and Sorority Experience

Sally G. Parish and Zach Carr

SERVICE AND PHILANTHROPY have been an integral part of the fraternal experience from the founding of American fraternal organizations. In many fraternal organizations, service is referenced in their mission, motto, or core values. Over time, that service and philanthropic commitment has evolved into more formalized experiences and in some cases official partnerships between fraternal and nonprofit organizations. The impact of service on the college student experience has long been studied and is typically referred to in both academic and student affairs communities as being a positive practice for student leadership, civic engagement, retention, moral development, and academic success. This chapter begins with a basic theoretical framework and research to lay the foundation of the importance and impact of service on the student experience, then will transition to what existing research indicates about that impact on the fraternal experience. The chapter will conclude with recommendations for practice.

Theoretical Frameworks

Volunteerism as a field of practice and study has proven to be extensive and impactful. Historians have traced early roots of service to Greek and Roman civilizations, and some scholars indicate that the creation of Campus Compact in 1986 was critical in incorporating service into the collegiate experience (Simha, Topuzova, and Albert,

2011) although service of fraternal organizations began long before Campus Compact's creation. While there is no singular definition of service in the literature, volunteerism is defined as a service that is willingly performed by a volunteer who acts out of social responsibility in response to a need (Simha et al., 2011). Philanthropy, in contrast, maintains a number of definitions in publication and practice. Scholar Marty Sulek compared the Webster and Oxford English Dictionary definitions and declared that both represent a recent shift in the historical meaning of philanthropy. Webster's most recent definition of philanthropy, "active efforts to promote human welfare," is broader than the OED definition, which describes philanthropy as "the generous donation of money to good causes" (Sulek, 2010, p. 200). Sulek posits that the meaning of philanthropy in both definitions may actually form a continuum, "ranging from ideal inner state of mind, to objective reality in the world, but with the current meaning strongly leaning toward the latter" (p. 200).

Volunteer contributions certainly have a significant benefit to the community, not only through the tangible help provided but also in the role service has in creating a caring and cohesive society (Taylor, 2007). Psychological literature indicates that the act of volunteering enhances the volunteer's self-esteem and well-being in addition to providing increased social support (Taylor, 2007). A number of higher education researchers and scholars have researched the impact of service (used interchangeably in the literature with volunteerism) and service learning, and widely agree on the positive impact the experience has on college students and their retention, academic success, and overall development.

Cocurricular Service Learning

Barbara Jacoby (2014) asserts that "co-curricular service learning engages students in activities outside the formal curriculum that address human and community needs together with structured opportunities for reflection designed to achieve desired learning outcomes" (section 5.1, para. 1). She asserts that although the student and community outcomes and the service and reflection activities may vary from those offered in course-based service-learning opportunities, the fundamental elements and impact still apply. These benefits include personal growth and interpersonal development, psychosocial and identity development, and growth in the areas of self-efficacy, emotional maturity, empathy, values clarification, sense of purpose, and greater awareness of individual identity components such as race, class, gender, sexual orientation, and ability (Jacoby, 2014). Recent research indicates that young adults engaged in volunteerism are associated with greater degrees of hope, self-efficacy, self-esteem, self-confidence, sense of meaning, and living up to one's own potential (Jacoby, 2014). Students engaged in cocurricular service learning also show gains in complex thinking, ethical and moral development, and clarity about their faith, and demonstrate a higher likelihood of degree attainment and greater satisfaction with their collegiate experience.

Student organizations also benefit from cocurricular service learning, as it creates strong student relationships, shared purpose, and a sense of community. According to Jacoby, "student groups can address a number of organizational issues, such as developing shared purpose, improving internal and external communication, working together across differences, organizational dynamics, and member recruitment and retention, by planning, organizing, and participating in service-learning" (section 5.4, para. 2). Jacoby also points out a variety of logistical benefits to cocurricular service learning compared to academic service learning, including the flexibility of scheduling, subjectivity of reflection, and the opportunity to potentially engage in more complex and challenging service. Jacoby also points out that cocurricular service learning is also more likely to be student led and student initiated, as is often the case in fraternal organizations, which provides a unique leadership and problem-solving opportunity to further advance student development.

Experiential Learning

Experiential learning theory (ELT) defines learning as "the process whereby knowledge is created through the transformation of experience. Knowledge results from the combination of grasping and transforming experience" (Kolb, 2005, p. 194). The ELT model includes the educational hallmarks of concrete experience, abstract conceptualization, reflective observation, and active experimentation. Kolb (2005) defines experiential learning as "a process of constructing knowledge that involves a creative tension among the four learning modes that is responsive to contextual demands" (p. 194). This process engages the learner in experiencing, reflecting, thinking, and acting. The learner uses their immediate or concrete experiences as the basis for observation and reflection, from which new actions or implications may be drawn.

While service and volunteerism are not always specifically integrated into the model as aspects of experiential learning, intentional service with a reflective component is a powerful experiential learning tactic, and ELT provides a useful model for student affairs practitioners to enact in their student volunteer experiences. This method not only engages students in a process of transformational learning, it also engages them in the act of taking ownership of their own learning and engaging in self-authorship to construct their own knowledge through their service experiences. Jacoby (2014) shares that "the framework of self-authorship reminds us that students come to service-learning at different points in their development that influence how they perceive people and situations, receive knowledge, engage in service and reflection, and understand the various complexities of service-learning" (section 5.2, para. 6). Jacoby also suggests that there are several aspects of Kolb's experiential learning model that apply directly to cocurricular service learning. She posits that service-learning experiences should be structured to offer a variety of opportunities for students to move through the learning cycle. She urges that it is important to recognize that students' varied learning styles will cause them to approach service-learning in different ways, and she also emphasizes that reflection is a critical and powerful vehicle for learning to occur through service.

High Impact Practices

Kuh identified 10 high-impact practices that positively impact the student experience, one of which is community service and service learning. These high-impact practices help to reinforce student engagement, deepen their learning, enhance their personal development, and retain them at the institution (Kuh, 2008). Kuh's research also demonstrates that these opportunities promote increased interactions with faculty and staff and the opportunity to collaborate with their peers, many of whom may be different from themselves. This experience has also been found to heighten a student's cultural and social awareness and perspective taking skills (Soria, 2017). Soria's (2017) research on service as a high-impact practice has also revealed that the three areas researchers have found most impacted by community service are student participation, multicultural competence, and leadership development. Soria's research also supports Astin's recommendation of integrating intentionally designed reflection as a mechanism to achieve multicultural competence through service experiences.

Impact

Student Development

As colleges and universities increasingly include in their educational mission the preparation of graduates as future citizens, it raises the question: what impact do colleges and universities have in the development of their students? Battistoni and Longo (Longo, Drury, & Battistoni, 2006) argue that higher education can exist to serve both workforce development and civic engagement to better create a strong society of engaged citizenry and that the two components are complementary visions for the future of higher education. This makes it very clear that student development is not just a learning outcome some institutions wish to integrate in a strategic plan, but an integral part of the overall college experience. When connecting the impact of the fraternity and sorority experience with overall student development, there are many factors to consider that influence how this community engages with and contributes to overall student development.

One contributing factor includes the extent to which alumni and administrators provide support and guidance for the organization. These campus stakeholders see the inherent value in the fraternity and sorority experience and work diligently to advocate for and provide development in areas such as leadership development, community and campus service and philanthropic activity, and engagement in campus life (Gregory, 2003, as cited in Hevel & Bureau, 2014). This support often takes an engaged advising approach to give members the tools they need to have an efficient membership selection and new member educational approach, including ensuring the chapters provide opportunities for members to understand personal and chapter values as well as employable skills (Jelke & Kuh, 2003). Evidence shows that support from the institution's administration is vital in creating holistic development opportunities, particularly in the areas of philanthropy and service that enhance members' dispositions toward community service and philanthropic pursuits (Bureau & Koepsell, 2017). These community and programmatic opportunities aid in students' development by living organizational values and developing skills to interact with and appreciate diverse communities (Martin, Parker, Pascarella, & Blechschmidt, 2015).

While higher education administrators play a key role in providing programming and resources to assist fraternity and sorority organizations' pursuit of socially responsible leadership development, one of the most important positive effects of fraternity and sorority membership is social capital. Whipple and Sullivan (1998) refer to social capital as the glue that holds societies together and includes the networks, norms, and trust that provides a foundation for individuals to work together for a shared goal. These shared goals include the values of service, civic engagement, and volunteerism, as research shows that group service interactions increase members' exposure to diverse perspectives, which in turn creates a broader worldview and a greater tolerance of differences among fraternity and sorority members (Perkins, Zimmerman, & Janosik, 2011). As the values and expectations of membership in a fraternal organization differ from the general student body, researchers found students that participate in organizations with an inherent value and expectation of community engagement and philanthropy are more likely than their peers to donate time and money to secular and/or religious causes. This research also determined the positive correlation between civic engagement and a commitment to lifelong learning.

Leadership and Career Development

Research shows that the career competencies employers desire in recent graduates include verbal communication, teamwork and collaboration, decision-making and problem-solving, and time management (National Association of Colleges and Employers, 2015). The National Association of Colleges and Employers identifies service as a unique pathway for students to develop the knowledge, skills, and values for collective action and civic engagement while simultaneously creating opportunities to gain skills and experiences employers seek from graduates entering the work force (Bureau & Koepsell, 2017).

Many universities introduce service-learning opportunities that are continuously connected experiences to develop ongoing community engagement commitments in an attempt to create greater community engagement to address community needs (Dooley, Frigo, & Morrison, 2017). While there is a level of involvement from higher education administrators and staff, many of these service opportunities are peer to peer, which creates an invaluable opportunity for student development through the planning and execution process. Development of verbal communication skills becomes a crucial part of this experience as fraternal student leaders can be relied upon to communicate effectively every step of the way; from the communication with community organizations, event and volunteer management, to leading a reflective discussion tied to learning outcomes. The opportunities for verbal communication skill development are endless (Collier & Voegele, 2013).

Research shows there is a "demonstrated link between service and leadership ability and the skills that contribute to teamwork, such as interpersonal skills, conflict resolution skills, and the ability to work cooperatively" (Astin & Sax, 1998, p. 251–263). The social change model of leadership development has become a guiding theory for a number of higher education institutions, as the model connects service involvement with the development and understanding of leadership. The social change model not only reinforces the development of self and community, but also focuses on group dynamics and the value of collaboration towards a common goal (Dooley, Frigo, Morrison, 2017).

Oftentimes students are more motivated by the intrinsic rewards rather than the traditional compensation model of the workforce. Students that have the opportunity to lead peer to peer service activities often deepen their understanding on leadership concepts and teamwork, two vital developmental skills that translate to the workforce, where teamwork or team chemistry cannot be mandated but must be developed (Dooley, Frigo, & Morrison, 2017). While leading a group of peers can foster the development of teamwork and collaboration, service can also play a major role in the development of students' problem-solving skills, especially when tied to an academic outcome or service learning course. When community service is structured and executed properly, it gives students a firsthand insight into the needs of the community in which they live. This provides an invaluable opportunity for students in fraternity and sorority communities to research and decide how to best tackle these issues and provide a solution for the disadvantaged community. At times there may be barriers to implementing a plan of action or service opportunity, which provides greater opportunity for real-world teamwork and problem-solving and continually developing these skills through the process. After the student or student leader completes the service experience, it is vital they include a reflective component for participating students or members. This allows for the processing and application of information to the community problems and solutions students have been working with firsthand, further developing the teamwork and problem-solving skills employers desire to see in graduates (Dooley, Frigo, & Morrison, 2017).

Academic Persistence and Graduation

Consistent research shows that student involvement in fraternal organizations has been positively linked to college satisfaction, retention, and persistence. Alexander

Astin (2000) further posited that membership in a fraternity or sorority has a significant positive effect on persistence, satisfaction with college, and satisfaction with both instruction and social life. Additionally, further findings suggest there is evidence that membership in a fraternity or sorority has a positive influence on members and their involvement with the greater community, especially for those organizations whose values, mission, and goals align with the higher education institution. This allows for further learning experiences, especially for out of class and experiential learning opportunities (Nelson, Halperin, Wasserman, Smith, & Graham, 2006).

Gregory (2003) presented overarching research on the involvement and development of students affiliated with a fraternal organization. His research concluded that affiliated students have a much greater tendency than the general student to engage in civic activities, which positively affects student retention and persistence to graduation. Gregory's research further concluded that this civic involvement carries over into students' post-graduation life, showing greater involvement and participation in service-oriented activities. Alumni of fraternal organizations are more likely to volunteer and to financially contribute to charitable organizations. These factors taken as a whole suggest that alumni who have participated in fraternities and sororities are more likely to remain involved in positive ways with their alma maters and their communities.

Recommendations for Practice

Jacoby (2014) indicates that in order for cocurricular service learning experiences such as those that fraternal organizations engage in to be successful, they must engage students in the practices of reflection and reciprocity. She identifies basic steps that cocurricular service leaders must adhere to in order to provide meaningful and successful service. In addition to connecting with the professionals on campus charged with planning service and volunteer opportunities, Jacoby suggests the following steps for developing cocurricular service learning experiences:

Step 1. Select Achievable Learning Outcomes

Articulate direct, achievable outcomes the students will experience as a result of their service experience. Jacoby recommends using concrete, measurable terms to articulate what the students should know, do, or be aware of as a result of their experience. It is important in this phase to identify learning outcomes that are rooted in service and not in philanthropy, and to be able to share the difference with participating students. For example, students may believe that five donated cans equates to five hours of service, which is not an accurate or ethical accounting of service provided. Clear outcomes will help to avoid this error in reporting and misinformed expectation of student engagement.

Step 2. Consider What Service Experiences Are Most Likely to Enable Participants to Achieve the Desired Outcomes

Prior to contacting community partners to begin planning a service opportunity, the student or staff member planning the service should consider what types of service are most likely to achieve the outcomes identified in the prior step. Considerations should include the type of service—direct, indirect, or non-direct—as well as the types of tasks involved, frequency, duration, and partners/sites involved.

Step 3. Approach Potential Community Partners

When planning service, Jacoby recommends that students should research local community organizations to see which organizations are the best fit for accommodating the time frame, schedule, expected attendance, and experience level of the student participants. When contacting a partner, the individual planning the service should be clear about desired outcomes and the type of students who will be engaged. A unique component of fraternal service engagement is that it often engages a large number of students in one site for one specific day/ time. It is important to convey that to the partner so they can accommodate the group's size and skill level without feeling as though the volunteers are presenting a barrier to their work or providing too much of a burden to the site to continue to function while they are present.

Step 4. Plan the Experience in Detail

The staff or students planning cocurricular service learning experiences for the fraternal community should engage in a planning process that includes: identifying goals and actions, assigning a point person for each task, establishing a clear time line, identifying available and needed resources, identifying and addressing potential barriers, establishing a communication plan, articulating what a successful service experience will look like, and identifying an assessment plan to measure success.

Step 5. Determine How You Will Prepare Students for the Experience

It is recommended that students are prepared prior to the service experience, which Jacoby suggests "may be more challenging than for curricular experiences that can rely on the structures built into the curriculum, such as syllabi, regular class meetings, assignments, and grades" (section 5.6, para. 6). If possible, the service coordinator should lead reflection prior to the experience, sometimes called "pre-flection," to assist participants in understanding expectations, site and population information, appropriate attire, and underlying social justice issues that inform their service work. Articles, videos, blogs, and speakers are all helpful to add context to the preparation phase.

Step 6. Select Activities That Are Appropriate and Meaningful for the Participants

According to Jacoby, "planning and implementing a cocurricular service-learning experience that participants view as worthwhile is critical if the desired outcomes are to be achieved" (section 5.6, para. 7). Service coordinators should consider if the volunteer population is appropriate or welcome at the site, as some sites provide gender or faith specific expectations for volunteer engagement. Coordinators should consider if the service type, direct or indirect, is the most meaningful in context of participant expectations and motivations to serve. If participants are not intrinsically motivated, engaging them with a vulnerable population may present risk, and an indirect option may be more appropriate.

Soria and Thomas-Card (2014) recommend that service coordinators seeking to stimulate lifelong civic responsibility, community service, and community engagement may be more successful if they first consider students' intrinsic and values-based motivations for participating in service rather than only motivating them out of organizational requirements. In their research, Soria and Thomas-Card (2014) found that students who "participated in service because it was required by their fraternity or sorority were less likely to indicate these experiences enhanced their desire to continue service" (p. 61). Researchers Ermer and McVaugh suggest that integrating opportunities to cultivate agency, choice, and personal competence may further develop intrinsic motivations for service, and coordinators of fraternal service experiences may explore opportunities to cultivate each throughout.

Step 7. Integrate Critical Reflection Throughout the Experience

Critical reflection should be integrated throughout the service experience culminating with a final, summative reflection. The service coordinator should consider when and where the reflection will occur, who will facilitate the reflection, whether it will be a group or individual reflection, what reflection tools they will use, and the specific prompts they will provide to encourage students in deep and meaningful reflection.

Step 8. Address Logistical Issues

As Jacoby suggests (2014), even one-time service experiences involve a large number of logistical pieces, which a campus-based volunteer or service learning center may be able to assist with. These may include background checks and required trainings or approvals, resources and tools, participant orientation and training, risk management and safety concerns, transportation, and so on. These should be organized and addressed in advance.

Step 9. Develop a Plan to Measure Achievement of Student and Community Outcomes

According to Jacoby, "if assessment and evaluation are not built into the initial plan, it is too easy for organizers of co-curricular service-learning experiences to do little or nothing in the way of evaluation or assessment" (section 5.6, para. 10). Service organizers should not only measure and report community impact such as hours served or the translation of service hours to monetary value, which may be coordinated using the standardized formula provided annually by Independent Sector (see www.independentsector.org), but they should also measure student learning outcomes affected by the cocurricular service experiences. This can be done through focus groups, surveys, and written reflections which should be implemented as part of the fraternal service experience.

Step 10. Seek Closure; Recognize and Celebrate Success

Cocurricular service learning is unique in that it can both start and finish in the same day, in comparison to curricular service learning experiences which can last the entirety of a semester. Even so, and perhaps more importantly, it is critical that the service experience receives closure so that students can reflect on what they experienced, answer any remaining big questions, and consider their next steps. Jacoby argues that "final reflection is essential even in one-day experiences, which may seem useless and irrelevant unless facilitators help students draw meaning from them" (section 5.6, para.11). Jacoby also recommends using formal and informal methods to recognize and celebrate students who engage in service. Options to consider include formalized opportunities like chapter and individual service awards and a cocurricular transcript detailing student service experiences. Informal options could include material shared in newsletters, social media, websites, and other community-based communication avenues.

Models in Practice

While most fraternal communities engage in some sort of service work, we have included four examples in this chapter of organizations, universities, and communities whose work excels in the areas of technology use, community partnerships, international service, campus-based experiences, and standing partnerships between international organizations and nonprofit service providers.

Use of Technology and Community Partnerships: The University of Memphis catalogs all student service experiences in an online database provided in partnership with a nonprofit volunteer center who vets and assesses all community partners for volunteer needs and capacity. The U of M's model provides one dashboard through which students, individually or grouped by organization, can log in with their university credentials to see service needs and sign up for them in real time, as well as track individual and organization hours and economic impact throughout the year. This provides safe, vetted, and expressed community needs for students to engage with and a mechanism through which to report hours for the fraternal community's standards of excellence assessment process.

International Service: The University of Tennessee Knoxville Panhellenic Community partners with Circle of Sisterhood and BuildOn to fundraise for and engage Panhellenic women in international service "Trek" trips to build schools for communities in need. Recent trips have sent 25 Panhellenic women from UT to Malawi and Senegal, where they not only engage in the groundbreaking of the school build, but students also stay with host families and participate in cultural immersion workshops. Since 2010, Circle of Sisterhood has constructed 16 schools in five international communities through partnerships with over 250 campus sorority communities.

Campus Based Service Experiences: A number of fraternity and sorority communities across the country fundraise and volunteer for local Habitat for Humanity house builds, connecting the concepts of philanthropy and volunteerism and channeling them to one community partner with the skills and resources to make a significant impact. While not an exhaustive list, Mississippi State University, Louisiana State University, Texas Tech University, Elon University, Middle Tennessee State University, Indiana University, George Mason University, and Northwestern University have all engaged in this work in recent years.

Standing Organizational Service Partnerships: A majority of fraternal organizations have a formal agreement with a specific foundation or nonprofit partnership through which members are encouraged to give back either in volunteer time or fundraising efforts. Examples of long-standing partnerships include Delta Delta Delta and Lambda Theta Alpha's organizational relationships with St. Jude Children's Research Hospital, Zeta Phi Beta's partnership with the March of Dimes, Alpha Phi Alpha and Sigma Phi Epsilon's support of Big Brothers, Big Sisters, Sigma Kappa's relationship with the Alzheimer's Association, Alpha Delta Pi's relationship with the Ronald McDonald House, Zeta Tau Alpha's long-standing partnership with the American Cancer

Society, Phi Sigma Kappa's support of the Special Olympics, and Iota Phi Theta's partnership with the American Red Cross, to name a few. Support varies chapter by chapter, but the standing relationships provide structure and opportunities for deep, meaningful, intrinsically motivated and mutually beneficial engagement between the organizations over time. A note to consider is whether or not partnering nonprofit organizations are comfortable with philanthropic endeavors including alcohol consumption, and we recommend that this is an area for exploration and future research.

Conclusion

In conclusion, service is a powerful vehicle for leadership, change, and engagement in fraternal communities. It is imperative that practitioners encourage fraternal values of service and philanthropy and connect students to resources on campus and in the community that will engage them in intentional and meaningful acts of each that are mutually beneficial for the student and for the community. Practitioners should consider ways in which they may more seamlessly weave this value of service into the fabric of the fraternal community and should provide opportunities for community engagement, reflection, sustained dialogue, intrinsic motivations to serve, and partnerships around service. Forced service and a disproportionate focus on philanthropic efforts should be evaluated in the context of the campus, community, and student population and perhaps reimagined to provide more intrinsically motivated and successful service experiences that will have a significant impact on not only the fraternal and surrounding communities, but also on the student's personal and leadership development during their collegiate years.

References

Astin, A., Vogelsang, L. J., Ikeda, E. K., & Yee, J. (2000). *How service learning affects students.* Los Angeles, CA: Higher Education Research Institute.

Astin, A. W., & Sax, L. J. (1998). How undergraduates are affected by service participation. *The Journal of College Student Development,* 39(3), 251–263.

Bureau, D., & Koepsell, M. (2017). *Engagement & employability: Integrating career learning through cocurricular experiences in postsecondary education.* Washington, DC: NASPA-Student Affairs Administrators in Higher Education.

Collier, P. J., & Voegele, J. D. (2013). Groups are fun, groups are not fun. In C. M. Cress, P. J. Collier, V. L. Reitenauer, and Associates (Eds.), *Learning Through Serving* (pp. 51–53). Sterling, VA: Stylus Publishing.

Dooley, J., Frigo, R., & Morrison, M. (2017). Developing employability skills through service and community engagement programs. In A. Peck (Ed.), Engagement and employability (pp. 373–398). Washington, DC: NASPA–Student Affairs Administrators in Higher Education.

Gregory, D. E. (2003). *The administration of fraternal organizations on North American campuses: a pattern for the new millennium.* Asheville, NC: College Administration Publications.

Hevel, M. S., & Bureau, D. A. (2014). Research-driven practice in fraternity and sorority life. *New Directions for Student Services, 147,* 23–36.

Jelke, T., & Kuh, G. D. (2003). High performing fraternities and sororities. In D. Gregory (Ed.), *The administration of fraternal organizations on North American campuses: A pattern for the new millennium.* Asheville, NC: College Administration Publications.

Jacoby, B. *Service learning essentials: Questions, answers, and lessons learned.* (2014). Jossey Bass. Retrieved from http://proquest.safaribooksonline.com.ezproxy.memphis.edu/book/college-planning/9781118944011/chapter-5-designing-and-implementing-cocurricular-service-learning/c05_xhtml?uicode=tbrdregt

Kolb, A. Y., & Kolb, D. A. (2005). Learning styles and learning spaces: Enhancing experiential learning in higher education. *Academy of Management Learning & Education, 4*(2), 193.

Kuh, George D. (2008). *High-impact educational practices: What they are, who has access to them, and why they matter.* Washington, DC: AAC&U.

Longo, N. V., Drury, C. & Battistoni, R. M. (2006). Catalyzing political engagement: Lessons for civic educators from the voices of students, Journal of Political Science Education, 2(3), 313–329.

Martin, G. L., Parker, E., Pascarella, E. T., & Blechschmidt, S. (2015). Do fraternities and sororities inhibit intercultural competence? Findings from a four-year longitudinal study. *Journal of College Student Development, 56*(1), 66–72.

Mathiasen, R. E. (2005). Moral development in fraternity members: A case study. *College Student Journal, 39*(2), 242–252.

National Association of Colleges and Employers. (2015). *Job Outlook 2016.* Bethlehem, PA.

Nelson, S. M., Halperin, S., Wasserman, T. H., Smith, C., & Graham, P. (2006). Effects of fraternity/sorority membership and recruitment semester on gpa and retention. Oracle: The Research Journal of the Association of Fraternity Advisors, 2(1), 61–73

Perkins, A. B., Zimmerman, J. D., & Janosik, S. M. (2011). Changing trends in the undergraduate fraternity/sorority experience: An evaluative and analytical literature review. *Oracle: The Research Journal of the Association of Fraternity/Sorority Advisors, 6*(1), 57–73.

Simha, A. S., Topuzova, L. N., & Albert, J. F. (2011). V for volunteer(ing)—The journeys of undergraduate volunteers. *Journal of Academic Ethics, 9*(2), 107–126.

Soria, K. M., & Johnson, M. (2017). High-impact educational practices and the development of college students' pluralistic outcomes. *College Student Affairs Journal, 35*(2).

Soria, K. M., & Thomas-Card, T. (2014). *Relationships between motivations for community service participation and desire to continue service following college.* Michigan Journal of Community Service Learning.

Sulek, M. (2010). On the modern meaning of philanthropy. Nonprofit and Voluntary Sector Quarterly, 39(2), 193–212.

Taylor, E. (2007). An update of transformative learning theory: a critical review of the empirical research (1999-2005). International Journal of Lifelong Education 26(2): 173–191.

Whipple, E. G. (1998). *New challenges for Greek letter organizations: Transforming fraternities and sororities into learning communities.* San Francisco, CA: Jossey-Bass.

CHAPTER 11

Making the Grade: Fraternity and Sorority Standards Programs

Daniel A. Bureau and James P. Barber

FRATERNITY AND SORORITY Community (FSC) standards programs have been a practice of campus administrators seeking to change fraternity (and sorority) culture for over three decades (Mamarchev, Sina, & Heida, 2003; Norman, 2003; Sasso, 2012; Schoper, 2009). These programs have been so much of a part of efforts by administrators, notably those responsible for fraternity/sorority advising programs (FSAP), that guiding documents such as the Council for the Advancement of Standards (CAS) FSAP Standards included content relative to the implementation of these types of programs as recommended practice for FSAP operations (CAS, 2015; Mamarchev, Sina, & Heida, 2003). However, the extent to which these efforts have influenced culture change, engaged stakeholders in a shared objective, and facilitated student and organizational learning and development is often called into question (Reikofski, 2008; Sands & Cucci, 2013), and with good reason: a number of these programs were developed without stakeholder input (Mamarchev et al., 2003; Sasso, 2012) and have had mixed results, sometimes resulting in abandonment based on a lack of institutional and chapter effort toward making implementation a success (Norman, 2003; Reikofski, 2008).

This chapter uses literature about these processes, which we call standards programs overall but often are termed differently depending on the intent (Sasso, 2012), and our own experiences as higher education professionals who have worked with fraternities and sororities in some way for over 20 years each to build on the recommendation by Sands and Cucci (2013) to implement an ethos of ongoing improvement. Our work as a campus administrator (Bureau, previously an assessment specialist and now assistant vice president) and a faculty member (Barber, who teaches courses in higher education assessment) has resulted in the conceptualization of a model that could enhance the outcomes of these standards programs by applying the Assessment Cycle (Suskie, 2009).

Author Positionality

Both authors have extensive background in working with fraternities and sororities. Dan Bureau served as a part of FSAP leadership from 1996–2006 on three campuses (University of Massachusetts, University of New Mexico, and University of Illinois) and has consulted with both campuses and international organizations on a range of FSC issues throughout the last 22 years, most recently serving on a number of external review teams for those FSAP completing a self-study using the CAS Standards. He served as President for the Association of Fraternity/Sorority Advisors during the launch of the *Call for Values Congruence* document and the umbrella group standards documents that followed. He has published and presented on a number of FSC and FSAP issues, including incorporating values congruence to change negative chapter culture.

For the last decade, Bureau has spent much of his time serving the fraternal movement with his affinity for assessment and planning. During the last decade, Bureau served as consultant for FSC assessment and planning, including use of the CAS FSAP Standards. Completing his doctoral work while working for the Center for Postsecondary Research (2006–2009) and the Center for the Study of the College Fraternity (2009–2010), Bureau has had numerous experiences with assessment. He became the Director of Student Affairs Learning and Assessment in February 2011, a role in which he served until 2016. He also serves on the Council for the Advancement of Standards (CAS). These roles have greatly influenced his views on assessment and planning in general and have strengthened his belief that FSAP must continue to improve their orientation toward assessment and planning, rather than enacting stand-alone standards programs for chapter recognition.

Jim Barber served in FSAP leadership between 1997–2004 on two campuses (Davidson College and Southern Methodist University). At both institutions he developed or revised standards programs for the fraternity community. Since 2004, he has served as a chapter and/or faculty advisor for chapters of his fraternity. He was an expert reviewer for the 2011 revision of the Fraternity and Sorority Advising Programs Standards and Guidelines for the Council for the Advancement of Standards (CAS).

As a Higher Education and Student Affairs (HESA) faculty member, Barber teaches a graduate level course on assessment and evaluation for student learning. His approach to assessment is rooted in Astin's (1993) Input - Environment - Output (I-E-O) Model, with a focus on the student environments and experiences that lead to learning.

Review of Literature

Rationale for and Evolution of Standards Programs

Norman (2003) explained the first fraternity/sorority standards program on record was at Dartmouth College, produced in approximately 1987. These programs from inception have been intended, at least in part, to address (possibly shared) expectations of fraternities and sororities. While a new tactic, the efforts of students, volunteers, headquarters staff, and educators invested in the success of these organizations have been attempting to right the wrongs of the fraternal movement for decades prior. For example, in honor of the 200th birthday of fraternity in 1976, the Bicentennial Commission on the American College Fraternity published *Fraternity for the Year 2000*, in which they outlined a number of steps to address the problems of fraternities and sororities (Owen & Owen, 1976).

As the 1980s came to a close, the relationship between institutions and their FSCs became increasingly antagonistic (Mamarchev et al., 2003). While the history of this relationship has been somewhat troubled, the behaviors of chapters post the release of the motion picture *Animal House* (Reitman, Simmons, & Landis, 1978), seemed to embrace the concepts of excess, privilege, and overconsumption in a way that administrators no longer could tolerate (Tampke, 1990). Many institutions developed relationship statements, which often dictated the terms of recognition (Mamarchev et al., 2003). These statements often were a part of or led to the development of standards programs (Sasso, 2012).

In the early 1990s, a number of standards initiatives were underway for fraternities and sororities across the country. National organizations and universities developed risk management policies to address high-risk alcohol consumption and other dangerous activities. Historically African American fraternities and sororities in the National Pan-Hellenic Council (NPHC) adopted the Membership Intake Process in 1990 to replace traditional pledging (Kimbrough, 2003), while a number of historically White groups, also categorized as social organizations, enacted programs to remove harmful pledging practices (i.e., Zeta Beta Tau's elimination of pledging [1989] and Sigma Phi Epsilon's Balanced Man Program [1991]). Even if individual organizations were not reconsidering their educational practices through member development program changes, there were collective efforts occurring to advance these change initiatives.

The Select 2000 initiative was launched among (inter)national fraternities and sororities, all of whom belonged to the National Interfraternity Conference (NIC; now known as the North-American Interfraternity Conference) and the National Panhellenic Conference (NPC). Among the number of initiatives in Select 2000 include standards and expectations to maintain higher grades and increasing participation in community service. What stood out most to people in this effort was the promotion of substance-free housing by 2000. A number of NIC and NPC member groups backed these initiatives, bringing forth a concerted effort to identify standards for chapters (Bode, 1997, May 5).

Thus, the Standards movement became part of a national and institutional effort to realign the actions of fraternities and sororities with their espoused values during the 1990s (Reikofski, 2008; Schoper, 2009). Schoper, who studied the implementation of one of the longest standing standards programs, in place since 1994 at the University of Maryland and known as "The Vision Statement," explained:

> Campus administrators have worked with chapters and their volunteers to establish institutional congruence programs, often resulting in the creation of recognition policies, required programming, and award systems intended to help chapters align with not only their values, but also the mission and policies of the institution. (p. 17)

Because higher education professionals who work with these organizations have an obligation to reconcile the day-to-day risks and benefits of fraternities and sororities, these efforts to focus on the conditions under which successful chapters operate is often the intent of a standards program (Sasso, 2012). As far back as 1996, CAS incorporated standards for FSAP that emphasized relationship statement development as well as ongoing assessment of the effectiveness of the FSAP in conducting activities that helped realize the outcomes espoused by fraternities and sororities. While newer versions have alleviated the push toward relationship statements and standards programs as an expectation for FSAP leadership, there are still recommended guidelines to implement these programs in the most recently updated FSAP Standards (CAS, 2015).

Those efforts continued into the early 2000s and went beyond the national organization and institutional approaches, engaging college and university presidents in the discussion through what became known as "The Call for Values Congruence." The Franklin Square Group (2003), named after the meeting place where they developed this document, called upon organizations to return to their founding values of scholarship, brother/sisterhood, and service to others. The Call for Values Congruence was a philosophical statement on the purpose of fraternity/sorority involvement, akin to the philosophical foundation for student affairs set out in the 1937 Student Personnel Point of View (American Council on Education, 1937; Hevel, 2012). The National Association of Latino Fraternal Organizations (NALFO), National Panhellenic Conference, National Pan-Hellenic Council (NPHC), and the North-American Interfraternity Conference (NIC), umbrella groups for over 100 organizations at the time, launched programs specific to each organization's membership in 2004 (Veldkamp & Bureau, 2012).

To some extent, standards programs emerged as a result of the increasingly litigious environment of higher education: stakeholders are clear that they will pursue legal actions against these organizations if they bring harm to members (Mamarchev et al., 2003). Ultimately though, these processes were enacted to help align chapter actions with their espoused and virtuous outcomes as well as position the institution to be appropriately collaborative with FSC stakeholders in achieving these goals (Veldkamp & Bureau, 2012). Factors that have influenced this concerted effort to promote values congruence include: (a) legal challenges have positioned fraternities and sororities as defending the meaning of its product; (b) fraternities need a distinctive niche in a flooded market of involvement opportunities; (c) college and university presidents told fraternal organizations they had to focus on this (Franklin Square Group, 2003); and (d) new member and intake programs have become more focused on concepts of student development, which coincidentally has components of aligning actions with values (see Patton, Renn, Guido, & Quaye, 2016). A more extensive examination of the recent history of the "values movement" can be found in Veldkamp and Bureau (2012).

Factors within student affairs work, not necessarily specific to fraternity/sorority life, were influencing the development of these programs as well. Within higher education, the early 2000s also saw a shift of how educators and fraternity staff viewed the responsibility to enact academic and social environments that facilitate student learning and development (CAS, 2015a). Over the last 20 years, the emphasis on student learning particularly within student affairs functions has become core to the work of campus administrators tasked with oversight to programs such as FSAP (Barber & Bureau, 2012; CAS, 2015a; Schoper, 2009). As fraternity and sorority members aspire to learn the skills to manage their organizations and work toward values review, development, and affirmation, the learning environment can be very rich in these organizations should the members wish to accept the opportunities that would help advance these educational goals (Barber, Espino, & Bureau, 2015; Hevel & Bureau, 2014).

There is a reason why standards programs continue to be identified as something to solve the problems of the FSC, and part of the reason is that few tactics have been successful in changing negative behaviors. With tragedies in 2017 resulting from continued problems such as hazing and alcohol misuse, as well as sexual assault, the question of support for self-governance of fraternities and sororities continues to be asked (Bureau & Barber, 2017). Ultimately, who should manage these organizations when they fail to hold themselves accountable? The answer often defaults to the FSAP, who implements one of these standards programs in order to "fix" things. Often the challenge comes when trying to identify the end states to which people are working when enacting these standards programs. Additionally, how these programs should influence the registration and recognition of fraternities and sororities is often considered (Sasso, 2012). Additionally, standards programs are a form of assessment as well as a road map for ongoing conversations for improving chapter operations, which requires a holistic and ongoing approach to their enactment. Such an approach can take a back seat to the day-to-day work of managing the latest FSC crisis (Mamarchev et al., 2003). Finally, staff turnover is a real problem in the administration of an FSAP: on average, staff members in the field of fraternity/sorority advising remain in their position (sometimes moving to something completely different or to a different campus doing the same thing) for less than three years (Stillman & Kopesell, 2016).

Types of Standards Programs

Sasso (2012) examined 31 fraternity/sorority standards programs to inform the development of a typology. Previous research from Reikofski (2008) helped to identify specific frameworks to incorporate into standards programs that Sasso incorporated into his analysis, including a focus on student development theory. Sasso used his experience with these programs, previously as a campus professional working with fraternities and sororities, to develop a rubric ("The Greek Standards Project Rubric") of outcomes one should expect these programs to support. The rubric assessed the extent to which each program (a) demonstrated a theoretical orientation which emphasized an administrative framework through which to identify the success of chapter operations (i.e., leadership development initiatives, program goal articulation, and encouraging involvement); (b) collected evidence of adherence to policy, including risk management, community standards or values, and compliance with FSC and campus policies, as well as local and Federal laws; (c) considered the user's overall experience on both administrative (i.e., use of resources, involvement of alumni) and chapter levels (i.e., forms and document submission to international headquarters and number of chapter members involved in operations in the chapter and across the campus; (d) clearly articulated the procedures of how the program was implemented and rewards were distributed; and (e) the extent to which programmatic and learning outcomes were infused into the standards program and how well they were used to facilitate an ongoing discussion with chapter leaders about success.

Through the use of the rubric, Sasso (2012) found that very few of the programs achieved all of the five goals identified as those of the FSAP when enacting these programs. He subsequently developed a typology for these standards programs. Those types and their primary outcome are (a) **evaluation:** mandatory processes designed to grade chapters on the extent to which they performed against a set of standards or criteria; (b) **minimum standards:** also mandatory and developed to provide a basic set of criteria that chapters must meet at some level to stay recognized; (c) **awards:** often voluntary and conducted to identify winners across councils and to present those chapters with awards at an annual reception/banquet; (d) **accreditation:** a mandatory program required in order for chapters to be recognized on an annual basis, often based on some set of minimum standards identified by the FSAP as well as goals developed by the chapter which they agreed to be evaluated against; and (e) **comprehensive:** to combine the best attributes of accreditation, evaluations, minimum standards programs, and also to provide awards for excellence.

Views on Effectiveness

The level of effectiveness of these programs has been explained as variable at best. Norman (2003) examined a single institution's five star chapter evaluation program to examine improvements since implementation in 1997. While chapter members' GPAs did increase, it was not significantly different from the general student population. An area of significant improvement did not occur for new members of these organizations. He found that over time, the number of judicial infractions increased and that members stated the process had not influenced behavior as intended. His study indicated that the desired outcomes of this institution's standards process were not entirely achieved.

Schoper (2009) also explained similar findings in her work studying the University of Maryland's Vision Standards. She explained that a primary goal was to motivate all chapters (at the time of her analysis, there were 57) to aspire toward the fulfilment of the Vision Standards. This goal has not been actualized within that institution, nor has it been realized within other institutions that have adopted standards programs (Reikofski, 2008; Sasso, 2012). Similar to Norman's (2003) research, the achievement of educational outcomes as a result of the Vision Standards effort appeared to be inconclusive: there was a moderate positive influence on some chapter GPAs as a result of this program, particularly in NPC sororities.

As one develops a standards program that meets the needs of a diverse FSC, there must be consideration of how the program can be universally applied: not all organizations operate the same (Reikofski, 2008). This is particularly true when examining how culturally based organizations should be evaluated against a set of standards that was likely developed by and for historically White, socially based organizations (those typically found in an Interfraternity or Panhellenic Council). Many who work with organizations grounded in a cultural identity argue that the application to their organizations is less salient based on founding principles, reason for existence, operations, and the language used (Chris Medrano, personal communication, December 2017; Symphony Oxendine, personal communication, December 2017).

Regardless of application across chapters and councils, the real problem may be the level to which these processes change culture, particularly if that is an expectation of implementation. Reikofski (2008) explained how a number of factors contribute to cultural change. Through his study of two institutions' efforts to implement a standards program, he found that stakeholder buy-in, staff commitment and retention, and a lack of planning were primary factors in the viability of standard programs. He called for a more ongoing consideration in operational planning within a FSC and recommended six essential actions: (a) identify the strength of institutional commitment to the implementation of the planning process and to the FSC in general; (b) develop policies and practices for standards that incorporate the needs of the institutional context; (c) conduct thorough research to ensure the right process is used for assessment and planning, specifically with attention to the history and functions of fraternities and sororities;

(d) identifying main priorities—what is it that the institution and other stakeholders wish to address, and of the many priorities, what matters most; (e) engage stakeholders throughout but absolutely prior to launch and implementation; and (f) adopt results as official policy or as a foundation for continued chapter recognition. Norman (2003) and Sasso (2012) both found that cultural change—shifting from a culture of negative behaviors and operations to one of positive and educational behaviors and operations within the FSC—was rarely achieved.

Using an approach such as Reikofski (2008) would permit for an FSAP to better plan for collecting the information needed to identify how an FSC is achieving, as well as what operations are outstanding and worthy of recognition. Additionally, Sands and Cucci (2013) explained the need to move from once a year assessment to a more ongoing approach to organizational improvement and operational planning. Reikofski promoted the use of operational planning to help chapters identify goals and assess the extent to which those were achieved. Sands and Cucci encouraged professionals to have an orientation toward continuous improvement. With this in mind, there needs to be a shift in how these programs are implemented as it is questionable how outcomes of these programs, either those identified by Mamarchev et al. (2003), Reikofski (2008), Sasso (2012), Schoper (2009) or any other that could be of interest when directing these organizations to become increasingly aligned with their organizational purpose, mission, and values, and the interests of the institution.

A Model for Continuous Improvement within FSAP Standards Programs

With calls for improving standards programs, the authors considered a range of recommendations that could help improve the development and implementation of standards programs. In order to best explain potential approaches (and counter ongoing challenges), we have chosen to use the assessment cycle as our framework. In previous writings, we have explained this cycle and the importance of its use in FSAP deliverance of programs and services (Bureau & Barber, 2017). There are many versions of the assessment cycle (e.g., Henning & Roberts, 2016; Roberts, 2015; Suskie, 2009). Some have as few as four steps and some as many as 15. Such variance often depends on how the person who developed the cycle views the need to map out each and every move versus categorize more broadly.

For the purposes of this chapter, we have selected the four-step model proposed by Suskie (2009): establish goals and outcomes, develop opportunities to achieve these goals, assess (through diverse approaches that are appropriate for the questions considered) how these opportunities enhanced the ability for these goals to be achieved, and use results for future improvements. Many of these who have written about these programs, including Sasso (2012) have explained the need to have a more comprehensive approach to collecting evidence of performance; such a call lends itself well to the concept of the assessment cycle, which focuses on continuous collection and use of evidence to inform strategies for enhanced operations (Suskie, 2009). This model can be broken up into tactics within each step, which can help lay the foundation for an approach to continuous improvement. Additionally, as you enact the steps, it is vital to address any potential shortfalls.

Before explaining the steps, we provide a word of caution about this cycle: it is never done. When applying this sufficiently, assessment is not something you only do four weeks or a few months during the academic year. It is a continuous examination of what our goals are, how we will know if we are successful, and what can we do together, with stakeholders across the FSC, to infuse an ethos of ongoing commitment to improvement. Those applying this cycle will find that they do give varying levels of energy toward the work across the span of a year, but they are always examining where they are in the cycle and identifying when it should "start over" or when you must backtrack. For the purposes of this section, we propose that one might think of this as a year process. As we explain the objectives of each stage, provide an overview of considerations, and address potential pitfalls, we also expand on a case of an FSL professional working on this step in the cycle, so that readers can understand the application.

Step 1: Establish/Revise Goals and Learning Outcomes

Intentionality matters in the work we do with students. One of the most essential ways that student affairs professionals are intentional is through the development of outcomes and objectives toward which their program will work. It is vital to determine clearly stated goals and essential learning objectives of a contributory and relevant fraternity/sorority experience (CAS, 2015; Reikofski, 2008).

There are a number of considerations in the development of these goals and learning objectives. First, there are many resources on how to develop good program goals and learning outcomes (i.e., Collins & Roberts, 2012; Schuh, Biddix, Dean, & Kinzie, 2016). Review of those resources can help a FSAP to author well-written statements of where it is they wish to go. Regardless of your approach to writing, the important first step is to determine priorities and scale of implementation: what is most important and at which intervals will you be able to say you have been successful?

When people are not involved in the creation, they may be less inclined to support the product. This is a lesson often learned by well-intentioned professionals who create a standards program in isolation from key stakeholders. When developing goals and outcomes in a FSAP, it is vital to engage stakeholders in a way that makes them feel valued and that their voice has been heard (CAS, 2015a). All too often when top-down programs are unveiled and no one had any input into its creation, there will be little to no adoption (Norman, 2003; Schoper, 2009).

Finally, there are a lot of possible goals and learning outcomes to incorporate into a standards program, but not all are equally important (and possibly some are not important at all in terms of expectations to be considered a high performing chapter). FSAP leadership should work with students, chapter advisors, and alumni/graduate members, and others with whom they have ongoing and meaningful interactions to identify the true priorities of a standards program (Reikofski, 2008). A standards program that prioritizes everything possible and with equal value assigned to each expectation will likely fail to help chapters in implementing the aspects of a positive fraternity/sorority experience because those completing the project are not tasked with thinking critically about what matters most in enacting member experiences. For example, if learning is an important part of the experience in a fraternity/sorority, then what learning outcomes should be prioritized: you could have 25 different learning outcomes focused on the many skills that one can learn through these organizations, but are they all equally important?

Some of the more effective evaluation processes to which we have been privy outline many ways to engage stakeholders. For example, Eastern Michigan University's Greek Standards and Assessment Program (EMU, 2018) recruits faculty, staff, alumni, and community members to meet with undergraduate members to review their standards materials and have a face-to-face conversation about recent performance and organizational goals. The reviews of these materials, as well as the personal meeting, are compiled and determine chapter awards and recognition.

In conceptualizing this over the course of a year, this step of goal and learning objective development should take about the first month to six weeks. This process, which will require conversations with a number of stakeholders, including institutional leaders, should start with identifying some framework which the FSAP may apply (i.e., use of CAS learning and development domains, division of student affairs already identified learning and programmatic goals) and seeing what is most pivotal for fraternities and sororities to implement. As explained in this section, engaging stakeholders and determining priorities among all of the options will be something that can delay this process.

Step 2: Provide Learning Opportunities

Suskie (2009) explained this step as making sure that every student has the opportunities and experiences to meet the learning goals we set. She noted, "if you are truly serious about ensuring that students achieve key learning goals, design the curriculum to ensure that students have multiple opportunities to develop and achieve these goals" (p. 43).

Relative to fraternity/sorority standards programs, the questions to ask here are "what events/experiences/resources will be necessary to demonstrate success against the standards process?" and "how do all chapters have access to these opportunities?" These questions get at what chapters will need to be successful. Depending on the model you use for administering your FSAP, there is a need to examine what experiences your department should provide against what chapters should provide and how to set these experiences up through good planning, advising, and collaborations. The CAS FSAP Standards can be helpful in providing direction as to how to establish priorities for all aspects of the department, including events and programs, as well as how to engage stakeholders in these efforts (CAS, 2015).

Standards programs often outline what a chapter should do to be compliant with expectations. Those who have written about Standards programs have lamented about the lack of success of these programs due to poor allocation of resources toward helping chapters to be successful (Reikofski, 2008; Sands & Cucci, 2013; Sasso, 2012; Schoper, 2009). The last thing you want is to put a chapter at a disadvantage to be successful in this process simply because of resources: time, talent, and treasure each contribute to the capacity for a chapter to focus on the work required to be successful. This is sometimes the argument that occurs when one standards program is cast across the diverse chapters of an FSC: if standards programs reward size and resources versus true priorities of the FSC, then many chapters will be left out of the race toward succeeding in the program. One of the shortcomings of these plans is when chapters do not have sufficient capacity to coordinate programs and events, as well as the culture to get students involved, that is needed to achieve the "high expectations" of this program. FSAP should work with stakeholders to conceptualize and possibly create the opportunities chapter members may need in order to do well with the standards program.

This step is important in creating an ethos of continuous improvement, because it engages FSAP staff with stakeholders in a way that says "we are going to be successful together." It is not as much a top-down "you must do this" kind of approach, but rather a "we are setting expectations (hopefully mutually developed during step 1) and we are going to work collaboratively to help chapters and the collective FSC to be as successful as possible."

A key consideration here is providing equitable experiences for all chapters, across all councils. Often the bulk of resources related to leadership programming, housing, recruitment, and overall campus advising attention goes to the historically White organizations affiliated with the North-American Interfraternity Conference (NIC or IFC), and the National Panhellenic Conference (NPC or simply Panhellenic), particularly at predominately White institutions. Historically, culturally based organizations are structured such that they may have similar if not better alumni support and engagement, but the operations of the undergraduate chapter can be negatively influenced by low membership numbers (Kimbrough, 2003).

Considering how this plays out over the course of a year time frame, it is important to remember that the cycle is always ongoing and that creating opportunities is really about planning tactics to achieve the programmatic and learning outcomes that have been determined as vital. Because chapters and FSAPs program plan events and provide services continuously throughout the year, it is important to figure out when are the times of year that permit staff and students to sit down and take audit of all the plans in place. This could be something that is done in the spring for the fall and the fall for the spring. Regardless of when opportunity planning occurs, you should always be working toward planning experiences and services that align to previously stated outcomes.

Step 3: Assess Goals and Outcomes

The next step in the assessment cycle is collecting information about whether and how students are achieving the learning outcomes. There are a variety of methods to assess student learning, including direct and indirect, formative and summative, and qualitative and quantitative approaches. The best ones for your FSC will depend on your campus context and goals. Suskie (2009) wrote, "every assessment strategy has potential value. Which are best for your particular situation depends primarily on the purpose of your assessment and the learning outcomes you are assessing" (p. 33).

Once you have goals and learning outcomes and have set up the opportunities for their achievement, this is where the instrument of the standards program comes into play: it is time to identify the evidence sources that will help a chapter and a standards review committee to know how well they did in implementation. To some extent, steps one and two precede the creation and subsequent revision of the standards program: yearly there should be a process of reaffirming the programmatic goals and learning outcomes, determining what levels of support are needed to help chapters enact them, and then revising the standards program expectations to ensure alignment.

As a part of the cycle, there is a continuous focus on collecting evidence of performance and using it to identify places for improvement in a more ongoing basis than just the submission of the packet of the standards program. This can require FSAP staff to continuously keep assessment in their minds as they work with students and stakeholders. Chapters and FSAPs who are engaged in the mutual goal of making the chapters successful in this process should talk through how sources of evidence can range. In some cases it is numbers, others it might be something else, but the ongoing relationship can help chapters to figure out how to demonstrate they have met a standard.

Once the FSL professional decides on the appropriate assessment methods and forms of evidence for the campus, it is important to plan out a detailed schedule for implementation. Start with the end date for when the assessment will be reported to the institution, FS community, and/or the public, and use backward mapping to determine when to begin the assessment process. On a university campus, it is essential to know when key dates including breaks, midterms, and exams fall. In working with an FSC, you will also need to note busy times such as recruitment or community-wide events such as a Dance Marathon.

Think of assessment as documenting student learning (see Collins & Roberts, 2012). You want to be able to show someone outside of the community—perhaps a parent, the university president, a board of regents member, or a state legislator—that students achieved the desired learning outcomes. How you document student learning helps you to tell that story to those outside of the fraternity/sorority community, both on and off campus. Such documentation leads us to the next step in the assessment cycle, sharing and using the results to improve the student experience.

Step 4: Use the Results

Too often in assessment, and particularly in working with student organizations, the results of the process are never used to improve the experience, now and into the future. This is such a shortcoming of most standards programs and of general assessment efforts in FSAP and across higher education.

Timing can contribute to this missed step. Fraternity and sorority standards programs often culminate at the end of a semester, either in December as most chapters install new officers, or in May at the close of the academic year. Although these times are ideal for recognizing achievements in a summative manner, the gap provided by the semester break can interrupt the organization from using the assessment process in a formative way. It is important for FSAP leaders to keep the results in the conversation after breaks or officer transitions so that the findings can be implemented to improve the overall chapter experience.

The campus-based fraternity/sorority advisor is often best positioned to assure that the results are used for improvement and don't remain untouched in a three-ring binder or on a jump drive. Engaging with chapter leaders, including alumni, in discussions during advising sessions about their standards program results—why they scored as they did and what all can do in order to improve in the future—is a great step toward using results to inform planning. Additionally, disseminating the findings widely will also help to make sure that the results are used. As we have explained the staff turnover of FSAP campus professionals can occur as early as each year or every few years (Stillman & Koepsell, 2016), the act of partnering with alumni chapter advisors, national headquarters staff, and senior university administrators can aid in use of results and the implementation of plans even when the front-line fraternity/sorority professional is in transition.

A good example of how a campus uses results is that of Worcester Polytechnic Institute (WPI). Their Chapter Excellence program helps organizations to identify goals in which they are interested while also addressing expectations for all chapters. They have created a cycle that is followed annually and that emphasizes chapter use of feedback to identify new goals and strategies for their achievement. The University of Rochester also has mapped out a yearlong process of identifying goals (of the chapter, the FSC, and FSAP), comparing those goals against evidence, and developing a plan for the FSAP to work with the chapter to maintain areas of strength and improve on areas of weakness.

Finally, remember that assessment is cyclic. This step of using the results feeds right back into the first step of establishing and revising student learning outcomes. The process does not end, but rather evolves each year based on the needs of the campus and the fraternity/sorority community. Assessment is intended to be an adaptive process. If your fraternity/sorority standards looks exactly the same today as it did 5–10 years ago, it is time to reevaluate and revise your process.

Conclusion

This chapter focused on how the enactment of standards programs typically does not achieve intended outcomes and goals. Such results undermine the intent of these efforts to improve the overall quality of chapters and the collective fraternity/sorority community. The experiences of fraternity and sorority members are often called into question, therefore improving the process to collect assessment and conduct planning in a more intentional and ongoing way to ascertain the real stories of members and chapters is vital. We applied Suskie's (2009) model of the assessment cycle and explained some of the important steps to take and avoid within each. It is our hope that using the assessment cycle as a framework for standards programs and FSAP advising in general will help practitioners to be more intentional and deliberative with their development, implementation, and ongoing attention toward standards programs.

References

American Council on Education. (1937). *The student personnel point of view* (American Council on Education Studies, Series 1, Vol. 1, No. 3). Washington, DC: Author.

Astin, A. W. (1993). *What matters in college? Four years revisited.* San Francisco, CA: Jossey-Bass Publishers.

Barber, J. P., & Bureau, D. (2012). Coming into focus: Positioning student learning from the student personnel point of view to today. In K. M. Boyle, J. W. Lowery, & J. A. Mueller (Eds.), *Reflections on the 75th anniversary of The Student Personnel Point of View* (pp. 35–40). Washington, DC: ACPA – College Student Educators International.

Barber, J. P., Espino, M. M., & Bureau, D. A. (2015). Fraternities and sororities: Developing a compelling case for relevance in higher education. In P. Sasso and J. DeVitis (Eds.), *Today's College Student* (pp. 241–255). New York, NY: Peter Lang Press.

Bode, G. (1997, May 5). Select 2000, a nine-part initiative to revitalize the Greek system, has some fraternity members questioning the program's need and how it should be enforced. Retrieved from https://dailyegyptian.com/46960/archives/select-2000-a-nine-part-initiative-to-revitalize-the-greek-system-has-some-fraternity-members-questioning-the-programs-need-and-how-it-should-be-enforced/

Bureau, D. A., & Barber, J. P. (2018). DSDM: Application to fraternity and sorority life. In M.A. Fredrick, P. A. Sasso, & J. M. Maldonado (Eds.), *The Dynamic Student Development Meta-Theory: A New Model for Success* (pp. 119–137). New York, NY: Peter Lang Publishing.

Collins, K. M., & Roberts, D. M. (Eds.). (2012). *Learning is not a sprint: Assessing and documenting student leader learning in co-curricular involvement.* Washington, DC: National Association of Student Personnel Administrators (NASPA), Inc.

Council for the Advancement of Standards. (2015). Fraternity and sorority advising program standards. In Council for the Advancement of Standards (Eds.), *CAS Professional Standards for Higher Education* (9th Ed.) (pp. 254–265). Fort Collins, CO.

Council for the Advancement of Standards. (2015a). The case for CAS. In Council for the Advancement of Standards (Eds.), *CAS Professional Standards for Higher Education* (9th Ed.) (pp. 1–9). Fort Collins, CO.

Eastern Michigan University. (2018). Greek standards and assessment Program. Retrieved from http://www.emich.edu/campuslife/greek-life/GSAP.php

Franklin Square Group. (2003). *A call for values congruence.* Washington, DC: Author.

Henning, G. W., & Roberts, D. (2016). *Student affairs assessment: Theory to practice.* Sterling, VA: Stylus.

Hevel, M. S. (2012, Summer). The enduring usefulness of philosophical statements for fraternity/sorority professionals. *Association of Fraternity/Sorority Advisors Perspectives,* 12–15. Indianapolis, IN.

Hevel, M. S., & Bureau, D. A. (2014). Research-driven practice in fraternity and sorority Life. *New Directions for Student Services, 147,* 23–36.

Kimbrough, W. M. (2003). *Black Greek 101: The culture, customs, and challenges of Black fraternities and sororities.* Madison, NJ: Fairleigh Dickinson Univ Press.

Mamarchev, H. L., Sina, J. A., & Heida, D. E. (2003). Creating a comprehensive worldview approach for managing a campus oversight plan: Do they work? What are the alternatives? In D. E. Gregory (Ed.), *The administration of fraternal organizations on North American campuses: A pattern for a new millennium* (pp. 347–355). Asheville, NC: College Administration Publications.

Norman, E. M. (2003). *Analysis of the Greek five star chapter evaluation program* (Doctoral dissertation). Retrieved from Dissertations & Theses: Full Text. (Publication No. AAT 3100109)

Owen, K. C., & Owen, S. M. (1976). Toward the year 2000: Perspectives on the American fraternity movement. In T. Schreck (Ed.), *Fraternity for the year 2000* (pp. 1–23). Bloomington, IN: American College Fraternity Bicentennial Commission.

Patton, L. D., Renn, K. A., Guido, F. M., & Quaye, S. J. (2016) *Student development in college: Theory, research, and practice* (3rd ed.). San Francisco, CA: Jossey-Bass.

Reikofski, S. H. (2008). *A comparative study of organizational change and planning efforts for fraternity system management: The University of Maryland, College Park and the University of Pennsylvania* (Doctoral dissertation). Retrieved from ProQuest. (AAI3322285)

Reitman, I., Simmons, M., (Producers) & Landis, J. (Director). (1978). *National Lampoon's animal house* [Motion picture]. United States: Universal Studios.

Roberts, D. (2015). Tenet seven: Develop assessment plans. In R. P. Bingham, D. A. Bureau, & A. Garrison Duncan (Eds.), *Leading assessment for student success* (pp. 81–94). Sterling, VA. Stylus Publishers.

Sands, T. L., & Cucci, A. (2013, June). Moving beyond assessment to continuous development and improvement. *AFA Essentials.* Retrieved from https://c.ymcdn.com/sites/afa1976.site-ym.com/resource/collection/0AF0F755-610D-4C20-8128-A307CF7A9924/Sands_Cucci_Essentials_June_2013.pdf

Sasso, P. (2012). Towards a typology of fraternity/sorority programs. *Oracle: The Research Journal of the Association of Fraternity/Sorority Advisors, 7*(1), 22–42.

Schoper, S. E. (2009). The impact of vision standards on fraternal learning environments. *Association of Fraternity/Sorority Advisors Oracle, 4*(1), 17–28.

Schuh, J. H., Biddix, J. P., Dean, L. A., & Kinzie, J. (2016). *Assessment in student affairs* (2nd ed.). San Francisco, CA: Jossey Bass.

Stillman, A., & Koepsell, M. (2016). The Association of Fraternity/Sorority Advisors membership: What we know about our members and why it matters. Retrieved from http://c.ymcdn.com/sites/www.afa1976.org/resource/resmgr/AU/AFA_WhitePaper_Spring_2016.pdf

Suskie, L. (2009). *Assessing student learning: A common sense guide* (2nd Ed.) New York, NY: New York University Press.

Tampke, D. R. (1990). Alcohol behavior, risk perception, and fraternity and sorority membership. *NASPA Journal, 28*(1), 71–77.

Veldkamp, S., & Bureau, D. (2012, Summer). Call for values reflection: Together forward. *Association of Fraternity/Sorority Advisors Perspectives*, pp. 12–15. Indianapolis, IN.

PART FOUR:

DIVERSITY & INCLUSION

CHAPTER 12

Embracing the Rainbow: Addressing Gender and Sexual Diversity (GSD)

Gary Ballinger, Jessica Ward, and Nathan Wehr

Introduction

As a social institution, the college fraternity and sorority can be viewed today as a vibrant organization, capable of expanding its boundaries to include a variety of students' needs and interests, hence, its diversity. However, that has not always been the case. While arguments can be made for a brotherhood and sisterhood of like-minded individuals in forming a fraternity and sorority, others would argue that it is diversity within each organization that makes it a social organization. It is the variety of fraternities and sororities within the social fraternity system that is a manifestation of vitality and viability of this institution. The college fraternity system is able to absorb students who have diverse perspectives and outlooks on life and come from a variety of social, economic, ethnic, religious, or racial backgrounds. A beauty of the system is its ability to meet the needs of a diverse student body (Torbenson & Parks, 2009).

According to Boschini and Thompson (1998), "diverse memberships expand the education and learning opportunities among fraternity and sorority members of different cultures, abilities, and backgrounds. Diversity in [these] organizations helps prepare members for working and living in a highly diverse society" (p. 22). Greek-lettered organizations have had to adapt and change over the years and must continue to do so. If they are to survive and flourish "within the modern college and university, it is imperative that they understand the importance of diversity" (p. 19). One way fraternities and so-rorities continue to evolve is in inclusion related to sexual identity.

Having students who identify within the Gender and Sexual Diversity (GSD) com-munity, which is a more inclusive term for the LGBTQQIA+ (lesbian, gay, bisexual, transgender, queer, questioning, intersex, and asexual) community, in a social fraternity or sorority on a college campus can make a difference in the acceptance of students who identify their sexuality differently from those who are heterosexual. Potential new mem-bers join fraternities and sororities to meet new friends, become involved, and connect to the social fraternity social scene on a university campus. Involvement could have an effect on being seen as more sociable and increase the individual's social status, but for some it is just an organization that provides activities and programs that are based on tradition, brotherhood and sisterhood, and community mixing (Welter, 2012).

Few researchers have identified reasons students who identify within the GSD com-munity join. The most notable is somewhat dated but provides useful insight. Case, Hesp, and Eberly (2005) conducted a quantitative study of 524 participants who identified as gay, lesbian, and bisexual (GLB) fraternity and sorority members on their reasons for joining. Both males and females listed three reasons for wanting to join social frater-nities, which were friendship/camaraderie, social life, parties, having fun, and support group/sense of belonging. Males reported leadership as a fourth reason to join. Only 3% of males indicated they wanted to join to find partners of the same sex (Case, Hesp, & Eberly, 2005). Men joined social fraternities to be among like-minded individuals, and gay and bisexual men have joined fraternities to develop friendships with like-minded individuals (Vary, 2004). Gay men have not desired to join social fraternities to find a date or romantic partner; they have joined fraternities for the same reasons any hetero-sexual male does; friends, development of leadership skills, the social aspect, and to be a part of an organization (Bossart, 1998).

Importance of Inclusion

A growing number of college students who identify in the GSD community enroll in higher education institutions (McKinney, 2005). Many choose to become affiliated with a social fraternity or sorority, and members, leaders, and supportive advisors and professionals should work to address the needs of all members (Case, Hesp, & Eberly, 2005). It is important that GSD-affiliated students know they are accepted for their sexual and gender identity due to the large amount of stress identifying with a minoritized population brings (Dewaele, Van Houtte, & Vincke, 2014). Dewaele et al. identified mental and physical consequences for GSD individuals who experience discrimination, worry about experiencing discrimination, or do not feel they are able to identify outwardly due to aspects of the fraternal environment. The high level of stress a student has by identifying in the GSD community makes them much more likely to experience stress-related mental health issues (Dewaele et al., 2014; Fingerhut et al., 2010; Irwin, 2002).

Understanding Campus Climate

The physical space and perceived openness of fraternal organizations are pertinent in the level of inclusion a student experiences (Patton, Renn, Guido, & Quaye, 2016; Strange & Banning, 2015). According to Strange and Banning, the physical space of the organization is critical for GSD members to feel accepted. If a fraternity has a transgender member and all of the restrooms are labeled for male use only, that member will not feel included or accepted. A better alternative would be to have gender-inclusive restrooms instead of gendered facilities. Similarly, if a lesbian is a member of a sorority who has a formal event coming up and all of the information is about taking a male date, including the picture of a man and woman on the shirt available for the event, that member may not feel included. The physical space that is created is extremely important for underrepresented members to fully feel that they matter within the organization.

Although the physical environment is important, the behavior of an affiliated member's peers is equally or more important. Rankin, Weber, Blumenfield, and Frazer (2010) found an overwhelming majority (92%) of GSD students experienced harassment by a peer while in college, and 68% of GSD students were the victim of derogatory remarks. Further, transgender students reported fearing for their safety, and a majority (72%) stated they did not feel comfortable disclosing their gender identity due to the fear of negative consequences. As a result of the negative experiences, more GSD students reported seriously considering leaving college than their heterosexual peers (Rankin et al., 2010). One of Rankin et al.'s participants stated that harassment came in the form of microaggressions, which the participant defined as, "death by a thousand tiny cuts" as a means of describing the uncomfortable mentally and physically unsafe environment (p. 89).

Visibility of GSD in Social Fraternities and Sororities

Researchers noted the small number of students who identify within the GSD community have affected stereotypes of the fraternity and sorority community (Aber, 2010; Case, Hesp, & Eberly, 2005; DeQuine, 2003; Lipka, 2011). Case, Hesp, and Eberly (2005) examined the visibility of gay, lesbian, and bisexual students in social fraternities and sororities. Their results showed visibility was hard to determine because students were still developing their sexual identities while attending college and most had not stated their sexual identity to fellow members of their fraternity or sorority. Even though the population of homosexual students in fraternities has grown, the responsibility of educating an entire university community that is lacking proper resources on gay issues to provide a supportive environment has fallen on students attending the institution (Lipka, 2011).

However, gay and lesbian individuals have yet to become completely welcomed within the fraternity community; Shane Windmeyer (2005), coeditor of *Out on Fraternity Row*, suggested that only 10% of males in social fraternities were homosexual, but many stayed closeted because of the fear of retaliation from heterosexual members with whom they shared common quarters. DeQuine (2003) noted that as more young individuals come out with their sexual identity in high school, they have assumed universities have a social climate that will align with their sexual identity. The researcher indicated homosexual individuals who are not comfortable in their identity when coming to college have a difficult time assimilating to the campus environment.

Inclusion Statements

While many colleges and universities have taken steps to be more inclusive of the GSD community, many are still searching for the best ways to provide the best options for their students. Renn (2010) noted that, "Improving campus climate for transgender students through nondiscrimination policies and gender-neutral facilities is a critical step-forward" (p. 136). Higher education institutions have been ill-prepared to provide for transgender students, and many are now rushing to adopt inclusive policies and practices and provide them with the services they require (Garvey & Rankin, 2015). However, some institutions have already taken steps to be more inclusive of transgender students, including being more conscious of the issues raised previously. As of 2014, 731 institutions had incorporated gender-inclusive statements into their nondiscrimination policies (Grewe, 2015).

While many inter/national organizations have not yet made statements concerning specific gender inclusivity, this does not necessarily mean they are not accepting of the transgender community. In addition, inclusivity and acceptance will vary by individual chapters, even within the same inter/national organization. To add to the complexity of the situation, "not every institution uses the same standards to determine an individual's sex and gender. These differing standards make it difficult to craft an inclusive policy" (Arrowsmith & Tran, 2014). Many organizations have recently adopted position statements regarding sexual orientation, but few have tackled the topic of gender identity. With more focus on the transgender community, especially in the media, this will be an important topic for years to come, as people become more accepting of the transgender population. McKinney (2005) noted,

> Much needs to be done if transgender students are to feel welcomed and included on college campuses. While the task seems daunting, student affairs

administrators can begin by educating themselves about the diverse range of issues and problems faced daily by transgender students. (p. 74)

Trans* Inclusive Fraternal Organizations

Alpha Chi Omega and Alpha Epsilon Phi, both National Panhellenic Conference (NPC) sororities, have developed policies that support women and individuals who identify as women joining their organizations. In an effort to encourage discussion among member organizations, the NPC also created a gender identity study group that surveyed the 26 member organizations on policy and questions generated around gender identity. The report concluded that more education on national and local college Panhellenic council levels was needed, case law was lacking regarding transgender membership, and the impact organizational policy may have on the college campus needed to be addressed; it also encouraged member organizations to begin dialogue on transgender membership (National Panhellenic Conference, 2017).

Founded in 2003, Gamma Rho Lambda sorority is a "multicultural social sorority for women, trans-women, trans-men and non-binary students of any race, culture, or sexual orientation (Gamma Rho Lambda, 2018). The sorority has embraced this policy since its founding and has experienced growth across the country as college students continue to embrace an environment that affirms individual identity and support. While older sororities may be struggling with identifying policy and concerned about the impact on older members and alumnae, newer organizations like Gamma Rho Lambda have the opportunity to be inclusive from their inception.

Several men's organizations have adopted policies that include those assigned male at birth and individuals who identify as male. The North-American Interfraternity Conference (NIC) is undertaking a study to examine transgender policies within their member organizations even though a few fraternities have affirming policies. One example of an inclusion statement is the following, released by Delta Epsilon Psi, Fraternity Inc. in the summer of 2017.

> In being true to our values and living our mission, Delta Epsilon Psi continues to be inclusive of all men, regardless of race, religion, creed, sexual orientation, nationality, citizenship, and ability. For this reason, our membership voted to become the first fraternity of our kind to extend membership to any individual who identifies as a man, regardless of their gender assigned at birth. Over the past few years, fraternities and sororities had had the need to re-evaluate what it means to be gendered organizations built on fellowship. As an organization built on a pillar of brotherhood, it

is imperative that we continue to advocate for more inclusive membership
while pursuing the vision of our founders, because, "in brotherhood lies our
strength." (Delta Epsilon Psi, 2017)

While several organizations have made efforts to develop policies or positions to be
trans inclusive, very few organizations have fully accepted transgender and non-binary
individuals.

Summary and Recommendations

Even though the population of GSD students joining fraternities and sororities has
grown, the responsibility of educating an entire university community that does not
have enough resources on GSD issues to provide a supportive environment has fallen
on students attending the institution (Lipka, 2011). Although the change has been slow,
the number of social fraternities and sororities belonging to governing councils that
have incorporated inclusive policies on transgender members continues to increase. The
Association of Fraternity and Sorority Advisors encourages organizations to be inclusive of transgender members, noting "decisions about membership should be based on
a member's character, values, and ability to form familial bonds with other members"
(Arrowsmith & Tran, 2013, p. 4). Following are some implementable recommendations
for practice.

Fraternity and sorority chapters should collaborate with GSD resource centers to
provide Safe Zone training for all chapter members. This training could provide education on inclusive speech, a supportive atmosphere for members who are within the
GSD community, and/or considerations about participating in recruitment or intake.
Having students who do not feel comfortable coming out to their chapter shows that
programs, such as ally training, which provides volunteers resources to be an ally for the
GSD community, are needed to provide a sense of safety (Aber, 2010).

Erikson (1968) stated that identity grows through the communication between a
person and their collective relationships. Erikson observed that society and culture
have impacted how individuals think about defining themselves. Membership within a
fraternity and sorority plays an impactful part in the development of the GSD students
who chose to join a fraternity or sorority (Erikson, 1968). Students affairs professionals
working with fraternity and sorority members should have an understanding of GSD
developmental theories. GSD students joining a fraternity or sorority may be at different developmental places when they join. Understanding these theories gives a better
depth of understanding of how to work effectively with an individual who is forming
their sexual identity.

References

Aber, N. (2010). Gay and Greek: The experience of being gay in a fraternity. *Michigan Daily*, pp. 1–7.

Arrowsmith, N. T. & Tran, S. V. (2013). Title IX empowers fraternities to include transgender members. AFA Essentials, B(3).

Arrowsmith, N. T. & Tran, S. V. (2014). Implementing a transgender membership policy. Fraternal Law, 132, 5–6. Retrieved from http://fratemallaw.com

Boschini, V., & Thompson, C. (1998). The future of the Greek experience: Greeks and diversity. In E. G. Whipple (Ed.), *New challenges for Greek letter organizations: Transforming fraternities and sororities into learning communities* (pp. 19–27). San Francisco, CA: Jossey-Bass.

Bossart, S. (1998, October 30). Homosexuals in fraternities The Chronicle of Higher Education, 1–2.

Case, D. N., Hesp, G. A., & Eberly, C. G. (2005). An exploratory study of the experiences of gay, lesbian, and bisexual fraternity and sorority members revisited. *Oracle: The Research Journal of the Association of Fraternity/Sorority Advisors, 1*(1), 15–31.

Craig, L. (Ed). *Brothers and sisters: Diversity in college fraternities and sororities*. Cranbury, NJ: Rosemont Publishing.

Delta Epsilon Psi, Fraternity Inc. (2017, July 25). Press release: Inclusive membership. Retrieved from http://deltaepsilonpsi.org/national/2017/07/25/inclusive-membership/

Dewaele, A., Van Houtte, M., & Vincke, J. (2014). Visibility and coping with minority stress: A gender-specific analysis among lesbians, gay men, and bisexuals in Flanders. *Archives of Sexual Behavior, 43*(8), 1601–1614. doi:10.1007/s10508-014-0380-5

DeQuine, J. (2003, March 17). Out of the closet and on to fraternity row. Time, 8.

Dozier, R. (2015). A view from the academe: Lesbian and gay faculty and minority stress. *Psychology of Sexual Orientation and Gender Diversity, 2*(2), 188–198. doi:10.1037/sgd0000105

Erikson, E. H. (1968). Identity: youth and crisis. Oxford, England: Norton & Co.

Fingerhut, A. W., Peplau, L. A., & Gable, S. L. (2010). Identity, minority stress and psychological well-being among gay men and lesbians. *Psychology & Sexuality, 1*(2), 101–114. doi:10.1080/19419899.2010.484592

Gamma Rho Lambda. (2018, January 14). Gamma Rho Lambda home. Retrieved from http://gammarholambda.org/

Garrett, D. (2002). The value of the Greek system: Should fraternities and sororities have a place on campus. *The Vermont Connection Journal, 19*, 22–29.

Garvey, J. C., & Rankin, S. R. (2015). Making the grade? Classroom climate for LGBTQ students across gender conformity. *Journal of Student Affairs Research and Practice, 52*(2), 190–203. doi:10.1080/194965591.2015.1019764

Grewe, M. (2015). Lesbian, gay, bisexual, transgender, queer, intersex, and asexual support systems within higher education. In W. Swan (Ed.), *Gay, lesbian, bisexual, and transgender civil rights: A public policy agenda for uniting a divided America* (pp. 275–295). Boca Raton, FL: Taylor & Francis Group.

Irwin, J. (2002). Discrimination against gay men, lesbians, and transgender people working in education. *Journal of Gay & Lesbian Social Services, 14*(2), 65–77.

Lipka, S. (2011, August 28). As they try to rein in fraternities, colleges stir debate. The Chronicle of Higher Education. Retrieved from http://chronicle.com/articles.

McKinney, J. S. (2005). On the margins: A study of the experiences of transgender college students. *Journal of Gay & Lesbian Issues in Education, 3*(1), 63–75. doi:10.1300/J367v03n01_07

National Panhellenic Conference. (2017). *NPC gender identity study group.* Indianapolis, IN: National Panhellenic Conference.

Patton. L. D., Renn, K. A., Guido, F. M., & Quaye, S. J. (2016). *Student development in college: Theory, research, and practice* (3rd ed.). San Francisco, CA: Jossey Bass.

Rankin, S., Weber, G. N., Blumenfield, W. J., & Frazer, S. J. (2010). *State of higher education for lesbian, gay, bisexual, and transgender people: Campus pride 2010 national college climate survey.* Charlotte, NC: Campus Pride.

Renn, K. A. (2010). LGBT and queer research in higher education: The state and status of the field. *Educational Researcher, 39*(2), 132–141. doi:10.3102/0013189Xl0362579

Strange, C. C., & Banning, J. H. (2015). *Designing for learning: Creating campus environments for student success* (2nd ed.). San Francisco, CA: Jossey Bass.

Torbenson, C. L., & Parks, G. S. (2009). Preface. In C. L. Torbenson & G. S. Parks (Eds.), *Brothers and Sisters: Diversity in College Fraternities and Sororities* (pp. 9–14). Madison, NJ: Fairleigh Dickinson University Press.

Vary, A. E. (2004). Rushing to come out. *Advocate, 924,* 1–6.

Welter, E. (2012). College Greek life: Perceptions and lived experiences of lesbian, gay, bisexual, transgender, questioning, and queer (LGBTQ) students. *Journal of the Indiana Academy of Social Sciences, 15,* 111–139.

Windmeyer, S. L. (2005). Brotherhood: Gay life in college fraternities, Los Angeles: Alyson Publications.

CHAPTER 13

Gender Performativity in College Social Fraternities and Sororities

Adam McCready and Scott Radimer

PROPONENTS OF THE fraternity and sorority movement often argue that fraternities and sororities provide undergraduates with the preeminent values-based experiences for learning and development growth (e.g.., National Panhellenic Conference, n.d.; North-American Interfraternity Conference, 2014). In addition, they assert that fraternities and sororities provide transformative experiences to foster better women and men through brotherhood and sisterhood, service to others, leadership opportunities, and community activism (e.g., Beta Theta Pi, n.d.). Despite the noble intent of these organizations, fraternity and sorority membership is linked to a number of troubling outcomes. Fraternity and sorority members are more likely to abuse alcohol than their unaffiliated peers (Wechsler, Kuh, & Davenport, 1996), and hazing is prevalent in these organizations (Allan & Madden, 2008). Fraternity men are more likely to commit sexual assault or be more supportive of sexual violence and rape myths than other students (Murnen & Kohlman, 2007; Seabrook, Ward, & Giaccardi, 2018), while sorority women are more likely than unaffiliated women to develop eating disorders as their undergraduate careers progress (Allison & Park, 2004). Although attitudes in America have significantly shifted over the past 20 years, fraternities and sororities continue to be associated with homophobia (Hall & La France, 2007; Syrett, 2009).

While some people would like to explain away this behavior as the result of these organizations recruiting "bad" people, or somehow being inherently flawed, a better, and more nuanced, explanation is that these outcomes are associated with gender stereotypes. An increasing number of scholars have argued that the outcomes associated with fraternity and sorority membership are the result of members' attempts to validate and prove their masculinity or femininity (e.g., DeSantis, 2007). The rest of this section will address the concept of gender performativity, the relationships of particular gender performances with fraternity and sorority member outcomes, and the potential implications of the extant literature on fraternities and sororities.

Gender Performativity

In her book *Gender Trouble: Feminism and the Subversion of Identity*, Judith Butler (1990) argued that gender is not something that it exists on its own, but rather is something that people are constantly *performing*. Gender is something that you *do*, rather than something that you *have*. Although this may strike many as a radical conception of gender, when one analyzes the idea further, it seems much less radical. Consider, for example, the emphasis that parents put into training their children to perform gender correctly. Little boys are constantly given messages around appropriate emotional expressions ("don't cry like a little girl"), appropriate toys ("boys don't play with dolls"), or projecting romantic feelings onto children too young to yet be feeling them ("oh look at all his girlfriends"), as are little girls (Pollack, 1998).

If gender was something that simply innately existed in people independently, there would be no point in coaching children how to appropriately act as their gender (e.g., "Be more ladylike," or "man up!"), because their behaviors and attitudes would be natural. If for some reason someone was not "correctly" acting as their assigned gender, what would be the point of trying to get them to change the way they acted, if it is innate? Furthermore, if gender were simply innate, why do men and women act differently across cultures? Why would kissing another man on the cheek be considered normal and masculine in Europe, but be taboo in America? Or what about differences across time? Men used to wear high-heeled shoes and wigs. Today those behaviors are considered feminine. If what is considered masculine was biological, those things should not change over time.

The differences across cultures and time illustrate how gender is socially constructed (Butler, 1990). Individuals' concern about making sure that others "correctly" act according to their gender confirms Butler's assertion. Gender is a performance shaped by our interactions with others and other social forces, and gender performativity is ever ongoing and evolving. It is not enough to simply do something masculine or feminine once, but rather it must be done over and over, to reaffirm one's commitment to their socially assigned role. This constant gender performance then works to create the illusion of an innate gender, because if everyone else is doing it, and it always follows the same socially-acceptable patterns, well then it must be natural. Gender performances become part of a self-reinforcing system. We conform to our gender roles because everyone else appears to be, which just further reinforces them.

There are particular normative conceptualizations of gender that serve as the benchmark for all other gender performances in our society. Because masculinities hold dominant standing over femininities, hegemonic masculinity is perceived to be the ideal gender performance standard in our society (Connell, 1987; Connell & Messerschmidt, 2005). To pursue and gain power, individuals often attempt to conform to hegemonic masculinity even though it is unobtainable for the majority. Once proved and validated, masculinity is a fragile construct that must constantly be reaffirmed through one's performances (Vandello & Bosson, 2013). Thus, individuals that conform to masculinity may engage in troubling or unhealthy behaviors to offer irrefutable proof of their identities and power (Courtenay, 2000; Vadello & Bosson, 2013). Finally, masculinity and femininity are routinely defined in opposition to one another, with the ambiguous boundaries of masculinity shaped by a fear of femininity (Kimmel, 1994).

Gender Performativity and Fraternities

Scholars have long argued that fraternities institutionalize hegemonic masculinity at colleges and universities (Kimmel, 2008; Martin & Hummer, 1989; Rhoads, 1995; Sanday, 1990/2007; Syrett, 2009). These organizations not only influence the gender performances of their members, but they may reify the conceptualization of manhood within the undergraduate experience and throughout society (Syrett, 2009). The power to influence the gender performances of members and other community members may rest in the men's-only environments of fraternities. Seabrook, Ward, and Giaccardi (2018) suggested that members of fraternities are under increased influence to adopt traditional masculinities because manhood is confirmed and reaffirmed by other men. Becoming "fraternity men" provides college men skeptical of their masculine identities with public opportunities to establish and display their manhood, while it also provides spaces for men to develop close, intimate relationships with other men that they often have difficulty establishing with peers (Sanday, 1990/2007; Syrett, 2009). In addition, inflicting and enduring hazing may serve as a beguiling means to denote a transition from boyhood to manhood. Thus, a fraternity badge or Greek-lettered shirt does not only confer membership in specific fraternity but indicates that a fraternity member is a real man.

A growing body of literature has associated the traditional masculinities performed by fraternity men with a host of problematic outcomes. Early research on this topic linked fraternity masculinity with misogyny (Martin & Hummer, 1989; Rhoads, 1995; Sanday, 1990/2007). Scholars continue to support the assertion that fraternity masculinity is framed by a fear of femininity and the marginalization of women. "In fraternities, manhood is affirmed, but at a cost: the devaluation of women" (Syrett, 2009, p. 287). It may be unsurprising then that traditional masculine norm adoption has been found to explain the relationship between fraternity membership and rape myth acceptance (Seabrook et al., 2018). In addition to reinforcing patriarchy, theory and research indicate that fraternity masculinities foster homophobia (Rhoads, 1995; Syrett, 2009), and relate to members' endorsement of hazing rationales (McCready, 2018). Fraternity masculinities may reinforce and exacerbate the troubling attitudes of their members.

The traditional masculinities espoused by fraternities may not only influence members' attitudes, but may affect their behaviors. The literature indicates that the conformity to hegemonic masculinity by fraternity men is associated with their alcohol use and alcohol-related consequences (DeSantis, 2007; Iwamoto, Cheng, Lee, Takamatsu, & Gordon, 2011; Iwamoto, Corbin, Lejuez, & MacPherson, 2014; McCready, 2018; Radimer, 2016; Sasso, 2015; Sweeney, 2014). Alcohol use may afford members with opportunities to prove and validate their manhood by serving as a means to take risks, compete with others (e.g., drinking games), and gain status in the collegiate party and hook-up culture. It may also afford members with opportunities to foster intimate, vulnerable relationships with other men that are often elusive to this population (McCready, 2018; Sasso, 2015). Alcohol is fundamental to fraternity masculinity.

In addition to alcohol use, others have associated fraternity masculinities with members' sexual promiscuity or conquests (Rhoads, 1995; Sanday, 1990/2007; Syrett, 2009), though this finding is not universally supported (Corprew & Mitchell, 2014). While limited to a single study, fraternity members' adoption of traditional masculinities may relate to members' obsession with athletic physiques and the devaluation of academics (DeSantis, 2007).

While the fraternity men's conformity to hegemonic masculinity may promote problematic attitudes and behaviors, not all fraternity men perform traditional masculine gender scripts (Anderson, 2008; DeSantis, 2007; Harris & Harper, 2014; McCready, 2018). Because hegemonic masculinity may be unachievable by fraternity members with marginalized identities, some members, particularly men of color and those from lower socioeconomic backgrounds, may limit their participation in the partying script, and pursue other endeavors to prove and validate their manhood (Sweeney, 2014). In addition, some fraternity chapters may promote more inclusive gender norm climates that reduce the pressure on members to engage in troubling behaviors or adopt problematic attitudes to prove their status as men (DeSantis, 2007; McCready, 2018). In short, the conceptualization of "fraternity man" varies between individuals, fraternity chapters, and even higher education institutions.

Gender Performativity and Sororities

The literature on the gender performativity of college students has overwhelmingly focused on college men and the relationships between masculinity and their behavior and attitudes (e.g., Harris & Edwards, 2010). The research examining the influence of college women's gender constructions on their outcomes is less prevalent. Mirroring this gender ratio, there has been much more research into the gender performance of fraternity men than there has been into the gender performance of sorority women.

The literature indicates that gender performance within sororities is that a specific kind of femininity is demanded throughout out the sorority experience, from recruitment until graduation. Sorority femininity is not a new social construction but has existed since the initial founding of these organizations in the mid-19th century. Rowen (2013) described how the performance of femininity has been a part of Kappa Alpha Theta, the first sorority, since its inception in 1870 until today. Rowen identified that in 1870, women were rarely allowed to attend college, and it was considered anathema to femininity to receive a higher education. In order to prove they belonged in college, but were not "unsexed," Kappa Alpha Theta's founders described the organization as contributing to a "nobler womanhood." This secret society helped women succeed in college at a time that society was very skeptical of women's education, by proving women as acceptably performing their femininity while also creating a safe space for women to support each other free of the judgement of male faculty and peers.

Boyd (1999) used a case study of rush at the University of Mississippi to investigate the performance of a very specific type of femininity required for acceptance into the National Panhellenic Conference sororities. The sorority women recruiting new members, and the women rushing, hoping to join, both performed the role of the "Southern Lady" or "Belle," while both parties seem to be aware that they were performing a script, rather than necessarily acting authentically. The script of "Southern Lady" covered the ways the women acted, how they dressed, as well as whom they knew and where they were from. While not happening in the South, Arthur (1999) described many similar dynamics of women in the sorority recruitment process in the Pacific Northwest. Women looking to join sororities constructed their femininity through adopting the dress style of the sorority (the sorority look), an idealized image of femininity as their gender role obligation. Only once the women were secure in their status as a full sister could women revert to adopting their more personal image.

The specific type of femininity that women in sororities perform extends beyond the recruitment process. Berbary (2012) interviewed and observed sorority women at a chapter in the South, and described a social structure where the discourse the women engaged in reinforced a very specific type of femininity among its members. The femininity discourse was shaped and enforced by women's stories about previous sisters who upheld or transgressed "ladylike" behaviors, and a social structure that required them to observe and police each other's behavior. These discursive practices also reinforced White and upper class social norms and values (Berbary, 2012). Along similar lines, Armstrong and colleagues (2014) examined the ways college women at a university in the Midwest used "slut discourse," or the labeling of other women as promiscuous to reinforce class divides and perform their gender. Most of the high-status women in the study were members of sororities, and they used slut discourse to differentiate their sexual behavior as socially acceptable and "classy," while the behavior of women from lower status groups were, in their eyes, acting slutty and socially unacceptable. Just as within Berbary's (2012) study, Armstrong and colleagues (2014) found the performance of gender by the high-status sorority women to be embedded within a construction of femininity that was racially White and socio-economically privileged.

Like Armstrong et al. (2014), DeSantis (2007) identified that members of high-status sororities promoted and reinforced rigid conceptualizations of traditional feminine gender performances. However, women in sororities with less status were provided more latitude in their gender performativity, and these individuals engaged in fewer problematic behaviors than their high-status sorority peers. Thus, DeSantis (2007) argued that gender performances were not the same among all sorority women in his sample, and that the adoption of traditional feminine performances aggravated the troubling attitudes and behaviors of these students.

Gender Performativity and Gender Inclusive Societies

While Greek-letter societies without gender restrictive policies have steadily increased in number over the past half century (e.g., Dartmouth College, 2016), researchers have yet to examine how members of these organizations enact gender. The dearth of literature on this population may be because these organizations tend to lack the power and privilege associated with gender-restricted fraternities and sororities, or because they are not broadly associated with problematic outcomes. However, as more students and higher education institutions push for gender inclusive policies among fraternities and sororities (e.g., Harvard University, 2017), scholars and practitioners should make concerted efforts to investigate and understand the influences of membership in gender inclusive societies on student outcomes.

Implications and Conclusion

Though additional research is needed, the literature indicates that fraternities and sororities socialize gender performances that affect the outcomes of their members (e.g., Berbary, 2012; Seabrook et al., 2018). In particular, fraternity and sorority socialization efforts that promote the adoption of traditional gender performances may exacerbate behaviors and attitudes associated with these organizations that draw the greatest ire from stakeholders. However, the extant scholarship on fraternities and sororities suggests that the social constructs of the "fraternity man" and "sorority women" identities are not monolithic across these populations, and they vary between individual members, chapters, and potentially other ecological systems (DeSantis, 2007; McCready, 2018). The climates promoted by fraternities and sororities exert pressure on members to conform to established gender performances, but no two members enact gender in the same way.

There are several implications of these findings for practice and research. Stakeholders who support fraternities and sororities should make concerted efforts to assess and understand how gender is performed by fraternity and sorority members in their communities and pay particular attention to the nuances of gender norm conformity among members, chapters, governing councils and other sub-communities (e.g., housed versus unhoused chapters). By understanding the ways that individuals, chapters, and other subcommunities that conform to traditional gender roles, practitioners may be able to identify at-risk individuals and groups and intervene prior to a troubling occurrence.

Because gender performativity varies among members and organizations, it is likely that broad, catchall intervention strategies will do little to mitigate the troubling outcomes associated with fraternity and sorority membership. Instead, practitioners should hone interventions that address individual and organizational traditional gender performances. For example, scholars have argued that mentors and role models are particularly important in the socialization of gender (e.g., Harris, 2010). A practitioner could design an educational initiative for new member big brothers or big sisters that incorporates interventions that address traditional gender performances. By role modeling less rigid conceptualizations of gender, the individuals may reshape the gendered climates of their organizations and communities.

There are also implications for future research on fraternities, sororities, and other Greek-letter organizations. While additional research is needed on the gender performativity of this population, the literature is particularly lacking on sororities and gender-inclusive organizations. In addition, while scholars have argued that outcomes differ among predominantly White fraternities and sororities, and fraternities and sororities that are predominantly students of color (e.g., Parks, Jones, Ray, Hughey, & Cox, 2015), no studies have examined how gender is enacted among the latter population. Because traditional masculinities and femininities often marginalize individuals of color, understanding the construction of gender in fraternities and sororities that serve predominantly students of color may help to address inequities and other structures of power and oppression within fraternity and sorority communities.

References

Allan, E. J., & Madden, M. (2008). *Hazing in view: College students at risk. Initial findings from the National Study of Student Hazing.* Retrieved from http://www.stophazing.org/wp-content/uploads/2014/06/hazing_in_view_web1.pdf

Allison, K. C., & Park, C. L. (2004). A prospective study of disordered eating among sorority and nonsorority women. *The International Journal of Eating Disorders, 35*(3), 354–358.

Anderson, E. (2008). Inclusive masculinity in a fraternal setting. *Men and Masculinities, 10*(5), 604–620. doi:10.1177/1097184X06291907

Armstrong, E. A., Hamilton, L. T., Armstrong, E. M., & Seeley, J. L. (2014). "Good girls": Gender, social class, and slut discourse on campus. *Social Psychology Quarterly, 77*(2), 100–122.

Arthur, L. B. (1999). Dress and the social construction of gender in two sororities. *Clothing and Textiles Research Journal, 17*(2), 84–93.

Berbary, L. A. (2012). "Don't be a whore, that's not ladylike": Discursive discipline and sorority women's gendered subjectivity. *Qualitative Inquiry, 18*(7), 606–625.

Beta Theta Pi. (n.d.). About Beta. Retrieved from http://beta.org/about/about-beta-theta-pi/

Boyd, E. (1999). Sister act: Sorority rush as feminine performance. *Southern Cultures, 5*(3), 54–73.

Butler, J. (1990). Feminism and the subversion of identity. Routledge; London.

Connell, R. W. (1987). *Gender and power.* Stanford, CA: Stanford University Press.

Connell, R. W., & Messerschmidt, J. W. (2005). Hegemonic masculinity: Rethinking the concept. *Gender & Society, 19*(6), 829–859. doi:10.1177/0891243205278639

Corprew III, C. S., & Mitchell, A. D. (2014). Keeping it frat: Exploring the interaction among fraternity membership, disinhibition, and hypermasculinity on sexually aggressive attitudes in college-aged males. *Journal of College Student Development, 55*(6), 548–562. doi:10.1353/csd.2014.0062

Courtenay, W. H. (2000). Constructions of masculinity and their influence on men's well-being: A theory of gender and health. *Social Science & Medicine, 50*(10), 1385–1401.

Dartmouth College. (2016). *Dartmouth College Office of Greek Life handbook & policies: September 1, 2016 to August 31, 2017.* Retrieved from https://students.dartmouth.edu/greek-life/sites/students_greek_life.prod/files/greek_life/wysiwyg/greek_life_handbook_2016_2017.pdf

DeSantis, A. D. (2007). *Inside Greek U: Fraternities, sororities, and the pursuit of pleasure, power, and prestige.* Lexington, KY: University Press of Kentucky.

Hall, J., & La France, B. (2007). Attitudes and communication of homophobia in fraternities: Separating the impact of social adjustment function from hetero-identity concern. *Communication Quarterly, 55*(1), 39–60.

Harris, III, F. (2010). College men's meanings of masculinities and contextual influences: Toward a conceptual model. *Journal of College Student Development, 51*(3), 297–318. doi:10.1353/csd.0.0132

Harris III, F., & Edwards, K. (2010). College men's experiences as men: Findings from two grounded theory studies. Journal of Student Affairs Research and Practice, 47, 43–62

Harris III, F., & Harper, S. R. (2014). Beyond bad behaving brothers: Productive performances of masculinities among college fraternity men. *International Journal of Qualitative Studies in Education, 27*(6), 703–723. doi:10.1080/09518398.2014.901577

Harvard University. (2017). *Unrecognized single-gender social organizations: Harvard College social organizations policy.* Retrieved from https://www.harvard.edu/media-relations/media-resources/popular-topics/unrecognized-single-gender-social-organizations

Iwamoto, D. K., Cheng, A., Lee, C. S., Takamatsu, S., & Gordon, D. (2011). "Man-ing" up and getting drunk: The role of masculine norms, alcohol intoxication and alcohol-related problems among college men. Addictive Behaviors, 36(9), 906–911.

Iwamoto, D. K., Corbin, W., Lejuez, C., & MacPherson, L. (2014). College men and alcohol use: Positive alcohol expectancies as a mediator between distinct masculine norms and alcohol use. Psychology of Men & Masculinity, 15(1), 29–39.

Kimmel, M. S. (1994). Masculinity as homophobia: Fear, shame, and silence in the construction of gender identity. In H. Brod & M. Kaufman (Eds.), *Theorising masculinities* (pp. 213–219). Thousand Oaks, CA: SAGE.

Kimmel, M. S. (2008). *Guyland: The perilous world where boys become men. Understanding the critical years between 16 and 26*. New York, NY: HarperCollins Publishers.

Martin, P. Y. (2016). The rape prone culture of academic contexts: Fraternities and athletics. *Gender & Society, 30*(1), 30–43. doi:10.1177/0891243215612708

Martin, P. Y., & Hummer, R. A. (1989). Fraternities and rape on campus. *Gender and Society, 3*(4), 457–473.

McCready, A. M. (2018). *Relationships among fraternity chapter masculine norms, organizational socialization, and the problematic behaviors of fraternity men* (Unpublished doctoral dissertation). Boston College, Chestnut Hill, MA.

Murnen, S. K., & Kohlman, M. H. (2007). Athletic participation, fraternity membership, and sexual aggression among college men: A meta-analytic review. *Sex Roles, 57*(1–2), 145–157. doi:10.1007/s11199-007-9225-1

National Panhellenic Conference. (n.d.). *About the National Panhellenic Conference*. Retrieved from http://www.npcwomen.org/about/

North-American Interfraternity Conference. (2014). *Position statement: Single sex organizations* [Position statement]. Indianapolis, IN. Retrieved from http://nicindy.org/wp-content/uploads/2016/07/Single-Sex-Organizations.pdf

Parks, G. S., Jones, S. E., Ray, R., Hughey, M. W., & Cox, J. M. (2015). White boys drink, black girls yell . . . : A racialized and gendered analysis of violent hazing and the law. *Journal of Gender, Race & Justice, 18*, 93–158.

Pollack, W. S. (1998). *Real boys: Rescuing our sons from the myths of boyhood*. New York, NY: Random House.

Radimer, S. (2016). *Masculine norms, ethnic identity, social dominance orientation, and alcohol consumption among undergraduate men* (Unpublished doctoral dissertation). Boston College, Chestnut Hill, MA.

Rhoads, R. A. (1995). Whales tales, dog piles, and beer goggles: An ethnographic case study of fraternity life. *Anthropology & Education Quarterly, 26*(3), 306–323. doi:10.1525/aeq.1995.26.3.05x0935y

Rowen, S. B. (2013). Nobler womanhood: An exploration of sororities and scripted femininity. *Emerging Theatre Research, 1*(1), 21–53.

Sanday, P. R. (1990/2007). *Fraternity gang rape: Sex, brotherhood, and privilege on campus* (2nd ed.). New York, NY: New York University Press.

Sasso, P. (2015). White boy wasted: Compensatory masculinities in fraternity alcohol use. *The Oracle: The Research Journal of the Association of Fraternity/Sorority Advisors, 10*(1), 14–30.

Seabrook, R. C., Ward, L. M., & Giaccardi, S. (2018). Why is fraternity membership associated with sexual assault? Exploring the roles of conforming to masculine norms, pressure to uphold masculinity, and objectification of women. *Psychology of Men & Masculinity, 19*(1), 3–13.

Sweeney, B. (2014). Party animals or responsible men: Social class, race, and masculinity on campus. *International Journal of Qualitative Studies in Education, 27*(6), 804–821. doi:10.1080/09518398.2014.901578

Syrett, N. L. (2009). *The company he keeps: A history of white college fraternities*. Chapel Hill, NC: The University of North Carolina Press.

Vandello, J. A., & Bosson, J. K. (2013). Hard won and easily lost: A review and synthesis of theory and research on precarious manhood. *Psychology of Men & Masculinity, 14*(2), 101–113. doi:10.1037/a0029826

Wechsler, H., Kuh, G., & Davenport, A. E. (1996). Fraternities, sororities, and binge drinking: Results from a national study of American colleges. *NASPA Journal, 33*(4), 260–279.

CHAPTER 14

Social Belonging for Students of Color in White Greek-Letter Organizations

Monica Galloway Burke and Alex Kennedy

HISTORICALLY, FRATERNITIES AND sororities existed in racial segregation and ascendancy, specifically within traditionally and historically white Greek-letter organizations (WGLOs). In fact, Black national fraternities and sororities were excluded from the National Interfraternity Conference (NIC), and thus organized the National Pan-Hellenic Council (NPHC) to meet their needs (Torbenson, 2005). WGLOs have a history of exclusionary practices and race clauses, with Delta Sigma Phi Fraternity being the first fraternity to have a stated Caucasian membership clause (Brown, 1923). Even after discriminatory statements were removed nearly 50 years ago, in most cases, there are still campuses that have not seen a student of color join a WGLO, especially in the deep south (Luckerson, 2013). Although traditionally and historically WGLOs no longer have discrimination clauses as a part of their constitutions, it is obvious that the "history" as a white organization and all the perceptions and precedent that comes with that label persists today, creating an unsure environment for ethnic minority student involvement (Thompson, 2000). Nonetheless, some racial diversification in traditionally White Greek-letter organizations can currently be seen on college campuses.

Although there is much research available on the impact of student involvement in college (Astin, 1984; Tinto, 1993), there is less literature discussing the involvement and experiences of students of color within predominantly/traditionally white fraternities and sororities. Hughey (2010) argued the little research that does exist treats student of color membership as the end—not the beginning.

Students of Color in WGLOs

Chang (1996) noted students of color who join historically White fraternities and sororities can be considered "integrationists and assimilationists" who negotiate their racial identity as they move through college, developing strategies and attaining positions through various experiences and relationships that enable them to move through racially diverse societies. However, after deciding to join WGLOs, they can face the "paradox of participation" (Hughey, 2010) —the process in which minority Greeks balance their relationships with their Greek brothers and sisters (in WGLOs) and members of their ethic/racial group. Students of color who do assimilate into the mainstream culture to avoid alienation are seen by members of their own race as having "sold out," "acting White," or abandoning their own cultural heritage so they could attain success (Banks & Banks, 2007; Nieto, 2004; Ogbu, 1994; Thompson, 2000). Tucker (1983) similarly noted difficulties for Black students who accepted membership in predominantly white organizations include facing ostracism and criticism from other Black students. Furthermore, in Thompson's (2000) research, minority students who joined WGLOs viewed their membership in a positive light, but some Black participants showed levels of dissonance in their responses. Hughey (2010) reported,

> the majority of respondents indicated that they felt genuinely accepted most of the time. Yet, simultaneously, most of the respondents were quick to point out that the strength and authenticity of the kinship bond was fragile. Racial tensions, as one respondent told me, always lurked beneath the surface. (p. 669)

This chapter aims to provide some perspective on the experiences and sense of belonging for women and men of color in WGLOs. To better understand the lived experiences of students of color in WGLOs, narratives were collected from twelve National Panhellenic Conference (NPC) and Interfraternal Council (IFC) affiliated members using purposeful homogeneous sampling, which is used to gain insight into a specific phenomenon within a particular context (Smith, Flowers, & Larkin, 2009). The narrative inquiry, a qualitative approach in which the researcher uses stories to study the impact of experiences (Clandinin, 2007), allowed the invited WGLO members to share their stories. The authors guided semi-structured interviews to provide intersections of personal narratives in a way of making meaning (Glesne, 2006) and to explore the experiences of the participants as well as obtain a more robust comprehension of their perspectives related to their social belonging and support in WGLOs (Creswell, 2007). To ascertain perceptions related to social belonging of a person of color in a WGLO, the interviews focused on the following:

1. What perceptions did they possess of their sense of belonging within their Greek experience?
2. What differences, if any, were there between the experiences relating to a sense of belonging of minority women/men compared to those experiences of White women/men?

Broad and general questions posed in the interviews were helpful in getting "a textural description and structural description of the experiences, and . . . provide an understanding of the common experiences" (Creswell, 2007, p. 61), which allowed for insight of their perceptions of membership and social belonging. The in-depth interviews were conducted with participants in face-to-face format, recorded with a digital voice recorder, and transcribed while ensuring confidentiality and the identity of the participants. Anonymity was ensured and therefore, names are not used in this chapter. Four of the WGLO members racially self-identified as Caucasian, four identified as Black, one as Black/Arab, one as Asian American, and two as Latino/a.

In the interviews, each participant communicated factors related to their experiences and perceptions of their membership in their respective WGLO sororities and fraternities. Each participant's subjective experiences were incorporated into a narrative by using their own language, enabling their story to be communicated in an authentic and descriptive manner (Auerbach & Silverstein, 2003). From the narratives, core themes and patterns materialized related to the research questions, which provided further insight on the sense of belonging for people of color in WGLOs. The sorting and coding of data were guided by research questions, describing the participants' reflections, conversations, and patterns that emerged (Bogdan & Biklen, 2003).

Telling Their Stories

The complex intersection of our identities (i.e., race, gender, sexuality, and class) accompanies each of us in every social interaction. Furthermore, the saliency of these identities becomes more apparent and poignant in situations where we are in a minority or subordinate status. On a predominantly white college campus, this manifestation is especially palpable as the campus culture can present challenges for minority students such as feeling marginalized and excluded from campus social networks to which their White peers had access and dealing with pressures to represent their race and assimilate to the majority culture of their campus (Lewis, Chesler, & Forman, 2000). Moreover, students of color can have lower satisfaction with campus climates and regard the general campus climate to be more negative than white students (Ancis, Sedlacek, & Mohr, 2000; Reid & Radhakishnan, 2003). As Pascarella and Terezini (1991) concluded in their research, students of color on predominantly white campuses live in a world significantly different in almost every aspect from their White peers academically, socially, and psychologically. Considering these factors, students of color who choose to become members of WGLOs on predominantly white campuses have put themselves in a position of being an enigma for many.

Thus, a key question becomes: how do students of color perceive their sense of belonging and experiences in WGLOs on predominantly white campuses? In telling their stories, themes emerged from what participants shared about their decision to join, challenges, experiences, sense of social belonging, and belief about their racial identity.

Reasons for Joining

The students of color provided details about their decision to join a WGLO. They reveal racial demographics of their hometown and upbringing; the approach of NPHC (National Panhellenic Council)—a collaborative organization of nine historically African American, international Greek lettered fraternities and sororities—toward recruitment; and their initial connection with WGLOs as factors in explaining the basis for their decision to join.

Comfort in Predominantly White Spaces

At the outset, the racial composition of the participants' hometowns and their upbringings, including interpersonal relationships, were deemed as influencing the majority of their decisions to join a WGLO as they were already comfortable operating in predominantly white spaces. As Tatum (1987) asserted, due to the demographic makeup of a predominantly white community, assimilation and friendships with Whites are common for a child of color, especially if that environment is the only one they have known. For example, an African American male member of Alpha Tau Omega indicated that being from a predominantly white community while growing up contributed to his "comfort in talking to White people." Furthermore, as revealed by an African American female member of Alpha Gamma Delta who grew up in a predominantly white community,

> Joining an NPHC organization never, ever crossed my mind. I had really negative experiences with bullying with Black girls in middle school and high school and was turned off by that . . . if Black girls don't like me, I'm not going to go out and decide to be around them.

A Black female member of Omega Phi Alpha also asserted that she did not feel like she belonged in the black community, and thus eventually joined a WGLO, since she knew herself and "didn't want to stray away from white friends." Moreover, a Latina member of Alpha Gamma Delta summarized, "You have to have a certain type of personality to get through a white sorority as you might be the only person in the room of color and you have to be able to get comfortable with it."

In spite of their comfort within the WGLO, several participants acknowledged that discussions about race and race relations within the organization or in general did not or rarely occurred. Some participants suggested that the lack of discussion about race was due to the desire of the group to not let race be the focus of a member's experience; the group's lack of awareness about the topic; the group putting more focus on the operations; and the group's aspiration to focus more on respect of all members. For example, a Latina avowed that there were not discussions "Because either we didn't care to talk about it, didn't know, or felt it was irrelevant. However, minority sisters wanted to talk about it but didn't want to make anyone uncomfortable."

Lack of Knowledge about and Disconnect with NPHC and MGLOs

Historically, NPHC organizations have been an integral part of higher education as they were influential in shaping the social, cultural, and academic experiences of Black students at predominantly white institutions (Whipple, Crichlow, & Crick, 2008). In the past, because Black Greek-letter organizations (BGLOs) were an avenue to obtain a support network to survive and thrive on a predominantly white college campus, there was not a need to recruit members because it was assumed everyone wanted to be a member; however, this ideology has changed as there are now more options for students of color (Johnson, Bradley, Bryant, Morton, & Sawyer, 2008). Accordingly, similar to other participants, another Black male member of Alpha Tau Omega associated an attitude of secrecy and exclusivity with Black-Greek organizations. While attending an informational meeting, he stated,

> They really treated me like I was just beneath them, until they found out my cousin was the president of a nearby chapter who Skyped in to speak with us . . . I don't have time for fake people. If you don't make me feel welcome off the bat, I don't want to be a part of that because you pay a lot of money to be in the organization and if I am going to pay to be part of something, I want to feel like you want me here other than just somebody else. So, they did not make me feel good about wanting to be a part of them, but ATO did.

Some of the participants alluded to the perception that the BGLOs' process and purpose were unfamiliar or not apparent to them and/or they had limited knowledge about their purpose on campus. For example, a Black/Arab male who is a member of Phi Gamma Delta explained that, "Even if I had wanted to join an NPHC organization based on friends, it was harder to see when they were having info sessions/intake." The idea of NPHC organizations being less transparent and accessible was echoed by a Black male who recalled while attending an orientation event,

more of the IFC and Panhellenic organizations were more engaged with
the incoming freshmen than the NPHC students. I remember within my
group I went with, it was just we felt more welcomed by the IFC and Pan
side than the NPHC side.

He further described how he saw WGLOs out on campus assisting with freshman
move-in and other first-week activities to assist students when he was a freshman moving on campus.

Cultural/Ethnic-interest Greek-letter organizations (e.g., Hispanic Greek-letter organizations, Asian Pacific Islander Greek-letter Organizations, etc.) or Multicultural
Greek-letter organizations (MGLOs), which were also founded to promote inclusivity
and level barriers among people while transcending differences (Wells & Dolan 2009),
were also not seen as an option for membership among some of the participants. A
Latina in Alpha Gamma Delta, who joined after being encouraged by a Latina friend in
a WGLO, contended she did not have an interest in joining a MGLO since she already
knew her culture and "didn't need to know it more." In addition, she found the MGL
sororities to be "standoffish." In a similar context, a Latino who is a member of Sigma
Nu expressed a disinterest in ethnic-specific groups, stating that, "I learned about their
[NPHC interest/informational] meetings and people were talking about those organizations, but it never crossed my mind."

Returns and Challenges

As within any group interaction and dialogues, the process of socialization, a core
aspect of an individual's development by which they learn the beliefs, values, and behaviors considered to be normative within their specific reference groups (i.e., racial,
ethnic, religious, etc.) (Harrison, Wilson, Pine et al., 1990) affects what each individual
brings to and how each interacts in intercultural dialogues (Pieterse & Collins, 2007).
Consequently, positive and negative experiences are likely to be perceived by each individual involved.

The most common positive return for being a part of a WGLO noted by many of
the participants was the leadership opportunities it provided within the organization
and/or on campus, which coincides with findings by Chang (1996), Byer (1998), Baier
and Whipple (2015), as well as Kuh and Lyons (1990). These studies also emphasized
that fraternities and sororities enhance and play a significant role in the college student
leadership development and participation in extracurricular activities. The benefit of
gaining leadership opportunities was conveyed by a Black male,

I want to say my overall experience definitely opened a lot of doors for me
in terms of leadership. It challenged me to do things that I never thought I

would ever do. I took on a lot of different leadership roles, not in my organization, but in other organizations that some of my brothers weren't involved in, which I never would have thought I would have done.

Acquiring increased confidence from leadership opportunities was also reiterated by a Latino member who stated,

> I felt like I was always leading the chapter. Being involved helped me become more confident. I felt like I was being recognized with awards on campus because I was Sigma Nu who was promoting community service, leadership, etc.

In contrast, experiencing microaggressions, stereotypes, and marginalization can negatively impact an individual's sense of belonging. Accordingly, some of the participants, as members of color in WGLOs, also noted there were some minor challenges.

Microaggressions

Microaggressions are subtle, denigrating messages which can be verbal, nonverbal, and/or visual, directed at people of color, often automatically or unconsciously, that can be brief, everyday exchanges (Solorzano, Ceja & Yosso, 2000; Sue et al., 2007). By nature, microaggressions put cultural differences and individuality to the forefront, and therefore can cause intrusive cognitions and have a psychological impact. For example, as a Black female explained,

> I never wanted to come off as overly sensitive when sisters would make comments such as "I've always wanted to be black, I just don't have the lips and nose." This was made even harder because I did not want to be seen as the "mean black girl."

She went on to explain her new member experience was especially difficult because others would assume she was angry or upset but understands that her sisters do not think about the impact their comments have on her and other minority sisters.

A Latino participant shared that there were offensive jokes that were never regarding him as an individual, but aimed at a group of people, grounded in stereotypes. He pointed out how he considered them brothers, and then they laugh at an inappropriate joke. He stated, "People made comments about not only my ethnicity, but also family/experiences. This was made worse during the Trump election. I got into arguments a few times."

In addition, the action or reaction of a member of color was sometimes used as a gauge to use language and/or engage in actions laced with prejudice, racism, and/or microaggressions. For example, one male participant explained that a lot of the members in his chapter were from Richmond, Virginia, which has a history as the former capital of the Confederacy, and the White members would make comments like,

> Let's put up Confederate flags up in our apartment/fraternity house. If [participant's name], the only person of color, has not said anything about it, then other people of color who come through the house also shouldn't have a problem with it.

In addition, another Black male member shared that some previous Black members in the fraternity had informed some White members in his chapter that it was acceptable to use the "N-word" in conversations with or around them. However, he reported that he candidly told them, "You can be drunk all you want to, but I will knock your teeth out if you use that word around me. You can call them that all you want to."

Racial Identity as a Member of a WGLO

The Model of Multiple Dimensions of Identity (MMDI) by Jones and McEwen (2000) emphasizes that salience related to a student's identity emerges through student–environment interactions as well as environmental factors and experiences (e.g., such as a race-related campus event or incident) which have influence on certain dimensions of identity (e.g., race, gender, etc.) being more salient than others. Students of color at predominantly white institutions, by nature, exist in an environment where their race/ethnicity is susceptible to saliency and the racial climate of the campus has influence on their decisions. In terms of Greek membership, Chang (1996) concluded that the racial climate on campus which influenced the participation of students of color in fraternities and sororities as well as their membership was based on the student of color's view of society and shared interests with WGLO members. In fact, many of the participants' perceptions of their racial/ethnic identity contributed to their ability to "fit in" at a WGLO. The most common reason was their ability to code-switch, the bicultural socialization process that enables a person of color to interact in both societies, often shifting between two (Barnett, 2004), and/or being the "right kind" of minority. As one Black participant emphasized,

> I have this ability to "fit in" with the white crowd. I'm well spoken, I've gone to good schools. I understand that culture, but I also have a lot of friends who are Black and only hang out in black circles. Their experience is entirely different. I can blend into both groups . . . Hearing so and so "wouldn't fit in." I could usually read into that code and know they were referring to what this person looks like.

In contrast, in a reflection, a Latino member reminisced, "In a way I did sacrifice my Latino values because I was in a fraternity. I lost my pride in being a Latino man."

Outside of recruiting and accepting the "right type," most participants reported that the topic of race did not come up often within their organization. As Hughey (2010) found, nonwhite members' ability to frame themselves as equal and belonging Greek brothers and sisters remain paradoxically tied to the patterned reproduction of their racial identities as different. An Asian American participant supports this idea by saying, "I wouldn't consider it [race] a topic they talk about. They focus on treating everyone as equal and with respect."

Members of color in WGLOs must constantly navigate and negotiate both the structure of the fraternal Greek world and the racialized climate and minority communities of campus (Hughey, 2010). Accordingly, some participants discussed the internal and external attitudes regarding their membership in a WGLO that were not so positive as they traverse the two worlds.

Acting White, Selling Out, and Serving as a Token Member

Externally, a student of color who is a member of a WGLO can appear to others as compromising or ignoring one's cultural heritage (i.e., selling out, acting out, or being an Uncle Tom). Such accusations can be delicate because as Tatum (1987) suggested, acceptance from same-race peers may be especially significant in predominantly white settings since same-race peers can provide a safe environment for students of color to explore aspects of their identity with individuals that may have similar cultural understanding in that environment. A Black female participant recounted, "My negative experiences came from outside the organization, from other black women, and others who asked why I was not in an NPHC sorority." Additionally, a Black male told stories about being questioned and acknowledged by Black Greeks,

> I was at home for a break during Thanksgiving and I went to Target with my lettered shirt on. As I was leaving, someone who was a member of Omega Psi Phi stopped me and asked, "what kind of academic organization is that?" I'm like, it's not; this is a social fraternity. He's says, "that's not a black fraternity" and I said, "I know." He then says, "oh, you think you are too good to be in a black fraternity? You have to be in that?" I said, no, if anything, they think they are too good for me, so I took the next best thing and went on with my business. It was a kind of tough because a lot of times, and sometimes I still do, kind of get that because some of my colleagues who are members of NPHC organizations . . . although they are better now, they kind of gave me a hard time because they would all be talking about being greek and I would say, I'm greek too, and they would respond, "you're not greek like us.

Internally, a student of color who is a member of a WGLO can appear as a token member. Based on a social and organizational foundation, a token is defined as a person, usually a woman or a minority, who is hired, admitted, or appointed to a group because of their difference from other members to serve as proof a majority group does not discriminate against such people (Zimmer, 1988). Token status brings forth performance pressure which is more evident when a person is underrepresented in particular contexts, as they can face negative experiences such as increased visibility and social isolation (Kanter, 1977). Additionally, such experiences are generally grounded in the attitude of members of an organization. For example, as a participant in a fraternity revealed,

> Members would say, "we have black kids." I also heard of an instance after I graduated. There was a Black guy who went through recruitment who asked if [the organization] is racist and the guy pointed to me on the composite: "How could we be racist if we have people of color in our chapter?"

Another participant in a fraternity recounted how there was a preference for minorities who "acted white" in the organization and how they were seen as a conduit to other minorities, stating "My roommates [fraternity brothers] would look at me and wanted me to be the bridge between NPHC/MGC organizations. People assumed I would serve as the connection to the black fraternities and sororities.

A few of the participants also mentioned that there were times they felt obligated to educate their brothers and sisters, formally and informally. For example, a Black male said,

> People have also said you don't act like the stereotypical black person. I stopped them and ask what do you mean. What is a stereotypical black person. We've got to fix that, because there are different versions of white people, Asian people, Hispanics; but, you've got to fix that person's perception.

A Black female also shared that she planned to host a program for her sisters that focused on the concept of microaggressions. She said, "I pride myself on having a diverse chapter, but I am sometimes disheartened that there is not as much inclusion."

Social Belonging

As social support is deemed an important determinant of college success and satisfaction (Brown, 2000), it can be a particularly advantageous avenue for students of color at predominantly white institutions. Strayhorn, Hurtado, and Harris (2012) asserted, "Students' perceived social support on campus, a feeling or sensation of connectedness, the experience of mattering or feeling cared about, accepted, respected, valued by, and important to the group (e.g., campus community) or others on campus (e.g., faculty, peers)" (p. 3). Furthermore, Whipple (1998) declared that being a member of a Greek organization means belonging to a group who cares about one another. Many of the members of color in WGLOs reported having social support and feelings of belonging within the organization. One member of a fraternity recalled, "I definitely did feel like I belonged. I don't know if everyone felt this same sense of belonging." For example, one Black male disclosed,

> My brothers provided me with a positive environment. Any ideas I had, they would support and if they did not support them, they would at least tell me why they wouldn't support them. But, I definitely would say they supported me because except for one position, everything I ran for, I got. So, I feel like I had their support in my leadership. In terms of campus involvement, I would say that they would support me. When I ran for Coming Home King, they were there in the crowd supporting me. So overall, I would say they created a positive atmosphere.

A couple of the participants did mention that in spite of their feelings of belonging, they were aware that at times, not everyone was comfortable with a person of color being in their organization. However, none indicated there were incidents that made them feel unwanted or unsafe, especially since they had the support from other brothers and sisters in the organization. However, as one participant described,

> I would definitely say that my race probably has been an issue for some of my other brothers within the chapter. Because some students are not very comfortable when it comes to the term diversity. So, that's kind of hard to say, but there are a lot of students who are very comfortable and vice versa.

Closing Thoughts

The students who shared their stories about being a student of color in a WGLO have given voice to a rarely discussed topic in Greek-letter organization literature, which is especially relevant in today's heightened political and racial climate. Such discussions not only give perspective for administrators and national organizations, they also re-mind us that it is important to not stop the concern and initiatives at the conclusion of the recruitment process but continue throughout their membership experience. Similar to other studies, what the narratives show is that while students of color in WGLOs may have positive experiences and a sense of belonging, there could still be a need for them to balance their identities internally and externally to the organization while facing pressure to think about the comfort of their White sisters and brothers and at times, needing to engage in teachable moments. In the end, their voices, as shown in this chapter, can offer a valuable insight of awareness, understanding, and guidance.

References

Ancis, J. R., Sedlacek, W. E., & Mohr, J. J. (2000). Student perceptions of campus cultural climate by race. *Journal of Counseling & Development, 78*(2), 180–185. doi:10.1002/j.1556-6676.2000. tb02576.x

Astin, A. W. (1984) Student involvement: A developmental theory for higher education. *Journal of College Student Personnel, 25*(3), 297–308.

Auerbach, C. F., & Silverstein, L. B. (2003). *Qualitative data: An introduction to coding and analysis.* New York, NY: New York University Press.

Baier, J. L., & Whipple, E. G. (2015). Greek values and attitudes. *NASPA Journal, 28*(1), 43–53. doi:10.1080/00220973.1990.11072186

Banks, J. A., & Banks, C. A. M. (2007). *Multicultural education: Issues and perspectives* (5th ed.). Boston, MA: Allyn & Bacon.

Barnett, M. (2004). A qualitative analysis of family support and interaction among black college students at an ivy league university. *The Journal of Negro Education, 73*(1), 53–68. doi:10.2307/3211259

Bogdan, R., & Biklen, S. K. (2007). *Qualitative research for education: An introduction to theory and methods.* Boston, MA: Pearson.

Brown, J. T. (Ed.). (1923). *Baird's manual of American college fraternities: A descriptive analysis of the fraternity system in the colleges of the United States* (10th ed.). New York, NY: James T. Brown.

Brown, T. (2000). Gender differences in African American students' satisfaction with college. *Journal of College Student Development, 41*(5), 479–487.

Byer, J. (1998). Fraternity members' perceptions of how involvement in a fraternity and involvement in student government has influenced their college experiences. (ERIC 421 956. 1–17).

Chang, M. J. (1996). *Race identity and race relations in higher education: Fraternity and sorority membership among students of color.* ASHE Annual Meeting Paper. Los Angeles: Higher Education Research Institute UCLA.

Clandinin, D. J. (2007). *Handbook of narrative inquiry: Mapping a methodology.* Thousand Oaks, CA: Sage Publications. doi:10.4135/9781452226552

Creswell, J. W. (2007). *Qualitative inquiry and research design: Choosing among five approaches* (2nd ed.). Thousand Oaks, CA: Sage.

Glesne, C. (2006). *Becoming qualitative researchers: An introduction* (3rd ed.). New York, NY: Pearson.

Harper, S. R., & Hurtado, S. (2007). Nine themes in campus racial climates and implications for institutional transformation. *New Directions for Student Services, 120*, 7–24. doi:10.1002/ss.254

Harrison, A. O., Wilson, M. N., Pine, C. J, Chon, S. Q., & Buriel, R. (1990). Family ecologies of ethnic-minority children. *Child Development, 61*(2), 347–362. doi:10.2307/1131097

Hughey, M. (2010). A Paradox of participation: Nonwhites in white sororities and fraternities. *Social Problems, 57*(4), 653–679. doi:10.1525/sp.2010.57.4.653

Johnson, R., Bradley, D., Bryant, L., Morton, D. M., & Sawyer, D. C. (2008). Advising Black Greek-letter: A student development approach. In G. Parks (Ed.), *Black Greek-letter organizations in the 21st century: Our fight has just begun* (pp. 437–458). Lexington, KY: University of Kentucky Press.

Jones, S. R., & McEwen, M. K. (2000). A conceptual model of multiple dimensions of identity. *Journal of College Student Development, 41*(4) 405–414.

Kanter, R. M. (1977). Some effects on proportions on group life: Skewed sex ratios and responses to token women. *American Journal of Sociology, 82,* 965–990. doi:10.1086/226425

Kuh, G. D., & Lyons, J. W. (1990). Fraternities and sororities: Lessons from the college experiences study. *NASPA Journal, 28*(1), 20–29.

Lewis, A. E., Chesler, M., & Forman, T. A. (2000). The impact of "colorblind" ideologies on students of color: Intergroup relations at a predominantly white university. *The Journal of Negro Education, 69*(1/2), 74–91.

Luckerson, V. (2013, September 16). University of Alabama moved to end segregated sorority system. *Time.* Retrieved from http://nation.time.com/2013/09/16/university-of-alabamamoves-to-end-segregated-sorority-system/

Nieto, S. (2004). *Affirming diversity: The sociopolitical context of multicultural education* (4th ed.). New York, NY: Longman.

Ogbu, J. U. (1994). Minority status, cultural frame of reference, and schooling. In D. Keller-Cohen (Ed.), *Literacy: Interdisciplinary conversations* (pp. 361–384). Cresskill, NJ: Hampton Press.

Pascarella, E., & Terenzini, P. (1991). *How college affects students.* San Francisco, CA: Jossey-Bass.

Pieterse, A. L., & Collins, N. M. (2007). A socialization-based values approach to embracing diversity and confronting resistance in intercultural dialogues. *The College Student Affairs Journal, 26*(2), 144–151.

Reid, L. D., & Radhakrishnan, P. (2003). Race matters. The relation between race and general campus climate. *Cultural Diversity and Ethnic Minority Psychology, 9*(3), 263–275.

Smith, J. A., Flowers, P., & Larkin, M. (2009). *Interpretative phenomenological analysis: Theory, method, and research.* London, UK: Sage Publications.

Strayhorn, T. L., Hurtado, S., & Harris, Q. (2012). *College students sense of belonging: A key to educational success for all students.* New York, NY: Routledge.

Solorzano, D., Ceja, M., & Yosso, T. (2000). Critical race theory, racial microaggressions, and campus racial climate: The experiences of African American College Students. *Journal of Negro Education, 69*(1/2), 60–73.

Sue, D. W., Capodilupo, C. M., Torino, G. C, Bucceri, J. M., Holder, A. M. B., Nadal, K. L., & Esquilin, M. E. (2007). Racial microaggressions in everyday life: Implications for clinical practice. *American Psychologist, 62*(4), 271–286. doi:10.1037/0003-066X.62.4.271

Tatum, B. (1987). *Assimilation blues: Black families in White communities, who succeeds and why.* New York, NY: Basic Books.

Thompson, C. D. (2000). *Factors that influence minority student participation in predominantly white fraternities and sororities.* Retrieved from ProQuest Dissertations & Theses Global. (304648105)

Tinto, V. (1993). *Leaving college: Rethinking the causes and cures of student attrition research* (2nd ed.). Chicago IL: University of Chicago Press.

Torbenson, C. L. (2005). The origin and evolution of college fraternities and sororities. In T. L. Brown, G. S. Parks, & C. M. Phillips (Eds.), *African American fraternities and sororities: The legacy and the vision* (pp. 37–66). Lexington, KY: University Press of Kentucky.

Tucker, A. C (1983). Greek life and the minority student: A perspective. In W. A. Bryan & R. A. Schwartz (Eds.), *The eighties: Challenges for fraternities and sororities*. Washington, DC: American College Personnel Association.

Wells, A., & Dolan, M. K. (2009). Multicultural fraternities and sororities: A hodgepodge of transient multiethnic groups. In C.L. Torbenson and G.S. Parks, *Brothers and sisters: Diversity in college fraternities and sororities* (pp. 157–183). Cranbury, NJ: Associated University Presses.

Whipple, E. G. (1998). *New challenges for Greek letter organizations: Transforming fraternities and sororities into learning communities*. San Francisco, CA: Jossey-Bass.

Whipple, E. G., Crichlow, M., & Click, S. (2008). Black and White greeks: A call for collaboration. In G. S. Parks (Ed.), *Black Greek-letter organizations in the 21st Century*. Lexington, KY: University of Kentucky Press.

Zimmer, L. (1988). Tokenism and women in the workplace: The limits of gender-neutral theory. *Social Problems, 35*(1), 64–77. doi:10.2307/800667

PART FIVE:

NATIONAL ORGANIZATIONS

CHAPTER 15

Latino/a Fraternities and Sororities: *Historia y Familia*

Mónica Lee Miranda, Cristobal Salinas Jr., and Manuel Del Real

LATINO/A FRATERNITIES AND sororities have affirmed a valuable place in the history of fraternities and sororities and Latino/a students in the United States. Latino/a students seeking a home away from home and a sense of *familia* [family] began finding both within student organizations (Beatty, 2015) and subsequently, Latino/a Greek-Lettered Organizations (LGLOs) (Johnson, 1972; Miranda, 1999). This chapter briefly introduces student organizations, how Latino/a students began forming LGLOs, expands on the four phases of LGLOs introduced by Munoz & Guardia (2009), and highlights the value of these organizations in the experiences of Latino/a college students today.

College Student Organization History

The history of college student organizations can be traced to the middle of the 18th century when college students developed clubs and debating societies in order to provide a cocurricular experience outside of the classroom (Cohen & Kisker, 2010). The majority had Greek-letter names such as Phi Beta Kappa, which became the "prototype of the college fraternity" when it was established on the campus of William and Mary College in 1776 (Torbenson & Parks, 2009, p. 20). The growth and formation of these student organizations can be attributed to how they allow students with common interests to come together, have access to housing, and opportunities to build a social network (Cohen & Kisker, 2010). The increase of students of color attending predominately White institutions, and the challenges they face, gave impetus for them to seek and participate in culturally-based student organizations (Quaye, Griffin, & Museus, 2015).

The influence and establishment of culturally-based student organizations, especially Latina/o student organizations, was due to the case of *Brown v. Board of Education* and the Civil Rights Act of 1964, which changed the political, social, economic, and educational landscape of the United States (Cohen & Kisker, 2010; Munoz & Guardia, 2009). Since the 1960s, there are hundreds of Latino/a student organizations on college campuses with mission statements advocating for social change and improving their communities (Beatty, 2015). Latino/a student organizations share a common set of goals and objectives that include:

- "To support students and increase academic achievement, recruitment, and retention."
- "To provide cultural awareness and education activities for members, the campus, and the larger community, increasing pride and understanding."
- "To provide service activities, for example, tutoring, literacy, mentoring, and other volunteer efforts, for students, youth, and other community members."
- "To conduct political education and advocacy about issues of concern to Latin@s to improve conditions for Latin@s on campus, in the community, and in the nation." (Davis, 1997, p. 231)

These goals and objectives highlight Latino/a student organizations as platforms for leadership development, connecting with other Latino/a students, addressing Latino/a issues, and overall Latino/a student engagement.

Overview of the History of Latino/a Fraternities and Sororities

While fraternities and sororities date back to the late 1700s with the founding of Phi Beta Kappa at the College of William and Mary in Williamsburg, Virginia in 1776 (Brown, 1923; Torbensen, 2005; Turk, 2004; Voorhees, 1945), culturally-based fraternities and sororities began a century later, in the late 1800s, with the first African American Fraternity Sigma Pi Phi, founded in 1871 (Kimbrough, 2003; Harris, 2005) and Alpha Phi Alpha in 1906, more commonly known as the first Black fraternity (Johnson, 1972; Kimbrough, 2003; Torbensen, 2005). The first Asian fraternity, Rho Psi, was founded at

Cornell University in 1916 (Johnson, 1972). The origins of Latino/a-oriented fraternities and sororities can be traced back to Sigma Iota, founded in 1904 at Louisiana State University and Phi Lambda Alpha in 1919 at Rensselaer Polytechnic Institute in New York, as limited numbers of Latino students entered colleges and universities and sought their own opportunities for involvement. In 1931 these two organizations merged to form Phi Iota Alpha Fraternity, Inc. (Guardia, 2006; Johnson, 1972; Kimbrough, 2003; Miranda, 1999; Miranda & Martin de Figueroa, 2000), which is still in existence today.

The first Latina sorority recognized in the United States, Lambda Theta Alpha Sorority, Inc., was founded in 1975 at Kean University in New Jersey (Guardia, 2006; Kimbrough, 2003; Miranda, 1999; Miranda & Martin de Figueroa, 2000). A more significant growth of Latino fraternities and sororities continued thereafter, between 1975 and 1990, with the founding of 20 fraternities and sororities, including one co-ed Latino/a Greek-lettered organization. The growth of the Latino/a student population on college campuses prompted the increased need to serve this population of students. Latino/a fraternal organizations fulfilled a need for students with their purposes to advance Latino/a cultural awareness, advocate for Latino/a goals, provide a familial, home-away-from-home atmosphere for Latino/a college students, and affirm an established Latino/a community (Miranda & Martin de Figueroa, 2000).

Five Phases of Latino/a Fraternities and Sororities

Researchers have noted that Latino/a students have been underrepresented, marginalized, oppressed, and have struggled for equality in higher education (Muñoz & Guardia, 2009; Salinas, 2015). While there is limited research on the history of Latino/a fraternity and sorority organizations (Muñoz & Guardia, 2009), there is a need to continue writing about the history of Latino/a student organizations to empower and explore the needs of these communities of people. Through a four-phase history description, Muñoz and Guardia (2009) provided an overview of the history of Latino/a fraternity and sorority organizations. The four phases of the history of Latino/a fraternity and sorority organizations include: The *principio* [the beginning] phase, the *fuerza* [force] phase, the *fragmentación* [fragmentation] phase, and the *adelante* [moving forward] phase. These four phases have provided a thoughtful frame to contextualize the past, present, and future of Latino/a fraternity and sorority organizations. In this chapter, the authors provide context on each of the four phases of the history of Latino/a fraternity and sorority organizations, and introduce a fifth phase, the *activismo* [activism] phase. The *activismo* phase provides context to the current challenges and opportunities for Latino/a fraternity and sorority organizations and expands and updates Muñoz and Guardia's (2009) work.

Principio [the Beginning] Phase (1898–1980)

The *principio* [the beginning] phase (1898–1980) consisted on the foundation of se-cret societies. For example, Phi Iota Alpha Fraternity, Inc., is traced to 1899 with origins of a group of Latin-American male students who formed a student organization for its members "to provide a cultural and intellectual safe" space for its members (Muñoz & Guardia, 2009, p. 108). Secret societies connected with various student organizations on college campuses across the country to start with the development of a "well-rooted organization" (p. 108) that later became fraternities. The *principio* phase is the founda-tion of secret societies that later became fraternities founded to provide cultural and intellectual spaces for Latino/a students.

Fuerza [Force] Phase (1980–1990)

The *fuerza* [force] phase (1980–1990) provided new opportunities for Latino/a col-lege students. During the *fuerza* [force] phase new Latino/a fraternities and sororities were founded and expanded throughout the United States. Muñoz and Guardia (2009) explained that three major events occurred during the *fuerza* [force] phase. The three significant events include: the foundation of Lambda Upsilon Lambda Fraternity, Inc. in 1982 as the first fraternity to be founded at an Ivy League institution; then, in 1985 Alpha Psi Lambda National Inc. was founded as the first and largest co-ed Latino fraternity at the Ohio State University; and in 1986 two organizations were founded, Lambda Theta Nu Sorority, Inc. was established at California State University – Chico, and Sigma Lambda Beta International Fraternity, Inc. at the University of Iowa; and in 1987, Kappa Delta Chi Sorority, Inc. at Texas Tech University. Throughout this phase, more fraterni-ties and sororities were founded throughout the country and created new opportunities for Latino/a college students.

Fragmentatción [Fragmentation] (1990–2000) Phase

The third phase, the *fragmentatción* [fragmentation] (1990–2000) "stage bought a sig-nificant amount of expansion . . . Latino students were arriving on campuses in search of a Latino fraternity or sorority" (p. 113). During this time, two Latino fraternities, as well as 17 new Latina sororities, were founded across the country. The expansion and growth of Latino/a fraternity and sorority organizations created new challenges and opportuni-ties for colleges and universities to build community, support, and work with each other. During this phase, two national umbrella organization were formed: first, in 1991, the first national Latino Greek Council (renamed as the *Concilio National de Hermandades Latinas* [CNHL; National Council of Latino Fraternal Organizations]; and then, in 1998, the National Association of Latino Fraternal Organizations, Inc. (NALFO) was formed.

During the summer of 1999, CNHL and NALFO continued to operate independently. Muñoz and Guardia stated that "NALFO was formed to answer the call for unity, and Multicultural Greek councils offered students an alternative resource for support on college campuses (p. 116).

Adelante [Moving Forward] Phase (2000–2015)

The fourth phase, *adelante* [moving forward] (2000–2015) is an important stage for Latino/a fraternity and sororities as it was a phase of development and growth for all. The "communication and collaboration among these organizations demonstrated strength and national unity" (p. 117) among Latino/a fraternities and sororities. At the same time the *adelante* [moving forward] phase created new opportunities for research and leadership in order to advance the understandings of Latino/a fraternity and sorority organizations. With regard to research during this phase, there were three peer-reviewed articles published on LGLOs and the member experiences, as well as seven dissertations exploring the experiences of LGLO members focused, primarily, on membership impact on student success and persistence. This phase also included a significant leadership moment with the first time a member of a Latino fraternal organization led the national professional association for fraternity and sorority professionals, the Association of Fraternity/Sorority Advisors (AFA), when Mónica Lee Miranda, member of Omega Phi Beta Sorority, Inc., was installed as the first person of color, first Latina, first culturally-based fraternity/sorority member, and first LGLO member to serve as AFA President in 2011. In July 2016, Dr. John Hernandez, member of Lambda Upsilon Lambda Fraternity, Inc., and Dr. Frank Sanchez, member of Sigma Lambda Beta Fraternity, Inc., were the first LGLO members to be named University Presidents at Santiago Canyon College and Rhode Island College, respectively. These national leadership appointments, along with a number of members serving in local city councils and government roles, demonstrate the influence and leadership capital members are now having across the country, and transitions easily into the next phase of LGLOs.

Activismo [Activism] Phase (2015–present)

To advance the work of Muñoz and Guardia (2009), the authors of this chapter introduce a new phase, the *activismo* [activism] phase (2015–present). While it is important to acknowledge that Latino/a fraternities and sororities are seeking to move forward and are helping advance their communities, these organizations continue to be challenged to create political, environmental, and social change. As stated earlier, Latinos/as continue to be marginalized, oppressed, and continue to struggle for equality within higher education and in society. Latino/a fraternities and sororities have demonstrated resiliency and have promoted activism within their organizations.

Latinos/as continue to fight for civil rights and human rights within the United States. As Latino/a fraternities and sororities have adapted community service and philanthropic causes, they are committed to raise awareness within and beyond their communities. For example, for the 2016 U.S. Presidential election, many of the Latino/a fraternity and sorority organizations partnered with VotoLatino.org to help eligible Latino/a voters to register to vote for political issues that affect their communities. In addition, Latino/a fraternities and sororities have united to support Deferred Action for Childhood Arrival (DACA) members of Latino/a fraternities and sororities and beyond. The Congressional Hispanic Caucus Institute (CHCI) partnered with Lambda Theta Phi Fraternity, Inc., to raise annual funds for their two-week civic engagement program for high school Latino students to learn about the federal government in Washington, DC (Lambda Theta Phi, 2018). There are many social justice topics that Latino/a fraternities and sororities have taken to the forefront when it comes to creating equality and change for historically marginalized Latino/a communities of people.

Another form of activism by Latino/a fraternity and sorority members has been speaking up against overt racism, discrimination, and disrespect toward these organizations. In 2017, at the annual Greek awards ceremony at Iowa State University, members of the Interfraternity and Collegiate Panhellenic Councils booed, made racial slurs, and imitated the calls of award recipients from the Multicultural Greek Council (MGC) and National Pan-Hellenic Council (NPHC) (Heftman, 2017). Five days following the incident with no public apology influenced presidents of the MGC and NPHC to write a letter of discontent, which also included similar incidents and students' expressing feelings of disappointment, isolation, anger, and exhaustion. The letter concluded with a call to action to the Office of Greek Affairs to dedicate themselves to building a Greek community among the four councils on campus. This is another example of how Latino/a fraternity and sorority members continue to be marginalized and oppressed on college campuses; yet, Latino/a fraternity and sorority members continue to demonstrate activism and resiliency.

The activism and resiliency of Latino/a fraternities and sororities has been demonstrated through their work on community and campus engagement, and in programs related to the environment, food drives, health, mentoring, and cultural awareness. Del Real (2017) highlights the work of five Latino fraternity chapters in the Midwest region of the United States. Those five Latino fraternity chapters have focused on various programs that address race, health, poverty, and access to education challenges. For example, the racial issues in the United States influenced one chapter to host a discussion specifically about the hate crimes at the University of Missouri, and another chapter hosted an educational programing to raise awareness about the experiences of undocumented people. Latino fraternity members of the chapters that participated in mentoring programs within their local school districts served as role models, especially to younger Latino males. Another chapter hosted a 5K philanthropy event to raise funds for an annual scholarship for other college students that need additional financial support. In addition, another example of activism and resiliency by Latino/a fraternity and sorority members is how they raised funds for a local assault care center and shelter through a bowling tournament. These types of programs and events are non-traditional forms of service within the fraternity and sorority community and highlight their activism and resiliency around the topics of race, immigration, and gender (Del Real, 2017).

Finding Value, *Familia,* and Success in LGLOs

The lack of common representation of a student's culture upon arriving on campus may prompt a distinct desire to retain the cultural connection to home and family background. Students can feel alienated by the dissonance between their desire to retain the connection to their identity and family and the pressures from their family to remain connected, while the pressures of going to college and connecting with that environment continued to challenge them (Gloria & Kurpius, 1996; Gloria & Rodriguez, 2000; Gonzalez, Jovel, & Stoner, 2004; Torres, 2003). Torres' (2003) study of Latino students addresses their need for connection to their culture reflected in the students' family experiences serving as one example of how the literature shows the desire to remain connected to family and one's culture, in some way, throughout the student's undergraduate experience. According to Marin (1993), familialism, or *familismo,* is "that cultural value which includes a strong identification and attachment of individuals with their nuclear and extended families and strong feelings of loyalty, reciprocity, and solidarity among members of the same family" (p. 184).

The importance of family is a significant aspect of a Latino/a student's cultural socialization process. The notion of *familismo* is useful to consider how Latinos engage with a collegiate environment, their familial influences, and those persons or groups who may mirror those of family units and are relevant to Latinos' experiences and identity formation and negotiation in college. Tierney (2000) argued that students' identity negotiation is a key to academic success, and ethnic identity literature and retention literature often has referred to familial influences, supporting the argument that families are a key factor influencing Latino college student experiences, as described in the aforementioned Torres' (2003) study.

These studies show that the family is a critical source of support and encouragement for Latino students that positively impacts persistence. The notion of *familismo* is consistent with Tierney (2000) and his theorizing of the importance of the connection of family to Latino student success. Initial dissertation studies and anecdotal research on Latino fraternity/sorority member experiences demonstrate the notion that membership in an LGLO promotes social integration and the sense of familial connection to peers and the institution, prompting increased involvement in campus activities as a result of their membership, which research shows would significantly lead to their academic success (Guardia, 2006; Mejia, 1994; Mendoza Patterson, 1998; Miranda &

Martin de Figueroa, 2000; Reis, 2004). Although initial research leads us to believe that a students' membership in LGLOs positively impacts their socialization processes and integration into the greater campus community, which subsequently prompts persistence, more research must be conducted to determine the long-term impact of membership in LGLOs.

Conclusion

Latino/a fraternities and sororities emerged from the challenges that Latino/a students faced in higher education. Latino/a college students continue to join these organizations to find cultural validation and a *familia*. To date there are over 25 Latino/a fraternities and sororities that have been founded across the United States, and most continue to validate and promote the success in college of Latino/a students. Table 15.1 provides a list of all Latino/a fraternities and sororities that have been founded in the United States; yet, not all of these organizations continue to be active. Many of these organizations have created a positive impact in the success of college students and have helped shape the perspectives of the *principio* [the beginning] phase, the *fuerza* [force] phase, the *fragmentación* [fragmentation] phase, the *adelante* [moving forward] phase, and the *activismo* [activism] phase. Throughout these organizations' philanthropy and educational and cultural awareness, many of their members have created an impact on their various communities by advocating and creating more inclusive spaces for students with various social identities. Nevertheless, continued research exploring the impact of Latino/a fraternities and sororities is critical to the continued advancement and success of this ever evolving community.

Table 15.1 Latino/a fraternities and sororities founded in the United States.

Latino Fraternities	Year Founded	University
Phi Iota Alpha	1931	Rensselaer Polytechnic Institute, Troy, NY
Lambda Theta Phi	1975	Kean University, Union, NJ
Lambda Sigma Upsilon	1979	Rutgers University, New Brunswick, NJ
Lambda Upsilon Lambda	1982	Cornell University, Ithaca, NY
Alpha Psi Lambda (Coed)	1985	Ohio State University, Columbus, OH
Lambda Alpha Upsilon	1985	University of Buffalo, Buffalo, IA
Sigma Lambda Beta	1986	University of Iowa, Iowa City, IA
Omega Delta Phi	1987	Texas Tech University, Lubbock, TX
Gamma Zeta Alpha	1987	Chico State University, Chico, CA
Nu Alpha Kappa	1988	California Polytechnic State—San Luis Obispo
Gamma Phi Sigma	1992	Temple University, Philadelphia, PA
Sigma Delta Alpha	1992	San Jose State University, San Jose, CA
Lambda Kappa Kappa	1994	Texas Christian University, Ft. Worth, TX

Latino Sororities	Year Founded	University
Lambda Theta Alpha	1975	Kean University, Union, NJ
Chi Upsilon Sigma	1980	Rutgers University, New Brunswick, NJ
Lambda Theta Nu	1986	California State University, Chico, CA
Kappa Delta Chi	1987	Texas Tech University, Lubbock, TX
Sigma Lambda Upsilon	1987	Binghamton University, Binghamton, NY
Lambda Pi Chi	1988	Cornell University, Ithaca, NY
Lambda Phi Delta NYS	1988	State University of New York, Buffalo, NY
Omega Phi Beta	1989	University of Albany SUNY, Albany, NY
Alpha Pi Sigma	1990	San Diego State University, San Diego, CA
Sigma Lambda Gamma	1990	University of Iowa, Iowa City, IA
Sigma Iota Alpha	1990	Stony Brook University SUNY, Stony Brook, NY
Gamma Phi Omega	1991	Indiana University, Bloomington, IN
Delta Phi Mu	1991	Purdue University, West Lafayette, IN
Lambda Pi Upsilon	1992	University of New York Geneseo, Geneseo, NY
Gamma Alpha Omega	1993	Arizona State University, Tempe, AZ
Alpha Rho Lambda	1993	Yale University, New Haven, CT
Phi Lambda Rho	1993	California State University—Stanislaus, Turlock, CA
Zeta Phi Gamma	1993	Texas Tech University, Lubbock, TX
Delta Tau Lambda	1994	University of Michigan, Ann Arbor, MI
Pi Lambda Chi	1994	University of Colorado, Boulder, CO
Sigma Delta Lambda	1996	Southwest Texas State, San Marcos, TX
Sigma Omega Nu	1996	California Polytechnic State, San Luis Obispo, CA
Alpha Sigma Omega	1997	Syracuse University, Syracuse, NY
Alpha Beta Sigma	1998	University of Buffalo—SUNY, Buffalo, NY

Puerto Rico	Year Founded	University
Phi Zeta Chi	1958	University of Puerto Rico—Mayagüez, Mayagüez, PR
Eta Phi Zeta	1969	University of Puerto Rico—Arecibo, Arecibo, PR

References

Beatty, C. C. (2015). Latin@ student organizations as pathways to leadership development. In A. Lozano (Ed.), *Latina/o college student leadership: Emerging theory, promising practice*. Lanham, MD: Lexington Books.

Brown, J. T. (1923). *The Baird's manual of American college fraternities: A descriptive analysis of the fraternity system in the college of the United States* (10th Edition). New York, NY: James T. Brown Publisher.

Cohen, A. M., & Kisker, C. B. (2010). *The shaping of American higher education: Emergence and growth of the contemporary system*. San Francisco, CA: Jossey-Bass.

Davis, M. A. (1997). Latin@ leadership development: Beginning on campus. *National Civic Review, 86*(3), 227–233.

Del Real, M. (2017). *Living the creed: How chapters of Sigma Lambda Beta International Fraternity, Inc., contribute to civic engagement*. Graduate Theses and Dissertations. (15510) http://lib.dr.iastate.edu/etd/15510

Gloria, A. M., & Kurpius, S. E. R. (1996). The validation of the cultural congruity scale and the university environment scale with Chicano/a students. *Hispanic Journal of Behavioral Sciences, 18*, 533.

Gloria, A. M., & Rodriguez, E. R. (2000). Counseling Latino university students: Psycho-sociocultural issues for consideration. *Journal of Counseling and Development; 78*(2); 145–154.

Gonzalez, K. P., Jovel, J. E., and Stoner, C. (2004). Latinas: The new Latino majority in college. In A. Ortiz (Ed.), *New Directions for Student Services, No. 105. Addressing the Unique Needs of Latino American Students* (pp. 17–27). San Francisco, CA: Jossey-Bass.

Guardia, J. R. (2006). *Nuestra identidad y experiencias [Our identity and experiences]: Ethnic identity development of Latino fraternity members at a Hispanic-Serving Institution* (Unpublished doctoral dissertation). Iowa State University, Ames, IA.

Harris, W. (2005). The Grand Boule at the dawn of a new century: Sigma Pi Phi Fraternity. In T. L. Brown, G. S. Parks, and C.M. Phillips (Eds.), *African American Fraternities and Sororities*. Lexington, KY: The University Press of Kentucky.

Heftman, N. (2017, April). Greek council's response to Vespers, host joint meeting. *Iowa State Daily*. Retrieved on November 24, 2017 from http://www.iowastatedaily.com/news/student_life/article_423d5c6a-1a70-11e7-babe-23ace6d5614f.html

Johnson, C. S. (1972). *Fraternities in our colleges*. New York, NY: National Interfraternity Foundation.

Kimbrough, W. M. (2003). *Black Greek 101: The culture, customs, and challenges of Black fraternities and sororities*. Madison, NJ: Fairleigh Dickinson University Press.

Lambda Theta Phi. (2018). *Lambda theta phi Latin fraternity, Inc.* Retrieved January 3, 2018 from http://www.thelambdas.org/?page_id=1333/

Marin, G. (1993). Influences of acculturation on familialism and self-identification among Hispanics. In M. E. Bernal & G. P. Knight (Eds.), *Ethnic identity: Formation and transmission among Hispanics and other minorities* (pp.181–196). Albany, NY: SUNY Press.

Mejia, A. (1994, October). Hispanics go Greek. *Hispanic, 7*, 34.

Mendoza-Patterson, M. (1998). *Latina Sisterhood: Does it promote or inhibit campus integration?* (Unpublished dissertation). University of Southern California, Los Angeles, CA.

Miranda, M. L. (1999). Greek life … with a little sazon: Fraternities and sororities get a Latino twist. *The World and I Magazine*, 190–197.

Miranda, M. L., & de Figueroa, M. M. (2000). Adelante hacia el futuro [Forward to the future]: Latino/Latina Greeks: Past, present and future. *Perspectives*, pp. 6–8.

Muñoz, S. M., & Guardia, J. R. (2009). Nuestra historia y futuro [our history and future]: Latino/a fraternities and sororities. In G. S. Parks & C. Torbenson (Eds.), *Brothers and sisters: Diversity within college fraternities and sororities* (pp. 104–132). Madison, NJ: Fairleigh Dickson Press.

Quaye, S. J., Griffin, K. A., & Museus, S. D. (2015). Engaging students of color. In S. J. Quaye & S. R. Harper, *Student engagement in higher education: Theoretical perspectives and practical approaches for diverse populations*. New York, NY: Routledge.

Reis, M. L. (2004). *Latina college student success* (Unpublished dissertation). Phoenix, AZ: Arizona State University.

Salinas, C. (2015). Understanding and meeting the needs of Latina/o students in higher education. In P. Sasso & J. Devitis (Eds.), *Today's College Students* (pp. 21–37). New York, NY: Peter Lang.

Tierney, W. G. (2000). Power, identity, and the dilemma of college student departure. In J. M. Braxton (Ed.), *Reworking the student departure puzzle* (pp. 213–234). Nashville, TN: Vanderbilt University Press.

Torbenson, C. L. (2005). The origin and evolution of college fraternities and sororities. In T. Brown, G. S. Parks, & C. M. Phillips (Eds.), *African American fraternities and sororities: The legacy and the vision* (pp. 37–66). Lexington, KY: University Press of Kentucky.

Torbenson, C. L., & Parks, G.S. (2009). *Brothers and sisters: Diversity within college fraternities and sororities.* Madison, NJ: Fairleigh Dickinson University Press.

Torres, V. (2003). Influences on ethnic identity development of Latino college students in the first two years of college. *Journal of College Student Development, 44*(4), 532–547.

Turk, D. B. (2004). *Bound by a mighty vow: Sisterhood and women's fraternities, 1870–1920.* New York, NY: New York University Press.

Voorhees, O. M. (1945). *The history of Phi Beta Kappa.* New York, NY: Crown Publishers.

CHAPTER 16

Reclaiming and Asserting our Nations through the Growth of Historically Native American Fraternities and Sororities (HNAFS)

Robin "Zape-tah-hol-ah" Minthorn and Natalie Youngbull

Introduction

> It is imperative the fraternity/sorority community dismantle structures reflecting colonization and that professionals within higher education educate themselves about the practices and policies that continue to perpetuate oppression – especially for minoritized communities including Native Americans. (Oxendine, 2017, p. 3)

The Historically Native American Fraternities and Sororities (HNAFS) movement grew out of a need for support and representation of Native students attending non-Native colleges and universities (NNCUs) (Shotton, Lowe, & Waterman, 2013). "The creation of HNAFS stemmed from Native American students recognizing the importance of retention and support of Native students, a need for cultural awareness, and an opportunity to expand and promote the Native community on their respective campuses" (Oxendine, Oxendine, & Minthorn, 2013, p. 67). HNAFS are strategically situated between the Native and Greek communities on campus. It is in this space that these unique organizations not only provide support to their members, but also educate the larger student body about the Native American community on campus. This chapter builds upon the first chapter addressing the HNAFS movement, including HNAFS's foundation and development in relation to the larger fraternity/sorority system (Oxendine, Oxendine, & Minthorn, 2013). The term *Historically Native American Fraternities and Sororities (HNAFS)* was established to denote Greek organizations founded on principles of Native American traditions and cultural ways of being to serve Native communities (Jahansouz & Oxendine, 2008). The founders of HNAFS "were intent on creating organizations rooted in tribal values, customs, and traits, as a way to decolonize the experiences of Native students within higher education" (Oxendine, 2017, p. 2). HNAFS's roots go back to the mid-1990s and it has blossomed to include seven organizations. Currently, there are seven HNAFS on NNCU and tribal college and university (TCU) campuses nationwide. In this chapter, we aim to provide a greater understanding of HNAFS through discussing these unique organizations' histories, structures, traditions, and cultural rites of passage. Lastly, we offer implications for practice in working with and advocating for the continued success of HNAFS.

Overview of Organizational History

The HNAFS movement began in the 1990s on NNCUs in the southeastern part of the United States, but the need for these organizations that center Indigenous students' experiences had been needed long before then. There are currently seven recognized HNAFS organizations on over 25 campuses across the United States. Since the first one was founded there has been a call for more to be created that reflect the tribal culture and values of a specific region or to fill a gap from the other HNAFS organizations. Each are unique and each have been a part of sustaining and retaining the Native American students on their respective campuses. The first Native American sorority can be attributed to Alpha Pi Omega, Inc., which was founded in 1994, and the first Native American fraternity, Phi Sigma Nu, was founded in 1996. We give thanks to those founders for their vision and for the other five HNAFS who have since been established. For this chapter we will focus on the organizational history of two HNAFS, Gamma Delta Pi, Inc. and Sigma Nu Alpha Gamma, Inc.

The vision and effort to create a Native American sorority on the campus at the University of Oklahoma began in the early 2000s. With a culmination of events between five Native American women who were in various stages in their undergraduate degrees, each of them decided to commit to the creation and development of Gamma Delta Pi, American Indian Sorority. The process in founding the sorority took over six months of consistent meetings and developing the vision, motto, mascot, and the essential pieces of what would make Gamma Delta Pi unique. These five women came to be known as the "Five Changing Women" who were named after a story known among the Navajo people. The mission of Gamma Delta Pi, Inc. is to be established for women "who are committed to creating a life-long bond among sisters while instilling character, an appreciation of the native culture, unity, respect, scholarship, and most importantly, the sisterhood of American Indian women and all others interested." The motto, colors, medicine, and symbolism of Gamma Delta Pi reflect the tribal culture of each of the five founders in some way. In the alpha class there were 16 Native American women who became sisters, and since then there have been over 250+ who are now a part of the sisterhood. Gamma Delta Pi, Inc. is now on four campuses across the United States, including Oklahoma, Nebraska, and Kansas, with more interest shown in other states.

During the early 2000s there was a decrease in the number of Native men at the University of Oklahoma. Many Native men were not persisting through higher education, and it was found that many felt they did not have a support system that could help them navigate higher education. Therefore in early 2004, a number of men met and discussed the creation of an organization that would support and empower Native men. Sigma Nu Alpha Gamma, Inc., or the Society of Native American Gentlemen, was founded in order to develop and increase the academic retention, cultural awareness, leadership skills, and personal integrity of Native American men by providing a fraternal brotherhood for support and encouragement. We do this through the incorporation of our Four Pillars: Academic Excellence, Cultural Awareness, Spiritual Well-being, and Physical Fitness (C. Still, personal communication, February 11, 2018).

As can be seen from the two most recently established national HNAFS organizations and taking into consideration the first established HNAFS, each have fulfilled a need that was not being met within the traditional Greek system. Each HNAFS had to conjure support from the Native American student affairs offices and others on campus, as well as find men or women who were interested in working to create an organization that would specifically fill a gap and in some ways resist the traditional Greek system to reflect the traditions of our tribes and Native American communities.

Structures

In HNAFS, there are varied structures that have been created to reflect the tribal cultures represented within each sorority and fraternity. The structures weren't meant to reflect the "traditional" structures in Greek systems; they were meant to be unapologetically Indigenous.

Gamma Delta Pi, Inc. was founded on August 27, 2001. The motto for Gamma Delta Pi, Inc. is "We are Leaders of Our Nations, We Rise to Glorify Our Roots." The structure and way it was built was based off the clan system, in which we have a Clan Mother that leads the sorority and then there are councils that fulfill the more traditional system positions such as vice president, secretary, treasurer, and historian. Each council represents one of the four colors that are connected to the medicine wheel and four directions. The structure was built to not be hierarchical except for the clan mother, who holds responsibility over the sorority but works closely with each council. There has been expansion in place through a butterfly board for the organization and currently there are four chapters in place, and three of them are active with more recruitment ongoing. There was a Gamma Delta Pi Alumnae group created which became stagnant, but over the course of the last two years Gamma Delta Pi, Inc. became incorporated and now has a national governance board. The Gamma Delta Pi, Inc. Governance Board will allow for oversight on a national level, as well as sustainability and growth. There is representation across chapters, alumnae, and founders. There is a Gamma Delta Pi, Inc. Annual Conference that is held around the time of the original founding date which centers on bringing sisters together and to conduct business needed for the sorority. We currently have an estimated 250 sisters who derive from various tribes across the United States. We have alumnae who are working in positions within a tribal, local, nonprofit, and national level. We also have sisters who are working in various fields including medical doctors, nurses, professors, lawyers, social workers, and many more.

Another example of structures is with Sigma Nu Alpha Gamma, Inc., which was officially incorporated in 2016. In 2012, the fraternity began to initiate the National Governing board and successfully continued their yearly National Conference and Summer Leadership Summit. The emblem is the Phoenix, their motto is "We Set the Standard," and they pride themselves in being a dry fraternity. They currently have three fully established chapters and a number of probationary and preliminary chapters. Sigma Nu Alpha Gamma has approximately 150 members. The retention rate of brothers across the fraternity is at 79% with a 70% four-year graduation rate. As far as alumni, there are 45% who have completed some level of graduate degree, and 18% are working or have a terminal or professional degree (C. Still, personal communication, February 11, 2018).

It is important to talk about the HNAFS structures and give examples as to why they are important to the respective fraternity and sorority. Each have a significant meaning to maintain and uphold the tribal nations and regions that are represented from that organization. Other Greek organizations who reside on their respective college campuses should be open and willing to learn of their uniqueness and find ways to advocate for their inclusion and acceptance in the broader Greek system (Sasso, 2017). This openness and advocacy means amending structures and providing necessary resources so that HNAFS can be honored for the cultures that are reflected in their foundation and processes.

Traditions

The traditions established by Gamma Delta Pi, Inc. and Sigma Nu Alpha Gamma, Inc. align with the teachings and symbolism found within their Native communities, and less with the traditional Greek community. It is important when we think of tradition and what that means within a mainstream Greek system and within HNAFS to begin to deconstruct the term to be open to reflect both perspectives. The founders of Gamma Delta Pi, Inc. represent 20+ tribal nations and were inclusive of incorporating traditions from each founder's tribal backgrounds, including the tribal stories of each tradition. The importance of this process relates to the mission of the sisterhood to honor the culture, provide support, and be open to others. One of the founders of Sigma Nu Alpha Gamma, Inc. shared about the origins of the organization's traditions. "All of our traditions are rooted in tribal epistemologies and ontologies. It can be seen in our new member process to various programs that have been initiated in the organization" (Still, C., personal communication). What Still references as tribal epistemologies and ontologies are the traditional knowledge and teachings shared by members to inform the traditions of the organization.

> Sigma Nu Alpha Gamma, Inc. varies from mainstream fraternities as there was never a push in the beginning to establish one. One of the ways that we see ourselves is as likened to many of our traditional warrior societies. Within these societies, men would join due to their acts or achievements be it through war or deeds done within the community. With the influence of higher education and its potential impact on our communities, many of our founders and older member saw to create that same type of society with[in] the context of higher education. As [an] "educational warrior" per se this society was formed as a way to honor, recognize, support, and encourage the work that Native men are striving to do to impact their communities in a positive way." (Still, C., personal communication)

Sigma Nu Alpha Gamma, Inc. stands apart from conventional fraternities by making a strong connection of traditional teachings through a contemporary interpretation.

The new member processes for both Gamma Delta Pi, Inc. and Sigma Nu Alpha Gamma, Inc. are infused with cultural ways of being and rites. The founders of Gamma Delta Pi, Inc. designed the new member process to honor the four stages of life, including tribal teachings and service activities hosted within the community related to each stage. The tribal teachings and service activities may differ through each new member process to represent the backgrounds of current members and needs of the community. The Sigma Nu Alpha Gamma, Inc. founders recognized the importance of being flexible in incorporating tribal cleansing ceremonies of current members in the new member process.

A large piece of our new member process is cleansing and during this we
utilize a number of ceremonies and traditions of tribes that are represented
in our organization. This could include ceremonies such as smudging, ce-
darings, water ceremonies, etc. A part of the fluidity of our organization is
that these ceremonies are not set in stone and can be changed to honor and
recognize the tribal representation of any given chapter." (Still, C, personal
communication)

The founders of these two HNAFS were intuitive in the development of their new member process by incorporating cultural ways of being and ceremonies, and being inclusive
and open to the tribal representation of their memberships.

Many fraternities and sororities have a national or international philanthropy that it
supports through events that raise awareness and fundraise for the cause. Gamma Delta
Pi, Inc.'s philanthropies have always been more locally-based to fill a need within the local and surrounding tribal communities. Since Gamma Delta Pi, Inc.'s recent expansion,
a greater common health and wellness need to address within tribal communities—dia-
betes awareness—was chosen and each chapter identified a specific organization doing
work in that area to serve as their philanthropy. Each chapter hosts an annual event to
fundraise and raise awareness of their philanthropy. For example, the alpha chapter's
annual men's and women's basketball tournament has served as a great fundraising event
and familiarized the sisterhood with the local and surrounding tribal communities
through those participants of the tournament.

The founders of HNAFS were aware that there has not historically been a strong
connection between fraternities/sororities and Native communities and recognized
that many Native American college students do not seek out membership in Greek
organizations on campus. HNAFS built off the beneficial qualities of the Greek system
and incorporated many aspects of the Native culture, traditions, and symbolism within
their missions and structure (Oxendine, Oxendine, & Minthorn, 2013). Thus, it was
necessary for cultural teachings and symbolism to permeate through the traditions of
Gamma Delta Pi, Inc. and Sigma Nu Alpha Gamma, Inc., especially through the new
member process and chosen philanthropy.

Cultural Rites of Passage

A cultural rite of passage for many is the process of becoming or coming out in a
ceremony. In tribal communities, many still practice or have historically had cultural
rites of passage that welcome a boy or girl into manhood or womanhood. There are
other cultural rites of passage in allowing that person to take part in a tradition in the
community such as fishing, hunting, gathering, dancing, and so on. These practices are
more in alignment in influencing the HNAFS in the creation of their cultural rites of

passage in welcoming of a new brother or sister than hazing, which is more often seen in mainstream Greek organizations. For HNAFS, the integration of Native American and tribal culture is included in the crossing over of brothers and sisters as a part of their cultural rites of passage. Symbolism is also a part of this, meaning that how we are represented as new members or interested brothers and sisters as well as within the community see the HNFAS as important and culturally relevant. For instance, our symbols represent our tribal cultures and region. Gamma Delta Pi, Inc. has attempted to embody this with our mascot, which is a butterfly, and relates that to the dancing that takes place in a powwow and the connection to Indigenous cultures in Mexico. Another piece that is representative of one of the founders is incorporating a medicine plant, which is not commonly found in fraternities and sororities. The medicine plant chosen is cedar because of the connection that a founder has to its meaning for her tribe and community. This medicine also holds a common sacredness in other tribal communities. We have also incorporated a jewel or stone, which is turquoise, because of the significance that it has for one of the founders who uses turquoise as a part of the economy and a central stone used within their community. These are just some examples of symbolism that have significant meaning and also become a part of our cultural rites of passage. When we have our initiation, we include pieces of these symbols and we host a ceremony of blessing as each new and older sister join together as an organization, and the medicine of cedar brings that cleansing and blessing through prayer. These interactions create meaningful relationships between sisters. There are similar cultural rites of passage in other HNAFS that take place to welcome a sister brother into their circle of relationships.

Implications for Practice

HNAFS were uniquely created and are situated within the Native American and Greek communities on campus. It is imperative for representatives from the Offices of Greek Affairs and Native American Student Services to be attentive to organizational needs and issues on campus (Sasso, 2017). HNAFS have been affected by policies regulating their establishment, such as membership capacity, academic requirements, and levels of involvement (Oxendine, Oxendine, & Minthorn, 2013). HNAFS bring diverse and cultural backgrounds, perspectives, and experiences to the Greek and larger campus community. Greek Affairs offices should be open to broadening the "traditional" structure of Greek fraternities/sororities and need to evaluate and update their policies and requirements for recognition through greater understanding of cultural competency and significance on campus. "In order to decolonize the system, institutions and practitioners must closely examine their infrastructure and confront the policies, processes, practices, procedures, and their own beliefs that are based in colonizing systems" (Oxendine, 2017, p. 3). An example of a modification of policy and advocacy is when some HNAFS have their initiation ceremonies on campus they do the cedar or blessing ceremony and have often been met with resistance from the campus facilities to make accommodations. To achieve this understanding, Greek Affairs offices need to build relationships with the Native American Student Services professionals on campus (Sasso, 2017). Native American Student Services professionals serve as representatives, liaisons, and advocates for the Native American student community; hence, it is important for these professionals to understand their responsibility in supporting the HNAFS establishment and recognition within the Greek and campus community.

As HNAFS continue to expand nationally, there is a need for these organizations at tribal colleges and universities (TCUs). The majority of TCUs are two-year institutions, but many have and are continuing to develop four-year programs. Though TCUs specifically serve Native American students within tribal communities and reservations, there is a need for the type of support and community that HNAFS can offer to TCU campuses and student populations. Gamma Delta Pi, Inc. recently expanded to a TCU and has experienced major growth within its first few years. This expansion can also bridge TCUs and mainstream institutions, which can positively impact retention, graduation, and transfer rates.

Conclusion

As more Native American students matriculate to higher education institutions, whether mainstream or TCU, the need for HNAFS will continue to grow. HNAFS offers the communal and family-type support, as well as the structure on campus that many Native American students seek out. HNAFS are unique organizations situated within the Greek and Native American community, and can serve to broaden understanding within each community. It is important that the Greek community be aware of how it can learn and adapt to be more inclusive of HNAFS. For Native American communities, being a HNAFS pushes against the mainstream Greek system in ways that assert who we are as tribal and Indigenous peoples and show that it is okay to be a part of these organizations that include our culture and ways of being and bring an Indigenous perspective into something that wasn't originally made for us.

References

Jahansouz, S., & Oxendine, S. (2008, Spring). The Native American fraternal values movement: Past, present, & future. *Perspectives*, p. 14.

Oxendine, D., Oxendine, S., & Minthorn, R. (2013). The historically Native American fraternity and sorority movement. In H. J. Shotton, S. C. Lowe, & S. J. Waterman (Eds.), *Beyond the asterisk: Understanding Native students in higher education*. Sterling, VA: Stylus Publishing.

Oxendine, S. (2017). A call to action: Disrupting assimilation and colonization in fraternity and sorority life. *Essentials E-Publication, 9*. Retrieved from https://c.ymcdn.
com/sites/afa1976.site-ym.com/resource/collection/4B214BB6-56CC-4091-AC03-
8B1CFBD8DADC/Oxendine_Oct_2017_Educator.pdf
Sasso, P. (2017). Supporting First-Nation/Native American undergraduate students at non-Native colleges and universities in historically Native American fraternities and sororities.
Essentials E-publication, 9. Retrieved from https://c.ymcdn.com/sites/afa1976.site-ym.
com/resource/collection/4b214bb6-56cc-4091-ac03-8b1cfbd8dadc/Sasso_Oct%202017_
Researcher.pdf?hhSearchTerms=%22oxendine%22
Shotton, H. J., Lowe, S. C., & Waterman, S. J. (2013). *Beyond the asterisk: Understanding Native
students in higher education.* Sterling, VA: Stylus Publishing.

CHAPTER 17

The North American Interfraternity Conference (NIC)

Gresham D. Collom

Background

The North American Interfraternity Conference (NIC), Inc. is a trade association representing 66 inter/national men's fraternities, consisting of 6,186 chapters on over 800 campuses. The NIC (formerly known as the Interfraternity Conference and National Interfraternity Conference) arose from a meeting proposed by George D. Kimball, a member of Sigma Alpha Epsilon, at the University Club in New York City on November 17, 1909 (Brown, 1923). Twenty-six fraternities attended the first of many interfraternity conferences to "discuss critical issues facing fraternities at the time" (Smithhisler, 2003, p.117), where they agreed to formally organize as a trade association to provide members with "organizational support, educational programs and services, networking opportunities, and legislative/legal support" (p. 120).

Following its inception, the NIC hosted an annual meeting in New York City. Delegates for early NIC conferences consisted of one representative from each fraternity. Each fraternity chapter received an equal vote (Brown, 1923). The NIC's annual meetings were organized to provide support and direction to its member fraternities on relevant issues.

The NIC operates democratically and follows a constitution and bylaws. The NIC "is not, nor has it ever been, a governing organization of its member fraternities"

(Smithhisler, 2003, p.118). Although the NIC's House of Delegates voted on resolutions, these have always been non-binding actions.

The most recent NIC Constitution states:

> The purpose of the North American Interfraternity Conference shall be to promote the well-being of its member fraternities by providing such services to them as the Meeting of Members may determine. These services include, but not be limited to, promotion of cooperative action in dealing with fraternity matters of mutual concern, research in areas of fraternity operations and procedures, fact-finding and data gathering, and the dissemination of such data to the member fraternities. Conference action shall not in any way abrogate the right of its member fraternities to self-determination. (North American Interfraternity Conference, 2018, Constitution)

Organization

The NIC has undergone several revisions of its organizational structure since its inception. In 1955 the organization created a House of Delegates consisting of an elected individual from each member organization (Smithhisler, 2003). The House of Delegates was tasked with voting on legislation during the annual meeting. The House of Delegates also elected a Board of Directors to serve two-year terms in voluntary, unpaid positions. Between annual meetings, the Board of Directors were charged with executive and operational responsibilities for the NIC (Smithhisler, 2003).

Since, the NIC has significantly grown both in size and its governing body. Today the NIC represents 66 fraternities, and over 380,000 undergraduate students and 4.2 million alumni. The NIC's current organizational structure consists of 18 full-time staff, a 25-member Governing Council, the annual Meeting of Members represented by the 66 member fraternities, and a Council consisting of elected and designated members.

Membership Requirements

The NIC upholds strict membership requirements for fraternities interested in becoming members of the conference. Fraternities applying for membership to the NIC must have no fewer than five chapters and at least three chapters which have been active for at least five years. Applying fraternities must also adhere to the NIC standards, which provide guidelines regarding academic enrichment, health and safety, (inter)national support for chapters, opportunities for new fraternities and responsible growth, supporting student choice, interfraternalism, and member GPA requirements (North American Interfraternity Conference, 2018, Constitution).

In addition, member organizations are also required to submit data from their fraternity to the NIC. This data is used by the NIC to create an annual report (NIC, 2018). Data collected include numbers of new and returning members, active chapters and chapter closures, active alumni chapters, leadership involvement, GPA, housing and property information, volunteer engagement and training, and expansion efforts (North American Interfraternity Conference, 2018, Constitution).

Meeting of Members

The Annual Meeting of Members is held at the annual NIC conference and comprises one representative from each member fraternity. The representative is often the Chief Staff Officer (CSO) for their member fraternity or an alternative representative chosen by the fraternity's board or CSO. During the Meeting of Members, each representative present receives one vote per chartered and active chapter for which the member fraternity has paid dues. According to the most recent NIC constitution, the Meeting of the Members are "responsible for the broad general policies of the Conference, for electing three members to the Council, for establishing the annual Council Financial Threshold (CFT) associated with designated Council membership and for instructing the Council as to activities on behalf of the Conference" (p.2).

Council

The Council holds the executive and administrative powers of the Meeting of the Members and is comprised of elected and designated members. The representative must be a member of a fraternity which has paid its dues and is in good standing. Three council members are elected to fill at-large year-long positions at the annual meeting, while all other Council members are designated at each Meeting of the Members by their member fraternity to serve four-year terms. The Council is responsible for "carrying out the purpose and policies of the conference, for slating candidates for election in the Council, for establishing such fees as may be required to support Conference services and for the employment of the CEO of the conference" (North American Interfraternity Conference, 2018, Constitution, p. 4).

The Council is also responsible for electing a president, treasurer, and secretary to serve as officers of the Conference and with forming committees they deem necessary for the work of the Conference. These committees are comprised of Council members who are appointed by the CEO. Furthermore, Council members can be chosen to serve on the Membership and Accountability Committee. This committee is responsible for "review and recommendations regarding applications for membership in the Conference, adjudication of disputes between member fraternities, the resolution of alleged violations of the Constitution and By-Laws of the Conference, annual review of Standards compliance and development of aspirational benchmarks for attainment above Conference Standards" (p. 5).

Governing Council

The Governing Council works in collaboration with the NIC staff to address the collective needs of the 66 member fraternities. The current Governing Council consists of 25 representatives. NIC member fraternities can become eligible to have a Governing Council representative by meeting an annual investment threshold for operations of the conference. Furthermore, three Governing Council representatives are elected by the Meeting of the Members and the Fraternity Growth Accelerator organizations.

NIC Staff

The NIC central office was established in New York City in 1956 and relocated to Indianapolis in 1971. From 1956–1965, the NIC was run by the President of the Conference and one hired assistant. In 1965, the NIC hired its first executive, Jack Anson (Smithhisler, 2003). Today, a staff of 18 manage the day-to-day operations of the NIC at their Indianapolis office.

Initiatives and Programs

The NIC has long been involved in addressing prominent issues concerning their member fraternities. Legislation passed by NIC often addresses issues such as hazing and alcohol use. The NIC also coordinates educational programming for students and alumni involved with member organizations (Smithhisler, 2003).

Hazing

The NIC organized their first resolution against hazing in 1962. In this resolution, which is still supported today, the NIC stated that they were firmly against any hazing practices in their member organizations (Smithhisler, 2003). Recently, the NIC, National Panhellenic Conference (NPC), HazingPrevention.org, Association of Fraternity/Sorority Advisors, and the Association of Fraternal Leadership and Values partnered with families affected by hazing-related incidents to create an anti-hazing coalition (North American Interfraternity Conference & National Panhellenic Conference, 2018). In a joint statement, the anti-hazing coalition stated their partnership would:

- Pursue state-based anti-hazing legislation that delivers greater transparency through stronger hazing reporting requirements, strengthens criminal penalties and encourages prosecution, calls for university accountability for bad actors, provides amnesty to encourage people to call for help, and calls for student education.
- Expand awareness and intervention education, including providing a platform for the parents of hazing victims to speak to tens of thousands of college students.
- Engage fraternity and sorority members in educating high school students to confront hazing and bullying.

Alcohol Use

As far back as 1947, alcohol use within fraternities has been a point of conversation during annual NIC meetings. Yet a formal resolution on substance-free housing was not adopted until 1995, when the NIC House of Delegates adopted a resolution which supported efforts of fraternities to create substance-free communities (Smithhisler, 2003). Similarly, in 1997 and 1998 the NIC House of Delegates passed resolutions which supported increased resources designated to address alcohol misuse, and called for partnerships between NIC, NPC, and the National Pan-Hellenic Council (NPHC) to address alcohol misuse.

Recently, the NIC adopted a more forceful approach to addressing alcohol misuse among their fraternities. On August 27, 2018, the NIC passed legislation which gave member fraternities a year to prohibit drinks with an alcohol content of 15% or more unless served by a licensed third-party vendor (Brown, 2018). This legislation was in response to recent publicized fraternity hazing and alcohol related deaths in the United States. In the associated press release, Judson Horras, the NIC President and CEO, stated:

> At their core, fraternities are about brotherhood, personal development and providing a community of support. Alcohol abuse and its serious consequences endanger this very purpose. This action shows fraternities' clear commitment and leadership to further their focus on the safety of members and all in our communities. (North American Interfraternity Conference, 2018)

Other Initiatives

The NIC currently coordinates four educational programs for fraternity members: IMPACT, LAUNCH, PRIME, and UIFI. Along with its four educational programs, the NIC also offers support to campuses through the Interfraternity Council (IFC) and the IFC Academy. Additionally, the NIC launched the Alumni Housing Summit in 2017/18, a training program for fraternity/sorority housing volunteers.

IMPACT

IMPACT is a weekend-long program designed to foster improved relationships among campus leaders. The NIC staff lead the program at the hosting college or university along with small-group facilitators from the host campus. IMPACT focuses on problem-solving, leadership development, values-based decision making, effective communication, and community development (Smithhisler, 2003). In 2017/18, IMPACT served 1,066 students at 22 campus sessions (North American Interfraternity Conference, 2018).

LAUNCH

LAUNCH is a one-day retreat that brings fraternity and sorority leaders from a single campus together before the beginning of each school year. The purpose of this program is to build relationships, explore individual and shared issues, and set goals to address them. LAUNCH is held on the hosting institution's campus and facilitated by a NIC staff member. During 2017/18, 1,085 chapter and council leaders on 24 campuses partook in LAUNCH (North American Interfraternity Conference, 2018).

PRIME

PRIME is a leadership conference which began in 2018 and is held by NIC in partnership with the Association of Fraternal Leadership and Values (AFLV), Northeast Greek Leadership Association (NGLA), and Southeastern Interfraternity Conference (SEIFC). The two-day conference is intended for the IFC President. The PRIME conference was created to prepare IFC Presidents for their leadership roles and provide them with the tools to "provide a safe, enriching and memorable fraternity experience." In its first year, 59 IFC Presidents attended the conference (NIC, 2018).

UIFI

The Undergraduate Interfraternity Institute (UIFI) is a five-day educational program open to any collegiate fraternity or sorority member. The program, which began in 1990, is offered during nine sessions in Bloomington, Indiana. The Undergraduate Interfraternity Institute was started as a response to concerns about fraternal organizations (Smithhisler, 2003). UIFI has been attended by over 20,000 graduates in its 29-year history (North American Interfraternity Conference, 2018). Today, the UIFI encourages students to explore critical issues and to facilitate their development as leaders. In 2017/18, 795 students from 189 campuses participated in UIFI (North American Interfraternity Conference, 2018).

Interfraternity Council (IFC)

NIC also offers support to its members through the Interfraternity Council (IFC). The IFC's purpose, according to the NIC webpage, is "to advance fraternity on campus and provide interfraternal leadership to the entire community . . . [provide] direct support, resources, and services to IFC officers, representatives, advisors and alumni to further the health and success of local fraternity communities." In addition to increased campus support, NIC also offers training for IFC officers during the IFC Academy. Member chapters and corresponding campuses can purchase campus support packages with varying levels of included support for their IFC and fraternity community on the NIC webpage.

Conclusion

The North American Interfraternity Conference has a storied past and vast network of members. As the largest representative body of fraternities in the United States, the NIC is a central figure in today's push to improve fraternity and sorority culture. As their webpage states, "Fraternities are at a unique time in our history. To thrive today and beyond, fraternal culture must evolve. This will require greater partnership, collaboration and support than campuses, fraternities, chapters and the NIC have ever had."

References

Brown, J. T. (Eds.). (1923). *Baird's manual of American college fraternities: A descriptive analysis of the fraternity system in the colleges of the United States*. New York, NY: James T. Brown.

Brown, S. (2018, September 4). No more hard liquor at fraternity houses, national group says. *The Chronicle of Higher Education*. Retrieved from https://www.chronicle.com/article/No-More-Hard-Liquor-at/244436

North American Interfarternity Conference [NIC] (2018). Constitution of the north american interfraternity conference. Carmel, Indiana: North American Interfarternity Conference.

Smithhisler, P. (2003). The role of the North-American Interfraternity Conference (NIC). In D. E. Gregory (Ed.), *The administration of fraternal organizations on North American campuses: A pattern for the new millennium* (pp. 117–133). College Administration Publishers.

CHAPTER 18

The National Panhellenic Conference

Cynthia Weston

Background

Established in 1902, the National Panhellenic Conference is the oldest Greek-letter umbrella association. It is an alliance of 26 national and international women's-only social sororities, representing almost five million members. All member organizations are autonomous, maintaining the right to determine their own governing policies and practices. Through the Conference they work closely on matters of common interest and concern and collaborate with other stakeholders (see "Relationship with Host Institutions and Others," as follows).

NPC was founded before women won the right to vote under the U.S. Constitution and at a time when only a quarter of students at American colleges and universities were female (*Report*, 1905, p. 1064). The oldest sororities (first called "fraternities"[Anson & Marchesani, 1991, pp. 1–12]) arose in the mid-19th century as support systems for the small number of women undertaking higher education. Several decades later, NPC's seven founding sororities recognized that emerging competition on campuses threatened their shared vision and purpose: the promotion of high standards of intellectual achievement, character, citizenship, and leadership, and their determination to prove themselves as worthy and able as men. The Conference's initial decisions, which set ground rules about membership and recruitment, built trust and opened the way for the sorority community to focus productively, for more than a century, on matters of broader importance.

In 2011 NPC adopted the following Values Statement: "We are committed to relationships based on trust through transparency, accountability and mutual respect. Innovation and our core values of friendship, leadership, service, knowledge, integrity and community guide us in fulfilling our mission" (*National Panhellenic Conference Manual of Information*, 2018, p. 7).

Precepts and Organization

Relationship with Host Institutions and Others

NPC's aims have historically aligned with those of its host schools, and the Conference both values and has sought to cultivate strong ties with college and university administrations. "Your students, our members" is a principle that has guided a cooperative view of advancing the progress and welfare of collegiate women and their campus communities. It remains a relevant philosophy today, as fraternal organizations and administrations seek to address problems like hazing, substance abuse, and campus sexual assault.

The Conference operates with the awareness that its chapters are invitees of the institutions where they are located. NPC member organizations seek to be responsive campus partners and work to demonstrate effective and responsible self-governing (NPC Standards, 2014). As private, voluntary organizations, they are guaranteed certain freedoms—at least at public institutions—under the U.S. Constitution and Canadian Charter of Rights and Freedoms (Bradford, Saul, & Scott, 2003, p. 139). The Conference believes in partnering on issues of general leadership, as well as student and chapter development, while preserving member rights as private organizations to enjoy freedom of association and oversee chapter management and internal functioning. Traditionally, NPC member organizations have high expectations and hold their chapters to high standards, independent of any university relationship documents (NPC Standards, 2014).

To further common goals, the Conference works with other stakeholders, including the North-American Interfraternity Conference, the National Pan-Hellenic Council, Inc., the National Multicultural Greek Council, the National Association of Latino Fraternal Organizations, the National APIA Panhellenic Association, the Fraternity Executives Association, the Association of Fraternity Advisors, and the National Association of Student Personnel Administrators. It is also allied with such issue-related organizations as the Coalition of Higher Education Associations for Substance Abuse Prevention, HazingPrevention.Org, Cultivating Safe College Campuses Consortium, It's On Us (sexual-assault prevention), and Vision 2020 (gender equality).

Unanimous Agreements (UAs)

From the start NPC was a conference rather than a congress. It claimed no authority to legislate, except in matters of its own governance and in a handful of precepts so basic that every sorority ratified them as binding upon every member and chapter. These precepts have evolved into a larger collection of similarly ratified and binding policies, known as the Unanimous Agreements, which are found in the *NPC Manual of Information* (2018). Today's UAs cover topics including ethical conduct, the sovereign nature of member organizations, College Panhellenic judicial procedures, and the right of sororities to remain women's organizations.

NPC develops two other types of guiding statements. "Best practices" are model methods of operation for College and Alumnae Panhellenics and are strongly recommended. "Policies" are standards and procedures created by a vote, usually to address recurrent issues. There is an expectation that they be followed; however, policies are not compulsory with the force of the Unanimous Agreements. All member organizations are required to abide by the UAs, and because College and Alumnae Panhellenic associations are chartered by NPC, their governing policies and procedures must be in compliance. Any decision enacted by a local Panhellenic that conflicts with the UAs is invalid.

Governance and Operation

NPC operates democratically, according to a set of bylaws. It convenes annually to conduct business, with intervening meetings of a board of directors. Each member organization has one vote and is represented by a delegate and up to three alternates. The delegate casts the vote for her organization and is its representative on the board of directors. She and the alternates also serve on year-round committees.

A five-person executive committee, all of whom are members of the delegate body, leads the Conference. Two officers (chairman and vice chairman) hold their two-year positions in a rotation based on the member groups' order of entrance into NPC. The three other positions—advocacy chairman, finance chairman, and Panhellenics chairman—are held by appointment of the NPC chairman with approval of the board of directors (*National Panhellenic Conference Manual of Information*, 2018, p. 11).

In 1984 NPC established a central office located in Indianapolis (*Historical Review*, 2007, p. 22). Its staff, led by an executive director, supports the efforts of the Conference in programming, operations, communications, advocacy, and special projects.

The 26 member organizations have more than 3,200 active collegiate chapters at more than 670 colleges and universities in the U.S. and Canada, as well as nearly 3800 alumnae chapters (Member Organizations, n.d.). Whenever a second sorority chapter is installed on a campus, NPC begins the chartering of a College Panhellenic association (CPH), to be made up of member organizations represented there. The CPH is a democratic student entity responsible for Panhellenic operations in accordance with NPC rules and protocols. NPC also charters Alumnae Panhellenic associations (APHs), community-based organizations whose purpose is to further the mission of NPC and its member groups. There are currently 176 active APHs.

Recruitment and Membership

NPC's earliest agreements concerned membership and recruitment. Many remain in effect: among them, that no one may belong to more than one NPC member organization.

Apart from the principles in the Unanimous Agreements, the Conference honors the right of member organizations to set their own eligibility requirements for joining. Each follows policies of non-discrimination on any basis prohibited by law.

NPC organizations entrust membership decisions to their undergraduates. Depending on campus and Panhellenic needs, recruitment ranges from informal to highly structured, always involving mutual selection between chapter and potential new member. In structured recruitments, interested students attend several rounds of get-acquainted events, during which time both chapters and prospective members narrow their choices. Recruitment programs and Conference guidelines are designed to "provide opportunities for the greatest number of women to become sorority members while protecting the rights and privileges of both individuals and the chapters" (*National Panhellenic Conference Manual of Information*, 2018, p. 89). The Panhellenic ideal is parity among sororities on a campus, so that all members have a successful experience. Toward this end NPC provides guidance on capping allowable chapter size and, on most campuses, assists with management of invitations through its release-figure methodology program. At schools where interest in sorority membership exceeds capacity, another member organization may be invited to establish a new chapter.

NPC is a values-based organization, and recruitment is a time when sororities and prospective members should make considered, lifetime choices. The presence of men and alcohol is prohibited. Since 1989, NPC has urged every college Panhellenic to adopt the standardized Potential New Member's Bill of Rights (*National Panhellenic Conference Manual of Information*, 2018, p. 113). The Conference has eliminated the term "rush" as a synonym for recruitment, due to its connotation of undue haste and, in 2015, reinforced its commitment to a recruitment model that eschews non-substantive elements such as skits, costuming, refreshments, and elaborate decorations.

Accountability

Every College Panhellenic association must have a judicial board. To ensure fairness and due process, the board is responsible for following the judicial procedures outlined in Unanimous Agreement VII. This protocol exists to address any violations of the UAs or the local CPH's own governing documents, such as its code of ethics, bylaws, or recruitment rules. The *Manual of Information* gives procedural details.

As befits an organization committed to personal development and constructive engagement, NPC encourages informal discussion and/or mediation as preferred methods of resolution. Procedures provide for a formal hearing and appeals when called for. The CPH has the authority to impose sanctions as appropriate but may neither deprive a member chapter of its right to vote nor impede its right to recruit.

Each NPC member sorority has an internal accountability process as well.

Initiatives and Programs

NPC has a structure of support for College and Alumnae Panhellenic associations. Annually it hosts the national College Panhellenic Academy, to give collegiate officers training in achieving excellence in their sorority communities. It offers Consulting Team Visits, wherein NPC representatives visit a campus for two or more days at the Panhellenic's invitation and offer expert assessment and recommendations on subjects of the CPH's choosing. Most important is the area advisor/coordinator program: every CPH and APH has a designated NPC volunteer professional to serve as a source of information and guidance year-round.

The Conference and its organizations have always taken an interest in social, educational, and health issues. Member groups develop their own programs and support a wide range of philanthropic efforts. Each year, *at a modest estimate*, NPC-affiliated collegians and alumnae donate more than $35 million to worthy causes in the name of their organizations or Panhellenics, provide $6 million in scholarships to women, and volunteer upward of 2.5 million hours in their communities (NPC *Annual Report*, 2017; Annual Survey Highlights, 2017).

Many of NPC's educational endeavors have been targeted to College and Alumnae Panhellenic associations. The Conference has formulated its own materials but also serves as a conduit for programs developed by member organizations and others. It has thus passed along valuable information while seeking to prevent duplication of effort.

Topics of relevance have evolved. NPC's first official social initiative came in 1914, when it made a $200 donation to an organization whose mission was to help place females in careers besides teaching (*Adventure*, 2017, p. 5). Since then the Conference and its constituent groups have addressed a gamut of subjects: voter awareness, safe and affordable housing for working women, sex education, mental health, self-esteem, cancer prevention, positive confrontation, conflict resolution, and many more.

Among its enduring concerns are academic achievement and the rights of women. In 2000 the Conference created the Month of the Scholar, observed on campuses across the U.S. and Canada and, in 2016, became an allied organization with Vision 2020, a coalition to make social, political, and economic equality a national priority through shared leadership among women and men.

In support of its academic and educational ventures, NPC established the National Panhellenic Conference Foundation, Inc. in 1996. The Foundation is recognized by the Internal Revenue Service as a 501(c)(3) tax-exempt organization. It has funded wellness and educational programs, academic scholarships, development grants, and the Women in Higher Education Achievement Award.

Challenges

NPC's philosophy of addressing ills such as substance abuse, sexual assault, and hazing reflects that these problems are interwoven and related to campus cultures. Member organizations believe that education, vigilance, and systems of support/accountability are crucial, and they actively oversee their chapters through local alumnae advisors and inter/national volunteers and staff.

One of the Conference's signature programs is "Something of Value," launched in 1995 and supported by the NPC Foundation. Staffed by visiting facilitators, it addresses campus climate and risky behaviors.

NPC's 26 organizations mandate substance-free housing, and all set forth detailed social-event regulations. All sorority new-member programs cover responsible use of alcohol and related safety topics, and many College Panhellenic associations coordinate such educational endeavors. Through NPC's partnership with the Coalition of Higher Education Associations for Substance Abuse Prevention, the Conference promotes National Collegiate Alcohol Awareness Week, participates on task forces, and shares topical material with students.

In 2017 NPC released the Sexual Assault Awareness and Prevention Toolkit, created by its Student Safety and Wellness Special Committee. The toolkit includes information about hotlines and online chats, as well as member organization-developed programming. NPC also disseminates the Prevention Navigator, a free online tool from the Rape, Abuse, & Incest National Network (RAINN) that provides college administrators and students a resource to identify and provide feedback about sexual-assault-prevention programs.

Hazing is antithetical to the precept of "mutual respect and helpfulness" set forth in the Panhellenic Creed (*National Panhellenic Conference Manual of Information*, 2018, p. 11). Unanimous Agreement IV, 9. states: "NPC supports all efforts to eliminate hazing" (*Manual*, 2018, p. 33). Each member organization condemns questionable practices and has procedures for investigating allegations and sanctioning violations. NPC is a member of nationally recognized HazingPrevention.Org (HPO), a non-profit organization that sponsors National Hazing Prevention Week and other efforts. Individuals associated with the Conference have served on HPO's board of directors. Additionally, several member sororities support a national anti-hazing hotline (1-888-NOT-HAZE or 1-888-668-4293), whereas others publicize hotlines of their own.

In early 2018, NPC officials issued a "Call for Critical Change" and held its first meeting with leading university administrators, national sorority leadership, and experts in risk prevention. Participants are charged with developing recommendations for ways the sorority community can contribute to improved campus safety. According to Camera (2018), sorority leaders are "keenly aware of the unique role they could play to help change the conversation and culture."

Legislative Interests

In 2016 NPC unanimously adopted a government-relations platform consisting of three primary pillars: preservation of the sorority experience, financial parity and college affordability, and student and campus safety (*Annual Report*, 2017). Each spring the Conference participates in a visit to Capitol Hill, which has afforded thousands of students an opportunity to speak with legislators and their staffs about issues of concern.

NPC supports legislation to fight campus sexual assault and hazing. It favors transparency in reporting of incidents while protecting due process and survivors' rights.

It also endorses federal legislation to preserve the rights of single-sex student organizations. Among other protections, it asserts that an institution should not penalize students simply for being members of such groups.

NPC is a longtime advocate of the Collegiate Housing and Infrastructure Act (CHIA). When passed, the bill would permit donations to non-profit house corporations to be tax-deductible to the same extent as donations for university-owned housing. Supporters of CHIA, including more than 100 colleges and universities, maintain that it would enable much-needed safety and other upgrades to campus housing nationwide, help reduce student debt, and create thousands of jobs (Shapiro, 2015).

Outcomes

Since the inception of fraternities for women, members have attested to the long-term value of belonging to a sorority, including development of interpersonal and organizational abilities, encouragement of goal-oriented behavior, and cultivation of altruism. Gains in confidence, leadership, and other transferable skills, and a more holistic view of self are among the benefits they continue to cite (Walker, 2016). Moreover, campus professionals have perceived that sorority membership provides an environment where students can gain work values, reflect on life cycles, and balance formal and informal roles, all of which can positively affect future experiences (Walker & Havice, 2016).

In 2014 the Gallup-Purdue Index surveyed 30,000 college graduates to examine the relationship between college experiences and life after graduation. Controlled for factors such as gender, race/ethnicity, and socioeconomic status, the study found that fraternity/sorority alumni were more likely to be "engaged in their work" than non-Greek graduates, with a higher percentage also thriving in five types of well-being: namely, purpose ("liking what you do each day and being motivated to achieve your goals"), social ("having support relationships and love in your life"), financial ("managing your economic life to reduce stress and increase security"), community ("liking where you live, feeling safe, and having pride in your community"), and physical ("having good health and enough energy to get things done daily"). Fraternity/sorority alumni further reported a stronger sense of attachment to their alma maters. The study suggests that key factors of emotional support and experiential learning during college account for the differential (Busteed, 2014).

NPC-specific retention and persistence results, based on the same study, are that sorority members were retained from freshman to sophomore year at a higher rate than nonmembers (93% vs. 82%); graduated within six years at a higher rate (84% vs. 71%); and graduated within four years ("on time") at a higher rate (58% vs. 41%). After accounting for pre-college characteristics, such as high school grade point average and ACT score, as well as institutional differences, the differentials were even wider. Sorority members were three times as likely to remain after freshman year, two-and-a-half times as likely to graduate in six years, and twice as likely to graduate "on time."

According to the study, sorority membership did not affect final college GPA. This result is consistent with other research findings of more than two decades, as is the positive impact of membership on retention and persistence (Biddix, 2014).

In speaking of the Gallup-Purdue study, then-NPC chairman Jean Mrasek said: "For generations, our message has always been that sorority membership enhances the college experience and also provides lifelong support networks for members. The results of this index survey . . . validate what we advocate on a regular basis and what we know to be true—that sororities contribute to the overall well-being of women (Busteed, 2014)."

References

Adventure in friendship: A history of the National Panhellenic Conference. (2017). Indianapolis, IN: National Panhellenic Conference.

Annual Survey Highlights: Fast Facts. (2017). Retrieved from http://www.npcwomen.org

Anson, J. L., & Marchesani, Jr., R. F. (Eds.). (1991). *Baird's manual of American college fraternities* (20th Ed.). Indianapolis, IN: Baird's Manual Foundation, Inc.

Biddix, J. P. (2014). Sorority membership and educational outcomes: Results from a national study. Retrieved from https://www.npcwomen.org/wp-content/uploads/sites/2037/2017/10/Retention-Research-Results-2014.pdf

Bradford, L., Saul, B., & Scott, J. (2003). The role of the National Panhellenic Conference (NPC). In D. E. Gregory (Ed.), *The administration of fraternal organizations on North American campuses: A pattern for the new millennium* (pp. 137–161). Jacksonville, FL: College Administration Publications, Inc.

Busteed, B. (2014). National Gallup-Purdue Index reveals improved well-being among U.S. college graduates who joined fraternities and sororities. *Gallup Toolkit.* Retrieved from http://www.npcwomen.org

Camera, L. (2018, January 12). After tragedies, a call to change Greek life's culture. *U.S. News & World Report.* Retrieved from http://www.usnews.com

Historical Review. (2007). Indianapolis, IN: National Panhellenic Conference.

Member Organizations. (n.d.). Retrieved from http://www.npcwomen.org

National Panhellenic Conference manual of information (23rd Ed.). (2018). Indianapolis, IN: National Panhellenic Conference.

NPC annual report. (2017). Indianapolis, IN: National Panhellenic Conference.

NPC Standards. (2014). Retrieved from http://www.npcwomen.org

Report of the Federal Security Agency: Office of Education (Vol. 1). (1905). Washington, DC: U.S. Government Printing Office. Retrieved from http://books.google.com/books?id= 18ctAQAAIAAJ&pg=PA1142&lpg=PA1142&dq

Shapiro, T. R. (2015, April 29). Greek-letter college groups lobby Congress for housing tax code change. *The Washington Post.* Retrieved from http://www.washingtonpost.com

Walker, K. (2016). *How sorority alumnae remember acquiring the skills necessary to navigate their careers: A narrative inquiry* (Doctoral dissertation). Clemson University.

Walker, K. M., & Havice, P. A. (2016). Student affairs practitioners' perceptions of the career development of sorority members. *Oracle: The Research Journal of the Association of Fraternity/Sorority Advisors, 11*(1), 16–30. Retrieved from https://c.ymcdn.com/sites/ www.afa1976.org/resource/collection/0E038C73-3450-45DA-A3B4-C5C64D5ED39B/ OracleFall2016.pdf

CHAPTER 19

National Multicultural Greek Council

Tevis Bryant

THE NATIONAL MULTICULTURAL Greek Council (NMGC) originated in 1998. The NMGC serves as the national umbrella group that includes most multicultural-based fraternities and sororities. As a result of being the home of several organizations that view diversity and multiculturalism from different perspectives, the NMGC deemed it necessary to create a harmonious definition for the word multiculturalism. The council defines multiculturalism as not only diversity of membership, but a concrete commitment to acknowledge and celebrate all cultures equally through our programming, public service outreach efforts, and community education (National Multicultural Greek Council, 2018). Within the NMGC these individual groups are referred to as MGLOs, which simply stands for Multicultural Greek Lettered Organizations. This chapter provides a brief primer of the NMGC and background about each MGLO member organization.

Currently there are 11 organizations that are housed under the NMGC, only two of those organizations being fraternities. The member organizations are as follows: Delta Xi Phi Multicultural Sorority Inc., Theta Nu Xi Multicultural Sorority Inc., Mu Sigma Upsilon Sorority Inc., Lambda Tau Omega Sorority Inc., Lambda Sigma Gamma Sorority Inc., Omega Phi Chi Multicultural Sorority Inc., Psi Sigma Phi Multicultural Fraternity Inc., Phi Sigma Chi Multicultural Fraternity Inc., Gamma Eta Sorority Inc., Delta Sigma Chi Sorority Inc., and Delta Xi Nu Sorority Inc. Since the creation of the NMGC in 1998 and even prior, as some organizations were founded well before, these groups have spread the message of diversity, inclusion, and social justice across several institutions in the United States and abroad.

NMGC Governing Structure

The NMGC, like most national governing councils, has a standard executive board with positions such as President, Vice President, Secretary, and Treasurer. The executive board is the first level of the NMGC's governing structure. The council's executive board also features two and sometimes three unique roles. The frequent additional roles are the public relations coordinator and university liaison positions. Also, the executive board includes an appointed legal counsel. The second level of the governing structure is the standing committees. The current committees in place are: membership, programming, finance, research, and heritage. Each of these committees reports to the executive position that their tasks correlate with the most. For example, the financial committee reports to the treasurer. The third level in the governing structure in the NMGC is the representatives and the actual member organizations. Each organization has two NMGC representatives or delegates that attend the national meetings and provide the council with important advances within the organizations. In return, the NMGC provides the representatives with changes in the council to disseminate to their chapters.

Delta Xi Phi Multicultural Sorority Inc.

Delta Xi Phi Multicultural Sorority Inc. was founded April 20th, 1994 at the University of Illinois at Urbana – Champaign. There were 15 women who came together to start this organization in order to bring awareness on diversity, multiculturalism, and women empowerment to their campus. Delta Xi Phi has a unique beginning that has transitioned into a very well-respected sorority. In 1992, two separate women groups were working unknowingly of one another to establish a new sorority on their campus, and when the groups learned of one another it made sense for them to join forces and unite to hold a much stronger presence on the campus (National Multicultural Greek Council, 2018). Delta Xi Phi's mascot is the white Bengal tiger. The colors that represent the sorority are maroon and blue. Delta Xi Phi's flower symbol is the yellow rose of Texas and their stone is the white diamond. The organization has deemed The American Cancer Society as their national philanthropy. The organization seeks to aid this organization in gaining funding to conduct more research to discover more treatable solutions for cancer.

Theta Nu Xi Multicultural Sorority Inc.

Theta Nu Xi Multicultural Sorority Inc. was founded in North Carolina at the University of North Carolina-Chapel Hill campus. The sorority was founded by seven women who wanted to create an organization that they believed focused on scholarship, service, sisterhood, leadership, and the holistic idea of multiculturalism. The organization was founded on April 11, 1997 and was incorporated on April 29, 1999. Theta Nu Xi is one of the most rapidly growing multicultural organizations. Like the origin of most NMGC groups, Theta Nu Xi's founders felt a lack of options when looking into Greek Life. While historically Black and White organizations include some racial diversity, that is not the focus of these organizations. In order to capture the essence of diversity, this group of founders banded together to create this great organization. Theta Nu Xi chose their mascot as the butterfly, and in honor of that they refer to their founding sisters as the "Founding Monarchs." The organization's colors are lavender, Carolina blue, and black. The organization also has the sterling silver rose as its national flower. Theta Nu Xi's national philanthropy is Girl Up. Girl Up is an organization that was founded by the UNF in 2010 that seeks to give girls from various communities resources and a platform to promote change in their communities and to empower one another through leadership training.

Mu Sigma Upsilon Sorority Inc.

Mu Sigma Upsilon Sorority Inc. was founded November 21, 1981 at Rutgers University on the New Brunswick campus. Mu Sigma Upsilon is recognized as the first multicultural Greek-letter organization in the nation out of all known multicultural sororities and fraternities. Mu Sigma Upsilon is also known for being the sister organization of Lambda Sigma Upsilon Latino Fraternity. Mu Sigma Upsilon was founded by five women who are regularly referred to as the founding mothers by members of the organization. The organization suggests that multiculturalism is the belief that there's an instinctual value in uncovering, understanding, and appreciating the various ways in which people are different (National Multicultural Greek Council, 2018). Mu Sigma Upsilon's mascot is the Amazon Woman, to represent their strength and independence. The colors of the organization are baby blue and white. Mu Sigma Upsilon Sorority Inc.'s national philanthropy is "To Write Love on Her Arms," which is a nonprofit organization that helps individuals with depression, addiction, and self-injury.

Lambda Tau Omega Sorority Inc.

Lambda Tau Omega Sorority Inc. was founded on October 9, 1988 at Montclair State University. Sixteen women decided to come together to create a multicultural alternative that best connected to their ideals and values. A large emphasis in developing the organization was creating a space where women could promote one another and encourage academic enrichment and professional growth. Lambda Tau Omega uses the spelling of the word "womyn" instead of women, which holds great importance to the members of the organization. The mascot of Lambda Tau Omega is the Enchanting Mermaid, and their colors are royal blue and light gray. Lambda Tau Omega has several philanthropic initiatives all focusing on the welfare of children and providing them with opportunities to become successful.

Lambda Sigma Gamma Sorority Inc.

Lambda Sigma Gamma Sorority Inc. was founded on October 24, 1986 at Sacramento State University. Founding member Linda V. Fuentes spearheaded the movement by recruiting 26 other women who later became founding members of the sorority as well. The women came together to start the organization because they collectively realized that the institution did not have a holistic way of meeting the needs of female minorities on the campus. Lambda Sigma Gamma was the outlet for these women to bring the change on the campus that they very much desired. Lambda Sigma Gamma places an emphasis on both multiculturalism and early education intervention. Lambda Sigma Gamma is represented with the mascot of a tan teddy bear with a collared red ribbon. The organization's jewels are the emerald, pearl, and ruby, which also aligns with their national colors of green, white, and red.

Omega Phi Chi Sorority Inc.

Omega Phi Chi Sorority Inc. was founded November 9, 1988 at Rutgers University – New Brunswick. Omega Phi Chi was founded by eight women of various ethnic backgrounds which set the tone for the importance of diversity within their organization. Omega Phi Chi was one of the organizations that helped found and create what is now known as NMGC. The organization places importance on unity and getting involved with community affairs. Omega Phi Chi has several mottos that are used among its members that place a high level of importance on individuality and having respect for that. Omega Phi Chi is represented by the mascot of a Black Panther. The organization's flower is a lady's pink slipper also referred to as a Moccasin. Their stone is the Black Onyx. The organization's colors are Perfect Pink and Onyx Black. Omega Phi Chi participates in various service projects through their national philanthropy OPC C.A.R.E.S, which is an acronym for Omega Phi Chi Community Advocates Responsible for Educating and Serving.

Psi Sigma Phi Multicultural Fraternity Inc.

Psi Sigma Phi Multicultural Fraternity Inc. was founded on December 12, 1990 by 18 men seeking to bring a new and innovative type of men's fraternity to their campuses. The organization was co-founded at Montclair State University and New Jersey City University, which later came to be distinguished as the Patriarch Alpha Chapter and the Baronet Beta Chapter. Psi Sigma Phi seeks to develop young men in helping them become the best versions of themselves. Psi Sigma Phi Multicultural Fraternity Inc. has a mission of taking up leadership within the community while raising cultural awareness and promoting academic achievement and community service (National Multicultural Greek Council, 2018). Psi Sigma Phi Multicultural Fraternity prides itself on being the first nationally recognized and incorporated fraternity of a multicultural orientation and continues to grow and develop ways to support all students on various college campuses. Psi Sigma Phi's mascot is the Almighty Knight and their colors are black, silver, and white. The organization prides itself in the principles of service, brotherhood, education, and multiculturalism.

Phi Sigma Chi Multicultural Fraternity Inc.

Phi Sigma Chi Multicultural Fraternity Inc. was founded November 16, 1996 at New York City College of Technology. The organization was founded by six men who wanted to integrate diversity and inclusion into their Greek Life community in a very intentional way. In 2003 Phi Sigma Chi Multicultural Fraternity Inc. became a member group of the NMGC and helped ratify the council's constitution. Phi Sigma Chi has five philanthropic pillars, the main of which is the 363 campaign. This campaign is an initiative that is meant to help feed the homeless on every other day besides Thanksgiving and Christmas. Phi Sigma Chi is represented by the Phoenix as their mascot and their colors are Crimson and Gold.

Gamma Eta Sorority Inc.

Gamma Eta Sorority Inc. had a bit of a different origin than most of the NMGC member organizations. Gamma Eta Sorority Inc. was founded in the state of Florida on October 18, 1995, and originally began as a student recognized organization that was referred to as Gamma Eta Society. Gamma Eta was founded by 17 women who wanted to expand their mission of diversity and create a space for all women to feel accepted and supported. In 1996, the group initiated their founding class of members and was incorporated in 1999. In 2006, Gamma Eta became a member organization of the NMGC. Gamma Eta is represented by the mascot of the Sun and Fleur de Lis. The organization's flower is the sunflower and their colors are purple and teal. Gamma Eta's national philanthropy is Breast Cancer Awareness.

Delta Sigma Chi Sorority Inc.

Delta Sigma Chi Sorority Inc. was founded November 27, 1996 by four women who wanted to spread and continue a narrative of multiculturalism around their campus. The founding members of Delta Sigma Chi wanted to focus on building unity among the campus and providing women the option to join a group that empowers them. Delta Sigma Chi is the sister organization of Phi Sigma Chi Multicultural Fraternity Inc. Delta Sigma Chi is represented by their mascot, the white tiger. The organization's colors are Royal blue and Silver.

Delta Xi Nu Sorority Inc.

Delta Xi Nu Sorority Inc. was founded on October 7, 1997 at Texas A&M University. The five founding women wanted to create an organization where women of all cultures and walks of life felt welcomed while focusing on education and serving their communities. The founding mothers of the organization wanted to show everyone that it was their differences that made them stronger (National Multicultural Greek Council, 2018). The members of the organization go by the alias of "Xi Honeys," which has significance to their sisterhood. Delta Xi Nu is represented by their mascot, which is the butterfly. The organization's colors are Red and Silver, and their flower symbol is the red tulip. Delta Xi Nu's national philanthropy is Awareness of Violence against Women.

Programs & Initiatives

The NMGC has various initiatives that they are involved with; however, there is not a designated program that the council has adopted. The council is made up of 11 unique organizations which were founded even before the council, so maintaining non-partisan programming is important to the council. The NMGC collectively supports social justice issues and issues that face various students in college today. The council actively supports LGBT rights, and while individual member organizations are still developing more inclusive policies, the NMGC stands by all members of this community and seeks to support them in multiple ways. In 2018, various organizations in the NMGC came together to participate in the NYC Pride parade, showcasing support for the community and displaying council unity.

Future Directions

The National Multicultural Greek Council and its member organizations has its work cut out within the Greek Life community. The value of the member organizations is without a doubt at a high level; however, these organizations are recruiting in the same space as other organizations that have been around a hundred years or more and are more well-known. MGLOs must discover ways to recruit effectively and intentionally. Aside from increasing membership in all the groups, the council must continue developing the positions on the executive board and committee positions. A member of an NMGC organization had this to say, "What we do as a council from here on out has to make sense for us. We cannot do things just because IFC, NPHC, or NPC does them a certain way. We really need to own our uniqueness, and structure our council in that way." The National Multicultural Greek Council is still a growing organization, and with any organization there will be growing pains and struggles. NMGC is unlike any other representative umbrella organization, so it must begin operating in a way that maintains that individuality but works similarly to the longer standing council's blueprint.

References

National Multicultural Greek Council. (2018). National Multicultural Greek Council: About. Retrieved from http://nationalmgc.org

CHAPTER 20

National Asian Pacific Islander Desi American Panhellenic Association (NAPA)

Brian Gee and Hannah Seoh

Brief Overview of APIDA Organizations

Asian Pacific Islander Desi American (APIDA) students were historically discriminated against and barred from joining mainstream fraternities and sororities. In the same way that these organizations were formed for the students, the National APIDA Panhellenic Association (NAPA) formed largely in response to being left out of larger interfraternal conversations. NAPA in part provided legitimacy to Asian American Greek Letter Organizations (AAGLOs), not only on campuses but also in the larger interfraternal context.

Between 1910 and 1930, the first APIDA fraternities and sororities were established as support groups for small ethnic minorities (Chinese or Japanese) on Predominantly White Institutions. According to Kimbrough, as cited in the NAPA Resource Guide, APIDA fraternities and sororities mirrored their White counterparts by adopting Greek letters, forming a chapter, incorporating secret rituals, and developing their own traditions (Association of Fraternity/Sorority Advisors, 2013). Beginning in the late 1980s, the exploding Asian American student population, the rise in multiculturalism, and the advancement of technology combined to help usher in a fast-growing, national, APIDA fraternity and sorority movement. In the early 1990s, two organizations spearheaded national expansion efforts. Lambda Phi Epsilon Fraternity and alpha Kappa Delta Phi Sorority would become the first APIDA organizations to successfully start and sustain chapters in multiple states across the country. Their nationwide expansion forever changed the landscape of the APIDA fraternity/sorority movement.

By the mid-1990s, new organizations were founded with national aspirations. Pi Delta Psi Fraternity, Sigma Psi Zeta Sorority, and Kappa Phi Lambda Sorority were founded on New York campuses, and within five years, each had chartered several chapters. With the development of the Internet in the 1990s, it became easy for these new groups to find other organizations that shared similar ideals. While many existing single-chapter organizations chose to remain as local organizations, others such as Pi Alpha Phi and Sigma Omicron Pi chose to embrace the new paradigm of growing a national identity and began chartering chapters across the country.

Between 1990–2000, at least 35 APIDA organizations chartered across the country in 150 chapters. While most of their growth centered around the coasts, significant growth flourished at universities with large APIDA populations, such as the University of Texas and the University of Michigan.

Origins of NAPA

By the early 2000s, the boom in AAGLOs was becoming too large to ignore. In March 2004, the Chinese American Intercollegiate Conference held a panel on emerging cultural Greek organizations. Two of the invited panelists were Jeanette Moy, the President of Sigma Psi Zeta National Sorority, and Brian Gee, a former President of Pi Alpha Phi National Fraternity.

After the meeting, Moy and Gee discussed what they saw as the general state of the Asian Greek landscape. For all the great potential Asian fraternal organizations had to positively impact their members' lives and their communities, there also were serious concerns about the dangers and problems of Asian Greek life. The two leaders mapped out an idea of getting their groups to collaborate on one project: Asian Pacific Islander American (APIA) voter registration.

Janelle Hu, Executive Director of APIAVote, was also at the conference. APIA-Vote is a national nonpartisan organization that works with partners to mobilize Asian American and Pacific Islanders in electoral and civic participation. Hu attended the conference to promote APIAVote's youth voter registration drive for the 2004 U.S. Presidential Election.

A voter registration drive provided a tangible project for groups to work on collaboratively that utilized the groups' social and networking strengths. Voter registration was a non-controversial initiative that organizations could use to build a working relationship while promoting the common goal of civic engagement.

Moy reached out to organizations based in the East Coast. Gee reached out to groups in the West. After a few conference calls with potential participants, the group named itself the Asian Greek Alliance. From the press release:

FOR IMMEDIATE RELEASE

FRIDAY, JULY 30, 2004

Who: For the first time, Asian Pacific American Greek-lettered organizations nationwide are collaborating for a common goal, increased voter registration and turnout among APIA youth. **The APIA Greek Alliance (AGA) has partnered with APIA Vote**, a national coalition of non-partisan nonprofit organizations that encourages civic participation and promotes a better understanding of public policy and the electoral process among the Asian and Pacific Islander American community.

What: The cooperative campaign will **register and mobilize 20,004 young APIA voters** for the upcoming election. This will include **100% registration** among every member that is eligible to vote within the participating AGA organizations. Specifically, the AGA will lead APIA Vote's ongoing efforts to mobilize APIA youth networks across the nation. This will be accomplished by integrating voter registration and mobilization into the campus activities, recruiting APIA youth on college campuses to host coordinated voter registration drives on campus, and turning out the APIA youth vote in November.

The APIA Greek Alliance collectively represents over 2,500 undergraduates across the United States. This coalition aims to increase the number of registered APIA youth voters, by networking the Asian American university communities through our 149 chapters. Historically, our national organizations have never worked together on one concerted project. We are excited to begin a positive, working relationship through this worthy campaign, in one of the most critical elections years in recent history.

—JEANETTE MOY, APIA GREEK ALLIANCE COORDINATOR

APIA Greek Alliance partners included: alpha Kappa Delta Phi Sorority, Alpha Iota Omicron Fraternity, Delta Phi Lambda Sorority, Lambda Phi Epsilon Fraternity, Kappa Phi Lambda Sorority, Nu Alpha Phi Fraternity, Pi Alpha Phi Fraternity, Pi Delta Psi Fraternity, and Sigma Psi Zeta Sorority. The AGA resulted from this partnership and adopted the following mission statement in June 2005.

The APIA Greek Alliance serves to advocate the needs of its member organizations through the enrichment of the fraternal experience. The AGA
promotes and fosters positive interfraternal relations, communications, and
the development of all Asian Pacific American Greek Lettered organizations through mutual respect, leadership, integrity, professionalism, and
academic achievement. The AGA also recognizes the importance of community involvement.

Seeing the successful collaboration's positive impact on the APIA community and
on college campuses, several of the AGA leaders chose to continue the AGA on further
projects, including Tsunami Relief and Hurricane Katrina Relief. While there was not
necessarily a cohesive plan for the AGA, the members knew they wanted to do more.

On July 28–31, 2005, with support from OCA, a national organization dedicated to
advancing the social, political, and economic well-being of Asian Pacific Americans,
the AGA hosted the first-ever leadership summit between the various national APIA
fraternities and sororities. The summit provided the first in-person opportunity for these
organizations' leaders to engage in serious dialogue about the challenges and future of
the APIA fraternity/sorority community.

Attending the conference were members of alpha Kappa Delta Phi Sorority, Inc., Al-
pha Phi Gamma Sorority, Inc., Delta Phi Lambda Sorority, Inc., Pi Alpha Phi Fraternity,
Inc., Pi Delta Psi Fraternity, Inc., Sigma Beta Rho Fraternity, Inc., and Sigma Psi Zeta
Sorority, Inc.

At the conference, members of the aforementioned organizations had an opportunity
to meet with other APIA youth leaders and learn useful skills for working for change on
their campuses. By the end of the summit, recognizing the need for an umbrella organization for APIA fraternities and sororities, the attendees decided to formalize the AGA,
and member organizations agreed to meet via conference call on a monthly basis. Alice
Siu of Sigma Psi Zeta was elected to be the AGA's first chair.

Evolution of NAPA into a Collective Identity

Over the next year, the challenges of creating an umbrella organization became clear.
Many of the potential NAPA organizations had been in existence less than two decades.
They shared common problems such as being vastly underfunded and under-resourced
and struggled to keep alumni engaged.

In NAPA's early years, member organizations operated more like a federation of local
fraternities and sororities rather than a unified national entity. Unlike their counterparts
in the North American Interfraternity Conference (NIC), National Panhellenic Conference (NPC), and National Pan-Hellenic Council (NPHC), most APIDA fraternities and
sororities' national board members were young adults. Some even had undergraduates

serving on their national leadership. No member organizations had paid staff. They were all unpaid volunteers doing the best they could but without the training or the experience to adequately serve in the role of a national fraternity/sorority headquarters.

On the initial conference calls, the group organizers spent much of their time dealing with minutiae. Calls would get bogged down on membership criteria (e.g., requiring five chapters in one state or five chapters in a minimum of two states), whether to accept alumni chapters, whether to charge dues, and whether to change the name for the umbrella organization. In the course of 18 months, the group cycled through Asian Greek Alliance, National Asian Greek Alliance, National Asian Greek Council, and National APA Panhellenic Association (NAPAPA). Eventually, the council name was shortened to NAPA (although the NAPAPA listserv continued to be used until 2007). In the early days, every time the organizers felt that a decision had been locked, someone would reopen the discussion and another three to six months would pass before locking that decision in again.

Initially, not all the national APIA fraternities and sororities chose to join NAPA. Lambda Phi Epsilon Fraternity, the largest of the APIA organizations, was already a member of the NIC and did not see the benefits of joining an additional umbrella organization. While fraternities had the option of joining NIC, APIA interest sororities did not qualify for membership in NPC, NPHC, National Association of Latino Fraternal Organizations (NALFO), or National Multicultural Greek Council (NMGC). Sigma Omicron Pi Sorority joined NAPA in 2008 but left two years later when there was a change in their leadership. Sigma Phi Omega Sorority also was in conversations to join as a chartering NAPA organization, but ultimately did not pursue membership.

During the early years, NAPA was also looking for potential advisory board members. One of the leads turned out to be Mary Peterson. At the time, Peterson was serving as Executive Director of Sigma Lambda Beta International Fraternity, Inc. and Sigma Lambda Gamma National Sorority, Inc.—the largest Latino fraternity and sorority. As someone with experience in both student affairs and Latino Greek life, Peterson was uniquely qualified to have perspectives on how to build a new umbrella group. NAPA came into her life at a time when she was looking for a new challenge. In her first phone call with Brian Gee, she correctly identified the areas that the umbrella group was stalling on, which included a lack of trust among the member organizations, lack of a formal constitution, lack of standard membership requirements, and formalizing the name of the umbrella organization.

Peterson also asked: "In all the squabbling the past year, how have you helped your members? What is your purpose? To help each member organization be the best it can be. To help each member organization provide the best fraternal experience to its members." With Peterson's participation, in January 2007, NAPA suspended work on its constitution for six months. During that time, NAPA, with Mary's help, provided resources to help each member organization improve itself. These basic resources included documenting information on incorporation, building educational foundations, risk management policies, purchasing liability insurance, and working with campus-based Greek Life Offices. NAPA created a track record for membership buy-in so that within the next few years, the members could tackle heavier items, such as the long-term vision of NAPA.

Peterson introduced NAPA's leaders to other fraternal organizations: AFA, FEA, NIC, NPC, NPHC, and NALFO. She also utilized her network of contacts and introduced NAPA's leadership to various thought leaders and experts in their field. Friends of NAPA who contributed their time and expertise in NAPA's early days include David Westol in the field of risk management policy and fraternal law, Karyn Nishimura Sneath for personal and organizational development, and Shelley Sutherland for long-term strategic planning and assistance navigating the higher education and fraternal landscape. Each contributed and continue to contribute significantly to NAPA and its member organizations' growth.

In the mid- to late-2000s, NAPA continued to provide resources and spearhead initiatives to help improve the fraternal experience for its members. In October 2007, NAPA hosted its first training for member organizations' national boards. In 2008, NAPA worked with the Association of Fraternity/Sorority Advisors to create a resource guide to assist campus-based advisors working with NAPA chapters on their campuses. In April 2009, NAPA hosted an Asian Greek Summit. Attendees included a variety of stakeholders from national headquarters, campus Greek Life offices, undergraduates, and other interested parties. It was the largest event of its type to dialogue about issues affecting Asian Greek Life. In December 2013, NAPA, along with NALFO and NMGC, co-hosted a Cultural Greek Summit to discuss issues that affected all culturally-based Greek organizations. NAPA has also continued to unite its member organizations with collaborative initiatives, such as its Friends DO Make a Difference mental health campaign in 2014.

As NAPA has strived to become the gold standard for the APIDA fraternal community, benefits of membership have become clear to the APIDA fraternities and sororities. As of 2018, NAPA membership has grown to 18 organizations, including the largest organizations, such as Lambda Phi Epsilon Fraternity, which joined in 2010. NAPA has also made inroads in Desi fraternity/sorority membership, which by 2017 comprised half of the NAPA member organizations. The growing membership of Desi/South Asian fraternities and sororities in NAPA prompted the NAPA to change its name in 2017 to National APIDA Panhellenic Association.

The APIDA Greek landscape has changed significantly since Gee and Moy's first meeting in a cafe in Durham, North Carolina. From a few dozen chapters in 2004 to hundreds of chapters in 2018, NAPA has become the *de facto* voice of the APIDA fraternal movement. It has served to help its member organizations grow and develop into strong partners of the interfraternal community. As NAPA matured and embraced its role in higher education and the interfraternal community, its member organizations developed better operational practices and became more effective national entities. NAPA will continue to provide a voice to advocate for its members and work to make a positive impact on the APIDA community.

References

Association of Fraternity/Sorority Advisors. (2013). NAPA Resource Guide. Fort Collins, CO: Miranda, M., Gee, B.

A. Siu, personal communication, August 7, 2005.

The Association of Fraternity/ Sorority Advisors

Kara Miller McCarty and Lynda Wiley

History of AFA

Bureau (2006) recounted the first 30 years of the Association of Fraternity/Sorority Advisors (AFA) in the Association's magazine, *Perspectives*. The Association of Fraternity Advisors (AFA) began in 1976. The name was formally changed to the Association of Fraternity/Sorority Advisors in 2009 to more accurately reflect the work that our members perform professionally. According to Bureau (2006) campus professionals were organized through the Fraternity Advisors Association (FAA) prior to 1976. The National (now North American) Interfraternity Conference (NIC), Fraternity Executives Association (FEA), and Fraternity Advisors Association (FAA) were all meeting separately at this time. In 1976, these three groups met together in Williamsburg, VA, which is known as the birthplace of Greek-lettered organizations due to Phi Beta Kappa being founded on the campus of the College of William and Mary in 1776. An outcome of this meeting was the establishment of AFA, a vehicle to provide better communication between fraternity and sorority headquarter executives and staff members and those campus-based professionals who worked with sororities and fraternities.

Mission of AFA

According to Bureau (2006), the initial purposes adopted by AFA were:

- To share ideas and provide ways to share ideas among campus personnel who worked with fraternities
- To offer services to campuses and individuals with questions or problems related to fraternities
- To raise visibility and support for those advising fraternities and sororities at colleges and universities
- To encourage qualified individuals to aspire to take roles advising sororities and fraternities on college campuses
- To assist in maintaining positive relationships among campus-based personnel, fraternity and sorority executives and staff, and the North American Interfraternity Conference
- To cause educational programming and student development among fraternities and sororities
- To promote research related to sororities and fraternities

Bureau (2006) continued that in 1978, there were 185 professionals interested in belonging to AFA. As membership grew, AFA established a central office and employed one staff member. Over the years, AFA has moved locations and is currently located outside of Indianapolis, IN. There are six full-time employees that run the daily operations, plan programs, and ensure regular communication with members and constituents. Three of the six employees are shared with the Association of Fraternal Leadership and Values (AFLV). In terms of Association leadership and governance, the Association has also transformed over the years in the makeup of volunteers that serve on the Board of Directors. A majority of the Board of Directors are elected directly by the membership. As noted in the following, the addition of appointed members to the Board of Directors allows for a broad range of professional experience and insight. The Board of Directors utilize a traditional model of president, secretary, and treasurer for leadership within the Board. The Board of Directors sets the priorities and vision of the Association, and works with the Executive Director and staff to ensure these priorities are implemented and evaluated.

The current mission of the AFA website reads, "AFA provides exceptional experiences, a vibrant community, and essential resources for the success of fraternity/sorority advisors. We have an ongoing commitment to the professional development of our members, a deep appreciation of both academic and applied research that examines the entire spectrum of the fraternity/sorority experience and the advising profession, and a commitment to collaborations within and between the higher education and interfraternal communities. Through our programs and meetings, publications, networking opportunities, and other resources, AFA is the leading voice in aligning the fraternity/sorority and higher education experiences." Unlike other higher education/student affairs associations (such as ACHUO-I, NACA, ACUI, etc.), AFA focuses not just what occurs in a campus environment, but also the interaction and partnerships with (inter)national fraternity and sorority organizations. This presents both challenges and opportunities that are unique to AFA.

Core Competencies for Excellence in the Profession

Similar to other professional associations, AFA has established Core Competencies for Excellence in the Profession. These competencies were first established in the mid-2000s. In 2016, the Educational Resources Strategic Framework Workgroup recommended the Association revise and revisit the Core Competencies for Excellence in the Profession. A cross-section of professionals are currently working to develop the next iteration of AFA's Core Competencies. Their work is driven by the following concepts: an updated taxonomy including ways of thinking unique to fraternity and sorority life as well as professional skills essential to working in the field; a framework for continuous development; a progressive structure which recognizes each professional develops different competencies at different rates and times; a self-guided pathway which allows members to prioritize which abilities are relevant to their role and how to map their own professional development pathway; focus on progress which equips members with tools to identify needs and develop strategies for helping more professionals gain more abilities over time; and an opportunity to adapt which includes the notion that the Core Competencies are flexible in allowing the ability to include new knowledge, skills, attitudes, and ways of thinking that may become relevant in the future.

AFA Membership Data

The Association currently boasts 1570 members. Members are divided into five different regions of the Continental United States and Canada. The current membership categories available in the Association are: professional, graduate, affiliate, emeritus, and vendor. Professional members hold a full-time role at a college or university or at the inter/national sorority or fraternity office. Graduate members are enrolled part-time or full-time in a graduate or doctoral program but do not hold a current full-time position at a campus or inter/national organization. Affiliate members are those who are actively concerned about a sorority or fraternity but do not hold a full-time position at a campus or inter/national organization. An example may be a chapter advisor or a national president of a fraternity or sorority. Emeritus members were previously professional members who have since retired but remain active and interested in a fraternity or sorority. Finally, vendor members shall be those organizations, companies, or suppliers of goods and services—either for profit or not for profit in nature—that support the policies, purposes, and activities of the Association. All members can participate as a volunteer, but the members in the vendor category are not eligible to vote on Association business. All members can serve on the Board of Directors for the Association; however, only professional members who are employed by a campus can currently fill the role of President.

Evolution of the Board of Directors

Like many organizations that are relatively young, the role and philosophy of the governing board has evolved over time. In 2011, the decision was made for the AFA Board to move from an operation board structure to a governance board model. Embracing the style of a Carver model, the members began electing a President and electing up to four additional Board members to guide the strategic direction of the Association while also having the duty of ethical and fiduciary management of the AFA. The Board elects the Treasurer and Secretary internally. Two Board members are appointed by the Board with the end goal of filling any skill and experience gaps left after the election process. Appointed members may belong to any category of membership. The Board of Directors meets in person three times per year and regularly via electronic means. Members of the Board also serve as liaisons to various committees and work groups.

Strategic Framework

In 2014, the AFA Board set a strategic framework that remains in place today. The current strategic framework has four main categories. They are: research, educational resources, efficient operations and resource management, and communication. Each strategic framework area was assigned a group of volunteers to make recommendations to the Board in the summer of 2016. Many of the initiatives recommended are currently in action.

Research

The research committee generated a list of research priorities for those interested in the area of fraternity and sorority advising. More and more we are seeing the size of resources devoted to an office and benchmarking best practices as needs of senior student affairs officers (SSAOs). AFA seeks to be a leader in generating such information and encouraging more data collection and study. A partnership with the Council for the Advancement of Standards (CAS), the Center for the Student of Sorority and Fraternity Research (CFSR), and our own grant opportunities funded through the AFA Foundation will allow this strategic priority to flourish.

Educational Resources

Educational resources are a premier function of AFA. We currently offer: the annual meeting, Advance U, the Collective, Global Service Initiative, First 90 Days, and the Placement Exchange. We occasionally offer a program in partnership with another organization on a topic of importance, such as the Title IX conference in partnership with ASCA. We are revitalizing our Core Competencies for Excellence in the Profession and also conducting a needs analysis of our membership to determine what education is needed as well as what partnerships may exist to offer our members those educational opportunities.

AdvanceU is a virtual based classroom with educational programs specifically designed to enhance the alignment of the fraternity/sorority experience with the changing dynamics of higher education. AdvanceU programs provide AFA members the opportunity to engage on a wide range of topics with content experts who develop a curriculum with a specific set of learning outcomes geared at achieving higher levels of professional competence in our members.

Due to the generous support of Zeta Tau Alpha, AdvanceU is free to all members of the Association. This virtual classroom experience provides members with supplemental reading materials, a learning guide for each seminar, and the opportunity to engage with seminar participants following the program. The goal is to provide seminars that range from new skill development to the application of new concepts. Participants are exposed to new best practices in higher education and then encouraged to apply those new concepts to our work with fraternities and sororities. Every AdvanceU session provides members the opportunity to continually develop as a professional, is grounded in the Core Competencies for Excellence in the Profession, and continues to AdvanceU.

The Global Service Initiative takes place in Jamaica. Participants spend a week connecting with each other though service to the community and a guided curriculum focused on global citizenship and social justice. It is a partnership with Delta Upsilon Fraternity and members must pay to attend.

The First 90 Days program is designed to help new fraternity/sorority professionals acclimate to one of the most unique roles in higher education. Through a series of interactive web conference sessions and special projects, participants build their networks, understand their positions, and learn how to put their expertise into practice.

The Collective is a pilot program to help AFA members connect, support, and develop one another. The program was developed to respond to feedback that members want to connect in a smaller, more intimate format that allows for mentorship and deeper discussion of content areas. Participation in this program allows members to develop connections with professionals across their region that are likely experiencing similar successes or difficulties.

Efficient Operations and Resource Management

In order to be good stewards of resources of both members, vendors, and supporters, operating in a cost-efficient and cost-effective manner is critical. Mentioned previously is utilizing a shared-staff model with AFLV. Neither organization has a need for full-time staff in every area, so sharing staff allows both organizations to have high-quality staff that has different peak times of work throughout the year. In addition, AFA is currently participating as a member of the Center for Fraternal Excellence. This Center has a shared CFO and "back end" operations such a phone system, time tracking system, and expense system. This model allows the Association to offer competitive staff benefits while reducing costs for shared financial services.

Communication

AFA produces three publications. They are *Perspectives* magazine, *Oracle: The Research Journal of the Association of Fraternity/Sorority Advisors*, and *Essentials* e-publication. Each publication has a team of volunteers who contribute and editors who are chosen to lead their work in conjunction with the Director of Marketing and Communications.

Essentials is a monthly educational e-publication provided to AFA members to explore selected topics. Editions seek to start conversations around the way we approach our work and to illuminate innovative ways of pushing the fraternal movement forward. Editions are typically published on the second Wednesday of each month from February to November. Please note that pieces included in *Essentials* provide various perspectives across the field of fraternity and sorority life, and thus may not be reflective of the policies or positions of the Association.

Perspectives is the quarterly magazine of AFA. *Perspectives* provides a forum for research, ideas, and information related to fraternities and sororities that: is thought-provoking and innovative, shares new information, highlights best practices, and challenges thought.

Perspectives promotes the exchange of various angles, arguments, contexts, and experiences to stimulate a deeper understanding of fraternity and sorority advising, education, programs, and policies. *Oracle: The Research Journal of the Association of Fraternity/Sorority Advisors* is a peer-reviewed electronic journal dedicated to the study of fraternities and sororities. Finally, *Oracle* content is also available across multiple academic indexes with full text.

The AFA Foundation

The fundraising arm of AFA is the AFA Foundation. The AFA Foundation is a 501(c) (3) nonprofit organization. Its mission is to secure, invest, and distribute the necessary resources to support the educational objectives of AFA and other relevant research, scholarship, and educational programming that furthers the fraternity/sorority advising profession. The Foundation has its own Board of Directors who have a Chair and an executive committee. These are volunteer roles within AFA. AFA and the AFA Foundation share an Executive Director and Assistant Executive Director and headquarters. The AFA President is an ex-officio member of the AFA Foundation. The Board of Directors of the two groups have do not overlap.

Resolutions

The business of the Association includes a number of resolutions passed to inform the work of fraternity and sorority. Resolutions include topics such as position statements on hazing, risk management, and education, commitment to diversity and inclusion, alcohol-free housing, and a myriad of other contemporary issues related to the work of fraternity and sorority. All resolutions are passed by the membership and listed on the Association's website, which is http://www.afa1976.org. Honorary resolutions may also be made to honor anniversaries of individual sororities or fraternities, umbrella groups, or long-time work in the field by an individual member, often upon retirement.

Code of Ethics

AFA has a Code of Ethics that was developed in 2003. This code replaced the Statement of Professional Ethics for Fraternity Advisors created in 1993. An initiative of the current Board of Directors is to evolve our current Code of Ethics.

Awards and Recognition

It is not unusual for an association of our size to have a significant number of volunteers. AFA is fortunate to have over 150 volunteers that provide timely feedback, assist in program planning, and help execute large events such as the annual meeting. Each year, AFA recognizes outstanding contributions by our members/colleagues in a variety of categories. Named awards include: the Dr. Robert H. Shaffer, Jack L. Anson, and Sue Kraft Fussell Distinguished Service Awards, and the Dr. Kent L. Gardner Award. All named awards are given out at the closing event of our annual meeting and are designed to recognize the highest achievement in fraternity/sorority advising. Additional awards are also presented during the annual meeting and highlight excellence in specific areas, including research and specific volunteer roles.

Looking to the Future

The role of a fraternity/sorority advisor has always been both a challenging and rewarding professional position. The fraternal experience (if implemented correctly) is unmatched in terms of the positive opportunities it can create for the collegiate member and the positive force for good it can be on a college campus. Unfortunately, the experience is not always lived as it was designed to be, and students sometimes make decisions with harmful and even tragic consequences. Fraternity and sorority advising professionals are often the youngest, least experienced, and most underpaid staff members in a division of student affairs. AFA's charge has been and will continue to be how to best prepare these professionals to tackle ongoing challenges and advocate for themselves and their students as an important part of the college experience. We welcome the opportunity to change and evolve with the times and do whatever is necessary to provide our members with the highest quality professional development experiences, programs, and services.

References

Bureau, D. (2006, Winter). afa: The First 30 Years. *Perspectives*, 7.

CHAPTER 22

Through the Years: A Reflective Look at the Evolution of NPHC

Jennifer Jones and Stacey Jones

Introduction: What is The National Pan-Hellenic Council

The National Pan-Hellenic Council Incorporated (NPHC) serves as a coordinating body for nine historically African American fraternities and sororities. Since its inception NPHC has worked as a collective to elevate the needs of the community through service as well as serving as a sounding board for national issues that impact African Americans. Over the years the structure of NPHC continues to evolve in an effort to provide effective leadership to member organizations while promoting the idea of collective responsibility as modeled by the Council of Presidents, which consists of the nine international presidents of the member organizations.

History

The Black Greek letter movement as we know it began when six African American students did not re-enroll at Cornell University for the 1905–1906 academic year, and the remaining students formed a study and support group. The formation of this group was a direct result of African American students not being allowed to take part in the various organizations that were on the Cornell campus that would have provided them with a means of support. Among the members of this group were the founders of Alpha

Phi Alpha Fraternity, Incorporated. The success of the study group led the students to consider how they could make the organization more meaningful and permanent.

On December 4, 1906, Henry Arthur Callis, Eugene Kinckle Jones, Robert Harold Ogle, Charles Henry Chapman, Nathaniel Allison Murray, George Biddle Kelly, and Vertner Woodson Tandy created Alpha Phi Alpha Fraternity, Incorporated, the first continuous African American collegiate-based fraternity in America. These seven men, known as the Seven Jewels of Alpha Phi Alpha Fraternity, decided to base the ideals of the organization on the concepts of manly deeds, scholarship, and love for all mankind. Although Alpha Phi Alpha was founded on a White campus, the Seven Jewels knew that the issues that brought them together were everywhere. They decided to establish a second chapter at Howard University, the preeminent African American university in the country. Alpha Phi Alpha's example would catch on and spur the development of seven similar organizations over the following 14 years.

Between the years 1908 and 1922, seven African American collegiate-based organizations were established. All eight groups were founded on four campuses. Three of the four campuses were predominately White institutions, in which one organization was founded per campus.

Table 22.1 African American Collegiate-Based Greek Letter Organizations Founded at Predominately White Institutions

Year Founded	Organization Name	Campus Founded
1906	Alpha Phi Alpha Fraternity, Inc.	Cornell University
1911	Kappa Alpha Psi Fraternity, Inc.	Indiana University
1922	Sigma Gamma Rho Sorority, Inc.	Butler University

The remaining five organizations were founded at Howard University, which can be called "the cradle of Black Greek Civilization." The culture of student life at Howard was very strict and disciplined, and the students used fraternities as a means of student expression and escape.

The creation of African American Greek letter organizations was similar to that of traditionally White Greek letter organizations. They both evolved from scholarly organizations, such as literary societies. Where they differ is in the fact that collegiate-based African American fraternities were created in the early 1900s, during a period of time when the national climate in the United States upheld racial injustice and inequality.

Table 22.2 African American Collegiate-Based Greek Letter Organizations Founded at Howard University.

Year Founded	Organization Name	Campus Founded
1908	Alpha Kappa Alpha Sorority, Inc.	Howard University
1911	Omega Psi Phi Fraternity, Inc.	Howard University
1913	Delta Sigma Theta Sorority, Inc.	Howard University
1914	Phi Beta Sigma Fraternity, Inc.	Howard University
1920	Zeta Phi Beta Sorority, Inc.	Howard University
1908	Alpha Kappa Alpha Sorority, Inc.	Howard University

The existence of African Americans was marginalized by a doctrine of separate but unequal treatment (Patton & Bonner, 2001). Yet some African Americans dared to occupy spaces formerly occupied only by Whites by attending predominately White colleges. African Americans who attended predominately White institutions during this period of time were forced to deal with the frightening task of navigating in a space where they were unwelcome. They also became quite familiar with the experience of being treated as nonentities by their White counterparts. The formation of African American fraternities and sororities created a stable connection for African American students, thus creating a safe haven and a place of refuge in an otherwise hostile institutional climate. The climate of hostility was especially prevalent as African American students began the arduous task of desegregating predominately White Southern institutions.

NPHC is composed of nine International Greek letter Sororities and Fraternities: Alpha Kappa Alpha Sorority, Inc. Alpha Phi Alpha Fraternity, Inc., Delta Sigma Theta Sorority, Inc., Zeta Phi Beta Sorority, Inc., Iota Phi Theta Fraternity, Inc., Kappa Alpha Psi Fraternity, Inc., Sigma Gamma Rho Sorority, Inc., Phi Beta Sigma Fraternity, Inc., and Omega Phi Psi Fraternity, Inc. NPHC promotes interaction through forums, meetings, and other mediums for the exchange of information and engages in cooperative programming and initiatives through various activities and functions.

On May 10, 1930, on the campus of Howard University, in Washington DC, the National Pan-Hellenic Council was formed as a permanent organization with the following charter members: Omega Psi Phi and Kappa Alpha Psi Fraternities, and Alpha Kappa Alpha, Delta Sigma Theta, and Zeta Phi Beta Sororities. In 1931, Alpha Phi Alpha and Phi Beta Sigma Fraternities joined the Council. Sigma Gamma Rho Sorority joined in 1937 and Iota Phi Theta Fraternity completed the list of member organizations in 1996. The stated purpose and mission of the organization in 1930 was "Unanimity of thought and action as far as possible in the conduct of Greek letter collegiate fraternities and sororities, and to consider problems of mutual interest to its member organizations." Early in 1937, the organization was incorporated under the laws of the State of Illinois and became known as the "National Pan-Hellenic Council, Incorporated."

Growth of NPHC Organizations

The growth of NPHC fraternities and sororities, on both historically White and historically Black campuses, can be viewed in three distinct phases:

- **Post-World War I**
  Undergraduate chapters of NPHC affiliate organizations began to spread to major research universities admitting Blacks and to major historically Black colleges in the South. Graduate chapters were birthed in cities across the U.S. as civic and service organizations, due to blatant racism prohibiting African Americans from participating in general civic organizations within their communities after college graduation.
- **Post-World War II**
  NPHC affiliate chapters proliferated on southern historically Black college campuses. Many cultural traditions which differed markedly from historically White college traditions became refined and embedded within the African American tradition and culture (e.g., "lining" and public skits on campus as a part of "pledging").
- **Post-Civil Rights Act 1964**
  Many colleges and universities which had previously denied admittance to African Americans or which had small enrollments grew in their enrollment of African Americans and established chapters on their campuses. Such actions caused the numbers of NPHC affiliate organizations to swell to over 400 undergraduate chapters and just as many graduate chapters on the average for each organization. Presently, there are approximately 1.5 million members of undergraduate and graduate affiliate chapters served by NPHC.
- In 1993, at the National Convention, NPHC hired its first National Executive Director, Dr. Michael V. W. Gordon.
- The first international council was chartered in February 1995 at Nassau, Bahamas by Dr. Gordon.
- The organization hired its second National Executive Director, Virginia M. Le Blanc, in February 2001 to run the headquarters, and the international reach of the National Pan-Hellenic Council expanded to encompass the NPHC of St. Croix (June 2001).
- Under the direction of the Council of Presidents, NPHC was formally restructured in December 2007 to meet the needs of our Undergraduate and Alumni councils across the United States. The COP and the Executive Committee of NPHC revisited the mission of the NPHC,

"Unanimity of thought and action as far as possible in the conduct of Greek letter fraternities and sororities," and decided that the mission still stands true for why we were formed, and this restructuring was to accommodate that mission.

- In January 2008, Beverly Burks was hired as a part-time executive director. In January 2009, that position was made full-time with Beverly Burks remaining executive director until 2018.

Organization of the NPHC

The NPHC organizational structure consists of the following:

- The Council of Presidents is made up of each National/International President of the nine member organizations of NPHC. The Council of Presidents shall have authority on all matters. (Article III Section 1 of the NPHC Constitution and By-Laws.) The Council of Presidents is composed of the International President of each member organization. The Council of Presidents selects their Chair from the members of the Council of Presidents.
- The NPHC Executive Committee is committed to continue to move NPHC forward under the leadership and guidance of the Council of Presidents. We are here to be a resource to each and every one of the NPHC councils, both graduate and undergraduate, and university officials. We strongly encourage you to also utilize the website. We will make every effort to keep you informed though this medium. The NPHC Executive Board is composed of:
  - President
  - Vice President
  - Secretary
  - Treasurer
  - Parliamentarian
  - Alumni Chair
  - Collegiate Chair
  - Convention and Conference Planning Chair
  - Programming Chair
  - Chaplain
  - Immediate Past President
  - Webmaster

- Undergraduate Councils are composed of undergraduate chapters of the nine member organizations. The Undergraduate NPHC Council, as well as the individual chapters, is a valuable asset to the university. Fraternity and sorority members are more likely to be loyal alumni following graduation, and they tend to participate in alumni contribution programs at their respective institutions. In addition, many members of NHPC organizations are campus student leaders. NPHC Undergraduate councils provide:
  - Preservation of the cultural heritage of the historically African American Greek-letter Organizations
  - Adequate and effective representation of the African American Greek-lettered organizations
  - A forum for addressing items of mutual interest and concern to the NPHC organizations
  - A minority view on majority campuses
  - An experience of self-governance necessary to the development of the emergent leaders
  - An organization that does not base fines, assessments, and penalties on unrealistic membership goals or housing policies.
  - Uniform membership intake procedures and standards of conduct for NPHC organizations
  - A body able to recommend changes to the national body
- The Alumni Councils are composed of alumni chapters of the nine NPHC affiliate organizations. The alumni councils serve as the means by which the organized activities of the professional and intellectual leaders in the Black community become a reality. At a time when Blacks are afflicted with high poverty levels, large school dropout rates, and overall economic deprivation, the NPHC alumni councils carry the leadership banner in the minority communities. By combining resources, NPHC organizations make a much more significant impact. Among many other projects, the alumni councils provide:
  - A framework for joint community service projects and other activities and functions
  - A forum for the discussion of common goals and items of mutual interest and concern among the nine affiliate member organizations
  - A network for the promotion of continued social progress
  - A body able to recommend changes to the national body

Services Provided by NPHC

- Monitors federal and state legislative and regulatory activities and other matters of mutual concern to NPHC organizations.
- Spearheads joint action by NPHC member organizations, where appropriate, and maintains active and open communication with the executive offices of each of the nine member organizations.
- Publishes national newsletters, which allow NPHC undergraduate and alumni councils to exchange ideas and resources.
- Conducts national workshops and webinars on issues specific to NPHC member chapters and councils.
- Serves as a resource sharing body and engages in constructive discussions on areas of mutual interest with other Greek federations, associations, and university Greek administrators.
- Provides sample bylaws and rules of operations for alumni and undergraduate councils. The collegiate and alumni chair work directly with alumni councils and collegiate councils and advise on NPHC organization, shared standards, and constitutional revisions.
- Provides consultation to councils and universities on NPHC matters.
- Assists the nine member organizations in meeting their individual objectives, where requested.
- Conducts awards programs, which recognize councils and member organizations for outstanding service.
- Conducts a biennial national leadership conference, which provides the opportunity for NPHC members to exchange ideas and solutions to common problems.

The History of the NPHC Shared Standards

Out of a response to the efforts of the Franklin Square Group, this is a group of university presidents, the American Association of State Colleges and Universities, the National Association of Independent Colleges and Universities, the National Association of State Universities and Land Grant Colleges, and inter/national Greek organization executive directors, in the development of criteria to be used by campuses in defining campus expectations for Greek chapters, the NPHC shared standards were drafted.

NPHC felt that this was an opportunity to assist institutions of higher learning across the nation and abroad in understanding the history and function of Black fraternities and sororities, and the standards governing these organizations, and to continue to address issues of mutual concern.

Under the direction of President, Michael Bowie, the first draft of the standards were developed by First Vice President, Jennifer M. Jones, with the assistance of the National Executive Director of NPHC, Virginia LeBlanc, and National Executive Director of Kappa Alpha Psi, Richard Snow. Many revisions later, a final draft was distributed to the Council of Presidents for feedback and approval. The approved shared standards were disseminated to all NPHC councils.

National Initiatives of NPHC

NPHC promotes national initiatives, which are typically related to current social issues as well as promote collaboration between NPHC and various community partners. Current initiatives include but are not limited to:

- **Law & Your Community**
  The National Pan-Hellenic Council and The National Organization of Black Law Enforcement Executives developed a partnership in 2016. The National Organization of Black Law Enforcement Executives (NOBLE) represents chief executive officers and command-level law enforcement officials from federal, state, county, municipal law enforcement agencies, and criminal justice practitioners. Councils were encouraged to host Law & Your Community events in their area. The Law & Your Community is a nationally recognized hands-on interactive training program for young people ages 13–18 designed to improve their communications with law enforcement officers and their understanding of their federal, state, and local laws.

- **Get Out the Vote Initiative**
  In 2016, the Council of Presidents created a Social Action Taskforce consisting of each of the respective political and social action leaders of each of our member organizations. This committee was charged to work on a plan of action to identify all the work that needs to be done in this election process in partnership with the NAACP. The Social Action Task Force has been diligent in their work and are now ready to launch the election initiative. Attached you will find a letter explaining the goals of the initiative and a getting started toolkit. We also provided a webinar on the Task Force initiative. Should you have any questions, you may contact NPHC Programming Chair, Deena Weems Thornton.

- **#NPHCUNITED4SERVICE**
  The National Pan-Hellenic Council will promote a #NPHCUnited-4Service initiative from April 10, 2016 through May 10, 2016. This time was selected to coincide with the anniversary of the founding of the

NPHC on May 10, 1930. NPHC councils, NPHC member organizations, and members of NPHC organizations will be encouraged to engage in a day of community service project(s) during the designated period.

- **Congressional Black Caucus Forum**
  - The purpose of the forum is to bring together Members of Congress who are members of NPHC organizations and the presidents of NPHC organizations to discuss relevant civil rights issues and the most effective ways to combat them.
  - The sessions raise awareness and act as a voice to some of today's pressing issues in the African American community.
  - The Forum always includes a call to action for the presidents of the NPHC organizations to devise a plan to mobilize their membership to ensure that our voices are heard.
- **"All of Us" Research Program**
  The National Pan-Hellenic Council and several of its member organizations have partnered with the National Institute of Health on the *All of Us* Research Program. This program is a historic effort to gather data from one million or more people living in the United States to accelerate research and improve health. By taking into account individual differences in lifestyle, environment, and biology, researchers will uncover paths toward delivering precision medicine.

"Why the Tradition Must Continue on College Campuses"

To understand the need for and concept of the National Pan-Hellenic Council, Inc., one must first consider, understand, and familiarize oneself with the historical accounts and significance of predominantly Black Greek-letter organizations. While having their own distinct heritages, the nine member organizations of NPHC offer insight and a unique perspective into this understanding and the development of Black socioeconomic and cultural life.

Each of the nine NPHC organizations evolved during a period when African Americans were being denied essential rights and privileges afforded others. Racial isolation on predominantly White campuses and social barriers of class on all campuses created a need for African Americans to align themselves with other individuals sharing common goals and ideals. With the realization of such a need, the African American (Black) Greek-lettered organization movement took on the personae of a haven and outlet, which could foster brotherhood and sisterhood in the pursuit to bring about social change through the development of social programs that would create positive change for Blacks and the country. Today the need remains the same.

While NPHC affiliate organizations recognize the social aspect of Greek college life, the primary purpose and focus of member organizations remains community awareness and action through educational, economic, and cultural service activities. NPHC affiliates and their respective members have pledged to devote their resources to service in their respective communities, realizing that the membership experience of NPHC organizations goes beyond organizational membership during an individual's college career. A lifetime commitment to the goals and ideals of each respective organization is stressed. The individual member is also expected to align himself with a graduate/alumni chapter, following graduation from college, with the expectation that he/she will attend regular chapter meetings, regional conferences, and national conventions, and take an active part in matters concerning and affecting the community in which he or she lives.

The need to form campus-based councils to represent NPHC affiliate organizations is not motivated by a "separatist" philosophy. The establishment of councils assists in maintaining a distinct identity as "service based organizations," as opposed to organizations that may be strictly social in nature; NPHC, Inc. does not advocate a disassociation from NIC, NPC, or NALFO organizations on college campuses. The council's purpose is to promote unity and expose members to the "service for life" philosophy and foster leadership development and scholarship. Furthermore, the National Pan-Hellenic Council provides a forum for participation and interaction among the members of affiliate organizations and the organizations themselves. It provides for a stronger unified voice and a stronger unified body. The continued advocacy for the establishment of local councils not only stems from tradition, but also from the realization that many colleges and universities maintain organization registration policies requiring an organization to belong to a national organization, and that national organization to a national umbrella organization, in order to function on that respective campus.

It is the endeavor of NPHC, Inc. to foster a more stable environment on campuses for local NPHC councils, provide a forum for dialogue, and provide training for and management of its respective councils. Having such an entity in place to serve as an umbrella organization centralizes and provides a clearinghouse for information sanctioned by the NPHC Council of Presidents, whether on the university/college campus and/or in civic, social, and political arenas. It is essential to have such a voice to advocate concerns of local councils and assert the position of the national body, particularly in decisions or rulings that may have a negative impact.

We pay tribute to the past and current NPHC national presidents for their leadership and service. Because of their leadership NPHC has been able to thrive and remain relevant for Black Greek Letter Organizations for the past 88 years.

Table 22.3 Past and Current NPHC National Presidents.

Date	Name	Sorority/Fraternity
1930–1933	Atty. Matthew W. Bullock	Omega Psi Phi
1933–1936	Atty. J. Ernest Williams	Kappa Alpha Psi
1936–1938	Maude B. Porter	Alpha Kappa Alpha
1938–1940	William C. Pyant	Alpha Phi Alpha
1940–1941	Joanna H. Ransom	Zeta Phi Beta
1941–1943	Atty. George W. Lawrence	Phi Beta Sigma
1944–1946	Bertha Black Rhoda	Sigma Gamma Rho
1946–1948	Ellsworth J. Evans	Kappa Alpha Psi
1948–1950	Mae Wright Downs	Delta Sigma Theta
1950–1952	Atty. Victor J Ashe	Kappa Alpha Psi
1954–1956	Arnette G. Wallace	Alpha Kappa Alpha
1956–1958	Dr. Ernest Wilkins, Jr.	Kappa Alpha Psi
1958–1960	Geraldine Elliott	Zeta Phi Beta
1960–1962	Rev. Julius Simmons, Sr.	Phi Beta Sigma
1962–1964	Edna Douglas	Sigma Gamma Rho
1964–1967	Dr. Alvin J. McNeil	Phi Beta Sigma
1967–1969	Dr. Walter J. Washington	Alpha Phi Alpha
1969–1971	Carey B. Preston	Alpha Kappa Alpha
1971–1972	Mildred C. Bradham	Zeta Phi Beta
1972–1974	Earl A Morris	Kappa Alpha Psi
1974–1976	James T. Bailey	Omega Psi Phi
1976–1978	Dr. Alice M. Swain	Sigma Gamma Rho
1978–1983	Charles B. Wright	Phi Beta Sigma
1983–1985	Beatrice McGowens-Jett	Alpha Kappa Alpha
1985–1989	Dr. Gilbert H. Francis	Phi Beta Sigma
1989–1993	Dr. Ada J. Jackson	Alpha Kappa Alpha
1993–1995	Daisy M. Wood	Delta Sigma Theta
1995–1997	Carter D. Womack	Phi Beta Sigma
1997–1999	Gregory Austin	Omega Psi Phi
1999–2003	Cassandra Black	Zeta Phi Beta
2003–2007	Dr. Mike Bowie	Omega Psi Phi
2007–2017	Jennifer Jones	Zeta Phi Beta
2018–Present	Vanetta Cheecks Reeder	Sigma Gamma Rho

REFERENCES

Baird, W.R. (1991). *Baird's manual of American college fraternities* (20th ed.). Indianapolis, IN: Baird's Manual Foundation Incorporated.

Gregory, D. E. (2003). *The administration of fraternal organizations on North American campuses: A pattern for the new millennium.* Ashville, NC: College Administration Publications, Incorporated.

Johnson, C. S. (1972). *Fraternities in our colleges.* Manesha, WI: George Banta College, Incorporated.

Jones, S. L. (2007). *Narrating the history of African American Greeks at the University of Alabama: Voices from the past* (Unpublished Doctoral Dissertation). The University of Alabama, Tuscaloosa, AL.

Kimbrough, W. M. (2003). *Black Greek 101: The culture, customs, and challenges of Black frater-nities and sororities.* Cranbury, NJ: Associated University Press.

Patton, L.A., & Bonner, F. A. (2001). Advising the Black Greek letter organization (HBGLO): A reason for angst or euphoria? *NASAP Journal, 4,* 1.

Ross, L. C. (2000) *The divine nine: The history of African American fraternities and sororities.* New York, NY: Kensington Publishing Corporation.

Contributors

GARY BALLINGER is a doctoral candidate in Educational Leadership (Higher Education Administration) at Indiana State University. He serves as the Director of Fraternity and Sorority Life at Arizona State University. He has worked in fraternity and sorority advising at the University of Arizona, the University of New Mexico, and in the offices of two national headquarters. His research interests include college and university presidential leadership, fraternity and sorority life, and minoritized student experiences on college campuses. Gary is a member of Phi Delta Theta Fraternity and was a founding father of his chapter at Eastern Illinois University. He has been an active volunteer in the fraternity and sorority movement for nearly twenty years.

DR. JIM BARBER is the Clark G. and Elizabeth H. Diamond Associate Professor of Education at the College of William and Mary. He is an expert in the areas of college student development, assessing student learning, and integrative learning. His research has been published in the *American Educational Research Journal, Journal of College Student Development, Journal of Higher Education, Journal of Diversity in Higher Education, and Change* Magazine. He is currently writing a book, *Integration of Learning,* about how college students learn across contexts. Prior to his faculty appointment, he worked in student affairs administration for nearly a decade, specializing in fraternity and sorority affairs, residence life and student activities. He currently serves as the Editor of *Oracle: The Research Journal of the Association of Fraternity/Sorority Advisors.* He was previously on the Board of Directors for the Center for Fraternity/Sorority Research at Indiana University and is a Faculty Fellow for Sigma Phi Epsilon Fraternity at William & Mary.

DR. J. PATRICK BIDDIX is professor Higher Education and Associate Director of the Postsecondary Education Research Center (PERC) at the University of Tennessee. His research and teaching focus on research design and assessment, student engagement and involvement, and postsecondary outcomes. Dr. Biddix is the author of *Research*

Methods and Applications for Student Affairs (Jossey-Bass, 2018) and co-authored the 2nd edition textbook of *Assessment in Student Affairs* (Jossey-Bass, 2016). He serves as the Associate Editor for Books for the *Journal of College Student Development* (JCSD). In 2015, he received a Fulbright Scholar Award to study in Montreal, Canada. Dr. Biddix is a recognized expert in fraternity and sorority research. He has authored numerous publications and reports on membership correlates and has appeared in national media, including National Public Radio (NPR). In 2014, he co-authored *The Influence of Fraternity and Sorority Involvement: A Critical Analysis of Research* (1996-2013) (ASHE, Jossey-Bass, 2014). He has completed grant-funded research with the National Panhellenic Conference (NPC) and is currently working with North-American Interfraternity Conference (NIC) to evaluate their new Health and Safety Initiative (HSI). From 2010-2013, Dr. Biddix served as Editor of *Oracle: The Research Journal of the Association of Fraternity/Sorority Advisors*.

DR. DAN BUREAU is the Assistant Vice President for Student Affairs at the University of Memphis. He has worked in higher education for 22 years in a range of roles and has consulted on fraternity and sorority life matters for over 35 campuses. He received his PhD in Higher Education and Student Affairs from Indiana University in 2011. He is past president of the Association of Fraternity/Sorority Advisors and is widely recognized for his research on the fraternity/sorority experience.

TEVIS BRYANT is Director of Student Life at Plymouth State University and was previously Associate Director of Intercultural Affairs and Inclusive Programing at Lebanon Valley College. He is a member of Psi Sigma Phi Multicultural Fraternity, Inc. where he serves on their national board. He is also a doctoral student in the Higher Education program at Rowan University.

DR. MONICA GALLOWAY BURKE, an Associate Professor in the Department of Counseling and Student Affairs at Western Kentucky University, has 19 years of experience as a faculty member and practitioner in Student Affairs and Higher Education. She has served as the lead author for *Helping Skills for Working with College Students: Applying Counseling Theory to Student Affairs Practice* (Routledge), authored several peer-reviewed articles in scholarly journals, and contributed chapters to various books. Additionally, Dr. Burke has conducted numerous workshops and presentations at the international, national, regional, state, and local levels.

ZACHARY CARR serves as Associate Director, Center for Service Learning & Volunteerism at the University of Memphis facilitating specialized leadership and service learning programs and has extensive experience designing and facilitating programming for fraternity and sorority life students. Zachary obtained a Bachelor of Arts degree in Communication Studies at the University of Southern Mississippi and a Masters of Arts in Higher Education Administration at Louisiana State University.

GRESHAM D. COLLOM is a Graduate Research Assistant at the University of Tennessee, Knoxville at the Postsecondary Education Research Center. His areas of research interest include access to and experiences in higher education for underrepresented populations, public policy in higher education, and international higher education. Collom is a doctoral student in the Educational Leadership and Policy Studies program with an emphasis in Higher Education Administration. Gresham most recently served as the Residential Learning Advisor for University Housing at the University of Wisconsin – Whitewater. He also has experience in Multicultural Affairs, International Student Affairs, and First Year Experience.

DR. MANUEL DEL REAL has been a member of a Latino fraternity for 11 years and an active alumnus serving as an advisor for a local chapter and chairmen of the Rocky Mountain Alumni Network. Manuel Del Real is an Assistant Director of Student Life at Front Range Community College and is an Adjunct Faculty in the Ethnic Studies Department at Colorado State University. He previously was the Assistant Director for El Centro, the Latinx cultural center, also at Colorado State University. His dissertation was an exploratory case study of five chapters of a Latino fraternity in the Midwest region of the U.S., using critical race theory to illustrate how they contribute to civic engagement.

DR. BRYAN DOSONO earned his PhD in Information Science and Technology from Syracuse University in 2019. His research seeks to understand how Asian Pacific Islander Desi Americans (APIDA) construct and express their identity in online communities and his dissertation research uncovers the ways in which APIDAs negotiate collective action in the context of online identity work. He holds a Bachelor of Science degree with honors in Informatics (Human-Computer Interaction) from the University of Washington. Dosono is an initiated member of Phi Beta Kappa Society, Lambda Phi Epsilon International Fraternity, and has served on the NAPA Board.

ALLISON SWICK-DUTTINE has served as Director of Fraternity/Sorority Life at SUNY Plattsburgh since 1998 after receiving her M.A. in Student Affairs Counseling from Marshall University. She has served as a National Vice President for Sigma Sigma Sigma Sorority, the founding President of the HazingPrevention.Org Board of Directors, the editor of the Association of Fraternity/Sorority Advisors *Perspectives* magazine and a board members for the Northeast Greek Leadership Association Board of Directors.

BRIAN GEE has been a proud member of Pi Alpha Phi Fraternity, Inc., since 1988. He previously served as Pi Alpha Phi's National President and currently serves as its

Director of Risk Reduction. He cares deeply about hazing prevention and has been quoted on the topic on NPR's *Tell Me More* and the *Wall Street Journal*. He has worked with NAPA since its inception in 2004 and served as the Executive Chair from 2012-2014. He is proud to see the positive impact NAPA has made in the communities it serves.

DR. DENNIS E. GREGORY currently serves as Associate Professor of Higher Education at Old Dominion University in Norfolk, Virginia. He has more than 75 articles, book chapters, book reviews and other publications, and over 250 speeches, presentations, co-presentations, research paper presentations and key note addresses. He is a sought after speaker on the Clery Campus Safety Act, the First Amendment, Title IX, and other legal issues. He served as a Fulbright Fellow to Portugal in 2014 and as a member of a Fulbright Regional Selection Committee from 2015-2017. His book, *The Administration of Fraternal Organizations on North American Campuses: A Pattern for the New Millennium*, was published in 2003. Prior to becoming a full-time faculty member in 2000, Dr. Gregory served as a student affairs administrator for almost 25 years. He has extensive international experience and travels broadly doing research and speaking.

KELLY JO KARNES HENDRICKS currently serves as the Director of the Morris University Center, Student Success Center and Kimmel Student Involvement Center Southern Illinois University Edwardsville. She earned her B.S. in Elementary Education from Emporia State University and her M.S. in Higher Education Administration from the University of Kansas. Kelly Jo has worked in student activities, fraternity and sorority life, and leadership programs at the University of Kansas; Old Dominion University in Norfolk, VA.; and the University of Iowa. She transitioned to the Director of the MUC, SSC and Kimmel in 2016. She is originally from Lawrence, KS. Kelly Jo was the 2010 President of the Association of Fraternity/Sorority Advisors (AFA) and is a Co-Lead Facilitator for the LeaderShape Institute. She serves as a volunteer for her sorority, Sigma Sigma Sigma, and as a delegate to the National Panhellenic Conference (NPC). In her free time, Kelly Jo loves to spend time with family and friends, travel, cook/eat great food and watch college basketball. She also loves to spend time with her partner Harold and their daughter, Harper Jo.

DR. AARON W. HUGHEY is a professor and program coordinator in the Department of Counseling and Student Affairs at Western Kentucky University. He supervises the graduate degree program in student affairs in higher education as well as graduate certificate programs in international student services and career services. He was head of the department for five years before returning to the faculty in 2008. He also served as Interim Director of WKU's Knicely Institute for Economic Development. Before joining the faculty in 1991, he was the Associate Director of University Housing. He has authored (or co-authored) over 60 refereed publications on such subjects including higher education administration, student affairs, counseling and testing, diversity, leadership, teams, and management. Substance abuse disorders are one of his specialties; he regularly presents and conducts webinars on this issue. He also consults extensively with regional companies and schools and provides training sessions and programs on a variety of topics such as total quality, statistical process control, teams, diversity, leadership/supervision, change management and motivation.

JENNIFER M. JONES is the Executive Director of Student Life at Southern Methodist University where she has been employed for over 30 years, 16 of those years in various positions within Residence Life and Student Housing. She received both her BA in Sociology and Master of Liberal Arts both from Southern Methodist University. In various capacities, Ms. Jones has given workshops on college campuses across the country. She has served as the President of the National Pan-Hellenic Council for the past 10 years.

DR. STACY L. JONES has been a devoted Student Affairs practitioner at the University of Alabama for more than 20 years. At UA she serves as the Associate Dean of Students and an Adjunct Faculty member. She serves the community both locally and nationally as a motivational speaker, Secretary of the National Society of Collegiate Scholars, the Vice President of NPHC, an educational consultant, and is an active compassionate community servant. She has received numerous honors and awards for her hard work and dedication. Dr. Jones is a dedicated member of Zeta Phi Beta Sorority, Inc. where she has served as a local, state, and regional officer.

BRIAN JOYCE is the Director of Greek Life at Dartmouth College. He has served as a practitioner in Student Affairs for over 12 years with progressive leadership experience in fraternity and sorority life, student activities, and new student orientation. He obtained his Ph.D. in Education Leadership with an emphasis in higher education from Clemson University. His dissertation explored the socialization of race in traditionally and predominantly White fraternities. Brian is a proud member of Lambda Chi Alpha. He served his national fraternity as a Master Steward, in which he traveled the country to host training workshops for undergraduate fraternity men on topics such as recruitment, risk management, values congruence, and inclusivity.

ALEXANDRIA KENNEDY has worked in fraternity/sorority life for over 4 years, both as a campus based professional and a headquarters professional. Alex earned her B.A. in communication from Central Michigan University and her M.A.E. from Western Kentucky University. She is a proud member and volunteer of Alpha Gamma Delta International Women's Fraternity.

WENDI KINNEY joined the Geneseo staff in 2001 and currently serves as the Associate Dean of Students for Fraternal Life & Off Campus Services. Prior to her tenure at Geneseo, Wendi worked at Sigma Kappa Sorority's national headquarters in Indianapolis,

IN as the Associate Director of Finance. She earned her Bachelor's Degree in Medical Technology from SUNY Fredonia, where she was initiated into the Theta Iota chapter of Sigma Kappa, and a Master's Degree in Higher Education Administration from the University at Buffalo. In addition to her work with Geneseo fraternities and sororities, Wendi is involved in the fraternal movement at the national and regional level. Wendi served as the Executive Director of the Northeast Greek Leadership Association from 2010-2016 and is a former Region I Director for the Association of Fraternity/Sorority Advisors. Additionally, she served as the convenor and first president of the SUNY Fraternity/Sorority Advisors Association. Wendi is an honorary member of Order of Omega, Golden Key, Phi Eta Sigma, and National Residence Hall Honor Society. She was awarded the SUNY Chancellor's Award for Excellence in Professional Service in 2013, the Sue Kraft Fussell Distinguished Service Award from AFA in 2015, and the National Order of Omega Outstanding Professional Award in 2016.

DR. ADAM MCCREADY is faculty member at the University of Connecticut in the Higher Education in Student Affairs program. He earned his PhD from Boston College, studying the relationships among chapter-held masculine norms, organizational socialization, and the problematic behaviors of fraternity men. Prior to his doctoral work, he served as a campus fraternity/sorority advisor for 7 years, holding positions at Massachusetts Institute of Technology and the University of New Hampshire. Also, he served as international president of his fraternity, Theta Delta Chi, from 2007 to 2011.

KARA MILLER MCCARTHY is the Director of Sorority & Fraternity Life at Cornell University. She has worked in the field of sorority and fraternity advising full-time since 2003. She is a proud member of Sigma Sigma Sigma and currently serves on their Executive Council. Kara is a doctoral candidate in higher education at Colorado State University. She has volunteered for the Association of Fraternity/Sorority Advisors since 2002 and is the immediate past President of AFA for 2017-2018. Kara is a past volunteer with the Northeast Greek Leadership Association (NGLA).

DR. ROBIN ZAPE-TAH-HOL-AH MINTHORN (Kiowa/Umatilla/Nez Perce/Apache and Assiniboine), an Associate Professor at the University of New Mexico in Educational Leadership and Native American Studies. Dr. Minthorn is the coordinator for the Native American Leadership in Education (NALE) doctoral cohorts in the Educational Leadership Program and currently serves as the Kiva Club co-advisor. Her research interests include: Indigenous leadership in higher education, intergenerational Indigenous leadership perspectives and Native college student experiences. She is co-editor of the *Indigenous Leadership in Higher Education* published through Routledge and *Reclaiming Indigenous Research in Higher Education* published through Rutgers University Press.

MÓNICA LEE MIRANDA is the current Director for the Center of Student Involvement at the University of South Florida and is a doctoral candidate at the University of Rochester. As Director she provides leadership, strategic planning, assessment, and direct coordination for campus wide programming and student involvement that enhances student learning and engagement. She is also the first person of color to serve as President for the Association of Fraternity/Sorority Advisors. Monica is also one of the leaders within the Latinx fraternal movement.

DR. ERIC M. NORMAN serves as the Vice President for Student Affairs at Austin Peay State University. Dr. Norman is the former editor and associate editor for *Oracle: The Research Journal of the Association of Fraternity/Sorority Advisors*, and he remains on the Editorial Board. He was also a contributor to the ASHE Higher Education Report *The Influence of Fraternity and Sorority Involvement: A critical Analysis of Research (1996-2013)*. We is also the former Vice Chancellor for Student Affairs and Dean of Students at Purdue University Fort Wayne, the Associate Dean of Students at Louisiana State University, the Director for Fraternity and Sorority Life at Virginia Tech, and the Assistant Director for Fraternities, Sororities, Registered Student Organizations, and Leadership Development at the University of Delaware.

SALLY PARISH serves as the Associate Dean for Student Leadership & Involvement at the University of Memphis where she provides leadership and strategic direction to a department of 17 staff, three functional areas, and 100+ programs a year. Prior to her current role, Sally served as the founding director of the Center for Leadership & Service and as a Co-Coordinator of the Leadership Studies Minor both at the University of Tennessee Knoxville. A first-generation college graduate of the University of Memphis and former sorority chapter president, Sally also has her masters degree in Higher Education Administration from Florida International University and is pursuing doctoral studies at the UofM. Sally is a Certified Strengths Coach with over 10 years of consulting and training experience in the corporate, education and non-profit sectors. She is active as an adjunct faculty member, chairman of the board for a local non-profit volunteer center, and in a number of professional associations and volunteer roles.

DR. GREGORY PARKS is Associate Dean of Research, Public Engagement, & Faculty Development and Professor of Law at Wake Forest University School of Law. A lawyer and PhD psychologist, Professor Parks teaches courses, researches, and writes in the areas of civil litigation, race and law, and social science and law. After law school, Professor Parks clerked for The Honorable Anna Blackburne-Rigsby on the District of Columbia Court of Appeals and then for The Honorable Andre M. Davis on the United States Court of Appeals for the Fourth Circuit. Thereafter, he served as a Visiting Fellow at Cornell Law School and then an Associate in the Litigation Group at McDermott Will & Emery in their Washington, D.C. office. Professor Parks has published ten, scholarly books on topics ranging from black Greek-letter organizations to race in America to social science and law. His books have been published by the likes of Oxford University Press, NYU Press, The New Press, University Press of Kentucky, and the University Press of Mississippi. Professor Parks' works have also appeared in a range of law reviews, such as *Cardozo Law Review, University of Pennsylvania Law Review, Indiana Law Journal, Florida State University Law Review, Howard Law Journal,* and the *Cornell Journal of Law & Public Policy.* He's currently writing a book about the history of African American fraternity and sorority racial uplift work for NYU Press.

DR. SCOTT RADIMER is the Director of Research, Assessment & Planning at the University of Memphis for the Division of Student Affairs, as well as an Adjunct Faculty Member in the Leadership department in the College of Education, teaching the College Student Development graduate seminar. Dr. Radimer earned his PhD in Higher Education from Boston College, and completed his dissertation examining the relationship between gender norms, ethnic identity, and social dominance orientation and alcohol use among undergraduate men. He has presented at state, regional, and national higher education conferences on topics ranging from supervising new professionals, first generation college students and social media use, and undergraduate men's alcohol use. Prior to entering the doctoral program at Boston College, Scott worked in Residential Life at Bentley University and Vassar College. He earned his Masters of Science degree in Higher Education from the Florida State University, and was also the Assistant Swim Coach for the Men's and Women's team at Florida A&M University while in Tallahassee. Scott earned his Bachelor of Arts degree in Political Science from the University of Vermont.

TODD ROTGERS currently serves as the Senior Director of Undergraduate Services at Phi Gamma Delta's International Headquarters where he oversees all fraternity operations related to undergraduate chapters and colonies. Prior to his current role, he served as the Director of Education overseeing leadership development and health and safety initiatives. Prior to joining Phi Gamma Delta's staff, Todd served as a Graduate Advisor in the Office of Student Activities at Western Illinois University for the Panhellenic Council, National Pan-Hellenic Council, and Multicultural Greek Council. Todd has presented at the Association of Fraternity/Sorority Advisors, Association of Fraternal Leadership & Values (AFLV), and ACPA--College Educators International. He has volunteered his time for the North-American Inter-fraternity Conference educational programs and AFLV.

DR. PIETRO A. SASSO is Assistant Professor and Program Director of College Student Personnel Administration at Southern Illinois University Edwardsville. He has published over 40 scholarly articles and book chapters. He is the editor and author of 6 other texts, including *Today's College Students* (2014), *Higher Education and Society*

(2016), *Colleges at the Crossroads: Taking Sides on Contested Issues* (2018), and *The Dynamic Student Development Meta-Theory: A New Model for Student Success* (2018), and *Student Activism in the Academy: Its Struggles and Promise* (2019). His research interests include identity construction of traditional undergraduates (college student development), alcohol misuse in higher education (student health outcomes), the impact of the college fraternity experience, and masculinity in higher education.

DR. CRISTOBAL SALINAS JR. is an assistant professor in the Educational Leadership and Research Methodology Department at Florida Atlantic University. He coauthored the *Iowa's Community Colleges: A Collective History of Fifty Years of Accomplishment* book. Cristobal is the co-founder and Managing Editor for the *Journal Committed to Social Change on Race and Ethnicity*. His research promotes access and quality in higher education, and explores the social, political, and economic context of education opportunities for historically marginalized communities, with an emphasis on Latino/a communities of people.

DR. SARAH SCHOPER is an independent consultant and instructor. Prior to Sarah becoming a consultant and instructor she worked in a variety of positions such as advising the Student Government, advising Fraternity and Sorority Life, student organization student discipline/conduct issues, student leadership development programming, new student orientation, and student organization risk management and training. As an instructor Sarah has taught First Year experience courses, as well as a variety of courses including student development theory, organizational development theory, and helping skills. Sarah's main research area is on transformative learning and first-generation college students. Originally from Des Moines, Iowa, Sarah received her Bachelor of Science from TCU, Fort Worth, TX, and her Master of Science degree from Miami University, Oxford, OH. Finally, Sarah received her Doctorate of Philosophy from the University of Maryland, College Park, in Counseling and Personnel Services in 2011. Sarah is involved in ACPA—College Student Educators International serving as the research coordinator for the Coalition for (Dis)abilities, and as an expert speaker for the American Student Government Association (ASGA). She is a 2014 recipient of the Annuit Coeptis Award from ACPA, and a 2018 ACPA Foundation Research Grant award recipient. In addition to her professional work in Student Affairs, Sarah is a member of Pi Beta Phi fraternity (Past International Risk Management Officer and Chapter Advisor) and Mortar Board Honor Society.

HANNAH SEOH has an extensive volunteer history in the interfraternal world. She is the current Chair of the National APIDA Panhellenic Association (NAPA) and Director of Partnerships for the Delta Phi Lambda Foundation. She previously served on the sorority's national board from 2003-2013, serving as National President from 2007-2013. Additionally, Hannah has volunteered in various capacities for the Association of

Fraternity & Sorority Advisors, the Northeast Greek Leadership Association, and the Association of Fraternal Leadership & Values. Professionally, Hannah is the Director of Planning for the Center for Health Equity at the NYC Department of Health and Mental Hygiene. She earned a bachelor's in mathematics from the University of Cincinnati and a master's of public health and a master's of science, both from The Ohio State University.

SARAH J. SPANGENBURG is a law student at Wake Forest University School of Law and a 2016 graduate of John Carroll University. She was selected to be an Executive Editor for the Wake Forest Law Review for the 2018-2019 school year. She has been published as a co-author with Gregory S. Parks, JD, Ph.D, in the UC Hastings *Women's Law Journal*.

KRISTEN J. WAGNER is the Manager of Educational Initiatives at Alpha Xi Delta Fraternity Headquarters where she creates and manages educational programming and leadership development for undergraduate members. Prior to joining Alpha Xi Delta's staff, she served as the Associate Director of Student Activities at Simpson College overseeing and advising Fraternity and Sorority Life, Student Government, Campus Activities Board, student organizations, as well as New Student Programs. Prior to becoming a practitioner, Kristen served as a Graduate Advisor at Western Illinois University for the Interfraternity Council and Panhellenic Council. Kristen has presented at the National Association for Campus Activities (NACA) and has volunteered her time for educational programming and leadership institutes for multiple fraternity and sorority organizations.

DR. JESSICA WARD earned his doctoral degree in Educational Leadership (Higher Education Administration) at Indiana State University. She currently serves as the Assistant Director for the Office of Student Standards and the Coordinator for Gender and Sexual Diversity at Eastern Illinois University. She received her Master's degree from the University of Kansas in Higher Education Administration and her bachelor's degree in Rhetoric and Political Science from Georgia College and State University. Her research interest include transgender individuals within higher education and the inter-sectionality of identities within minoritized populations. She was a collegiate member of Gamma Sigma Sigma, and has enjoyed of fraternity advisement during her professional career.

NATHAN WEHR currently serves as the Interim Director of Fraternity and Sorority Programs at Eastern Illinois University. He received his Master's degree from Eastern Illinois University in College Student Affairs and his bachelor's degree in Public Relations and Advertising with an emphasis in Public Relations along with a minor in Communication Studies from the University of Southern Indiana. His research interest includes the support of LGBTQIAA students within a social fraternity and the fraternity and sorority experience. He is a member of Lambda Chi Alpha Fraternity and enjoys volunteering with his fraternity.

CYNTHIA ALLEN WESTON, a Phi Beta Kappa graduate of Emory University, is author of the history *Ordinary Miracles: 100 Years of Kappa Delta Sorority*. She has published and spoken extensively on topics related to women's fraternal groups. As a member of the National Panhellenic Conference delegation body, she has served on the Archives, College Panhellenics, Editorial, and Measurable Outcomes Committees.

DR. CAROLYN WHITTIER has been a higher education professional for over 19 years, specializing in fraternity and sorority life, student development, leadership programming, and event planning and implementation. Carrie is a graduate of DePauw University with a degree in music education, Ball State University with a master's degree in Higher Education Administration, a Master of Business Administration degree from Valparaiso University, and a Ph.D. in Education from Virginia Commonwealth University. Carrie currently works at Valparaiso University as the Assistant Dean of Students working with fraternity and sorority life, leadership programming, and volunteer programs. Previously Carrie has worked at Virginia Commonwealth University, Elon University, Randolph-Macon College and Centre College. Carrie is a member of Alpha Omicron Pi Women's Fraternity, Rotary International and served as the 2009 President for the Association of Fraternity/Sorority Advisors.

DR. LYNDA WILEY is the Executive Director of the Association of Fraternity/Sorority Advisors (AFA) and the AFA Foundation. Prior to coming to AFA, Lynda worked in student affairs at Ball State University from 1997 to 2017. She began as an Assistant Director of Leadership and Service Programs and advanced over 15 years to become an Associate Vice President, overseeing a variety of areas in student life and activities. Lynda was involved as a board member with both AFA and Gamma Sigma Alpha honor society. She holds a Bachelor of Science in Education from the University of Missouri and received a Master of Arts in Guidance and Counseling/Student Affairs from Southeast Missouri State University. While at Ball State, she received a Doctor of Education in Adult, Higher and Community Education. She is a member of Kappa Alpha Theta, and she currently is an advisor for the chapter at Ohio Wesleyan University.

DR. JAMIE L. WORKMAN is an Assistant Professor of Higher Education Leadership at Valdosta State University. She specializes in student affairs content areas including student development theory, social justice and inclusion in higher education, and current issues in student affairs. Her research focuses on undergraduate student success primarily from a major and career development perspective. Additionally, she has researched Living Learning Communities and student use of technology. She is the author or co-author of multiple publications in peer reviewed academic journals. She is a member of Phi Sigma Pi National Honor Fraternity, Omicron Delta Kappa, and has experience advising a fraternity council.

DR. NATALIE ROSE YOUNGBULL is a citizen of the Cheyenne & Arapaho Tribe of Oklahoma and descended from the Ft. Peck Assiniboine & Sioux tribes of Montana. She earned her Ph.D. in the Educational Policy Studies and Practice department with an emphasis in Higher Education from the University of Arizona. Her research focused on the experiences of American Indian Gates Millennium Scholars within institutions of higher education related to their non-persistence. Currently, she serves as the Faculty Development Program Officer where she administers fellowships to assist tribal college and university (TCU) faculty in the completion of their masters and doctorate degrees, organizes the annual TCU Faculty Research Convening and serves as co-editor of the *TCU Research Journal* (TCURJ). Natalie is a Gates Millennium Scholar alum and a member of the Gamma Delta Pi American Indian Sisterhood.